Patsy Mitchell

Diana Phipps's
Affordable Splendor

An Ingenious Guide
to Decorating Elegantly,
Inexpensively
and Doing Most of it
Yourself

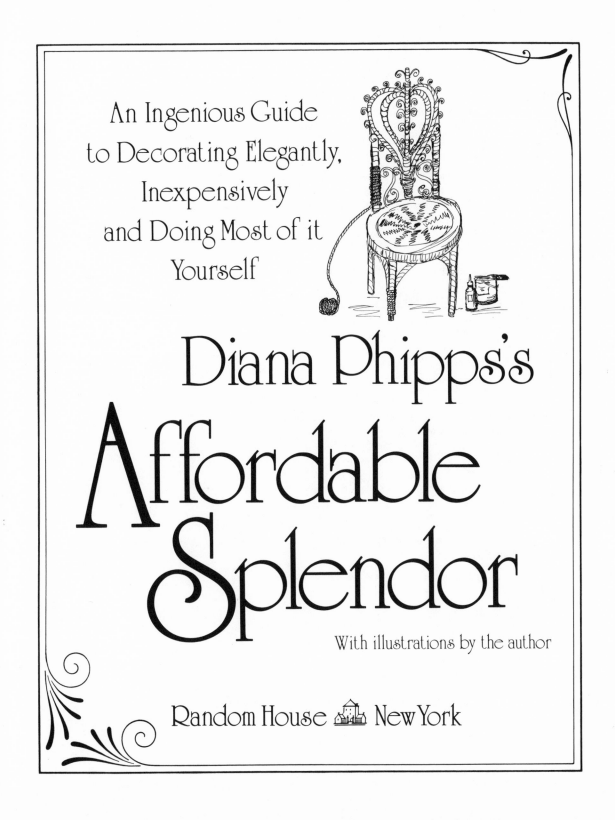

Diana Phipps's

Affordable Splendor

With illustrations by the author

Random House ⌂ New York

Grateful acknowledgment is made to B. T. Batsford Limited for permission to reprint previously published material: The drawing on page 272 is an adaptation of an illustration from *A Literary History of Wallpaper* by E. A. Entwisle. Reprinted by permission of the publisher, B. T. Batsford Limited.

Library of Congress Cataloging in Publication Data
Phipps, Diana.
Diana Phipps's Affordable splendor.
Includes index.
1. Interior decoration.   I. Title.
NK2110.P54   747'.1   80–6028
ISBN 0–394–50441–0   AACR2

Color insert between pages 150–151.

The photographs for the front and back cover and photographs 6, 9, 13, 14, 18, 19, 25, 49, 50 and 55 were taken by Derry Moore. Photographs 3, 7, 8, 20, 22, 23, 26, 27, 40, 41, 42, 43, 44, 51, 52 and 53 are by Michael Dunne. Photograph 12 is by Christopher Sykes, and 1, 2, 4, 5, 10, 11, 15, 16, 17, 21, 24, 28, 29, 30, 31, 32, 33, 34, 35, 36, 37, 38, 39, 45, 46, 47, 48, 54, 56, 57 and 58 are by Michael Boys.

Photographs 1, 5, 6, 9, 10, 16, 18, 19, 21, 24, 30, 31, 32, 33, 34, 46 and 55 have previously appeared in *Architectural Digest.*

Manufactured in the United States of America
98765432
First Edition

For my mother, Cecilia Sternberg

Acknowledgments

I would like to thank Jason Epstein for the title, Clive James for help with the grammar, Klara Glowczewski for the editing, and Jim Lambert for the design. I'm also grateful to Antonia Fraser, Jean Douglas and Evangeline Bruce for their advice and for reading the manuscript, Gore Vidal for the use of his house and Fran Bentley for being my assistant. I hardly need add that any eccentricities in either text or illustrations are entirely my own responsibility.

Thanks are also due to Derry Moore, Michael Dunne, Christopher Sykes and Michael Boys for the photography—and to Page Rense for so generously allowing me to reproduce those photographs already published in Architectural Digest.

Contents

Introduction 3

I   The Living Room 9

II   The Dining Room 77

III The Kitchen 133

IV   The Bedroom 159

V   The Bathroom 209

VI   One-Room Living 235

Index 273

Diana Phipps's
Affordable
Splendor

Introduction

This book, I hope, is not simply about interior decoration. At least not insofar as it suggests how things should look. It is more about house arrangements—my own sort of house arrangements. The rooms people choose to live in should be individual and suit their own ideas of comfort. Some people, the lucky ones, are sufficient to themselves and not dependent on their surroundings. They can wake up in a modern plastic box and not feel like ending it all. I can't. I am totally dependent on my backdrop for my state of well-being. And I like my backdrop luxurious, pleasing to the eye and extremely comfortable. To achieve this has always been more costly than I could afford, so over the years and in various countries I have devised ways of getting the surroundings I want by camouflaging what I have or improvising what I need. The shortcuts I have worked out to get the effects I want might be useful to other people whose purse, like mine, falls short of realizing their ideal setting.

There are many more qualified than I to be arbiters of taste. Already the language of decorating fills me with gloom. "Taste"—what does it mean? What my parents' generation found in atrocious taste I often find wonderful, and the spindly, dancing Louis XV chairs that were considered perfection then look awful to me today. "Style"—another ambiguous word. I believe that Edith Wharton, in her book *Decoration of Houses,* published in 1911, was the first to talk of style in the sense of it being something you could have. Her advice on what to do with your house to give it style seems remarkably outdated to me. (Sour grapes, perhaps, as she considered material-covered walls—which I love—both unattractive and unhealthy.) Style changes with general moods—political, economic, social. If ostentatious wealth is unpopular, out goes ornate furniture and in come plain shapes and natural woods. If a particular style becomes overpriced or too often seen, people will turn to a style that is still obtainable and occasionally affordable. Hence the present vogue for the nineteenth and early twentieth centuries, for Victoriana, Biedermeier, Art Nouveau and Art Deco. Fashions change with increasing speed. The tin can with which we litter today but which we already copy in plaster as an ornament our grandchildren will collect. The question is: Will they want the original or the ornamental copy?

My aim in this book is to show what I did myself to my own and to some other people's rooms, to show photographs of the results and the steps leading up to those results. Above all, I want to show the money I saved. By nature I am both lazy and untidy. A professional carpenter, upholsterer or painter could, with reason, find a great deal to criticize in my work. I know neither the orthodox way of doing things nor the correct terminology. In fact, I don't want to. I know what the professionals charge, the intimidating mystery they exude and above all how long they take.

The book is divided loosely into six sections: living room, dining room, kitchen, bedroom, bathroom and one-room living. Other bits of information cluster around these sections. But since many of the techniques I describe are applicable to every room, it is best to read the book all the way through. As I have lived, at different times, in four different places since moving to England, it may not be easy to identify which of the English rooms are in which house and to whom the house belongs. Because I hope the rooms could be anywhere, I don't think this matters, but it might surprise the reader to see the same pot or ashtray wandering.

For those who do not find the rooms in this book to their liking, the shortcuts could be adapted to most other tastes— except perhaps to the ultramodern, which calls for bare space and unblemished newness. There, alas, my messiness, which I hope to prove can be an asset, would only be an obstacle. Grand and old is more easily reproduced than simple and new. Time is the ally. What time has done to an old wall, a piece of furniture or a piece of fabric, I can do too. A modern structure of steel and glass I can't do at all. Even if I could design such a thing, I couldn't make it myself. And I wouldn't be able to afford to have it made.

There are centuries of the past displayed before us to copy —or at least to take ideas from and adapt to the present day. Art is, for the moment, in fashion. Excellent museums, exhibitions, even lectures, are there to tell us how people lived, what they saw and admired. Those who believe that the present

A

shouldn't steal from the past but should start afresh have a point. Yet access to the past is open, and the cost of innovation prohibitive.

I lived what I think are called my formative years in a castle. My mother, an indefatigable "arranger" of houses, made some charming and to my eye totally beautiful rooms in it. But the house was large and there were many rooms she did not get to. These remained gloomy horrors that haunted my early child-hood. Perhaps this is the reason rooms matter so much to me. Changing political and financial circumstances played havoc with our living habits. Within the first ten years of my life, my parents twice lost and once regained their properties from occupying military forces, losing them first to the Germans, then to the Russians. After that came various stages of poverty. When we finally became emigrants to the United States, at last, once again, I had a room of my own. It was in an ugly and very small house. There I first began "making do." I built my furniture out of cardboard boxes from the grocery store. Over the boxes I glued blue-and-white gingham bought at Wool-worth's. I tented my bed with the same material and had masses of ruffled cushions on the floor when floor cushions were not yet the fashion. They were stuffed with clothes waiting to be ironed. (A)

Thirty years later I'm still doing more or less the same thing, but now the gingham occasionally also covers a grand chair. Although mine may be exaggerated, the nesting instinct in human beings is strong. Still, having been uprooted a few times in my life, I tend to make things that are, for the most part, portable. I can turn the cardboard boxes around, pack and leave.

I hate to throw anything away. I want to keep the old—no matter how tired, ugly or worn—and cover it with the new. As a child, I helped my mother scrape a wall in order to uncover a particular shade of old paint hidden under many new layers. Clumsily, I scraped too deeply, only to uncover a still much earlier fresco. This taught me that covering instead of starting afresh can not only save time but perhaps give someone somewhere a great pleasure—the pleasure of discovery. Even if it's only as ordinary as finding an old tattered piece of material hiding under a new cover. That is, for me, in fact, the most important thing about decoration: the fun of it. The fun of discovering a broken-down nothing and turning it into something. An anonymous room turning into "your own" room.

Decoration is hard work—no use pretending otherwise. Indecision and change of mind are the most costly. Best is to just charge ahead with confidence, enjoyment and a sharp pair of scissors for cutting corners.

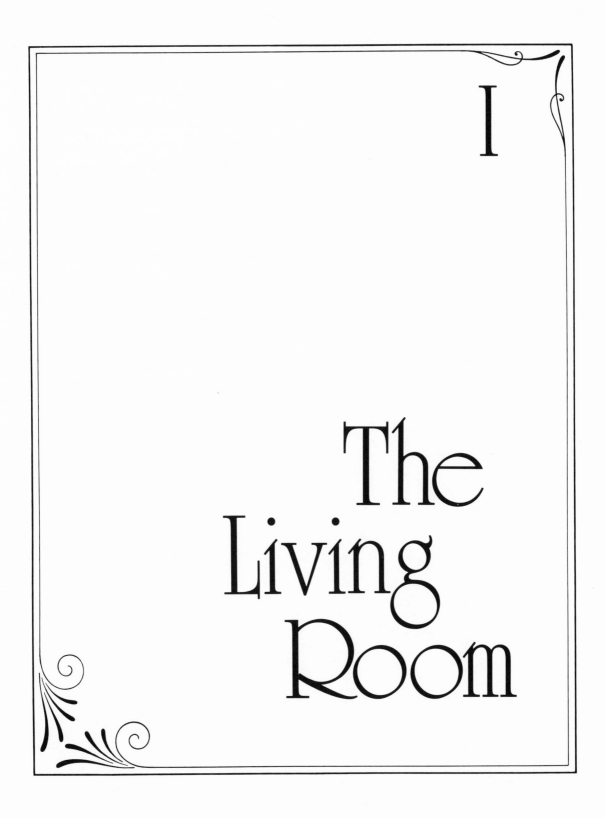

I

The Living Room

The living room I would like to start with in this chapter is my own, in London (photographs 1–5). It could be anywhere: any country, in the city or out, in a modern apartment or in an old one. It could be part of a house (as it, in fact, is in this case) or a glorified studio apartment with the alcove—curtains drawn for privacy—used for sleeping (photograph 1).

When I first saw the house, its floors were divided into apartments. The floor that is now the living room was two rooms, kitchen and bath—or what the unfortunate tenants must have been deceived into believing was a kitchen and bath. (A) The neighborhood was considered unsmart, the building was in deplorable shape, the proportions were ugly, and the few friends I was unwise enough to show my find to were frankly appalled.

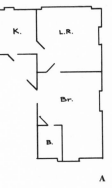

A

But the price was right. Opportunities for camouflaging layers of peeling wallpaper, misproportioned doors and windows were limitless. It took me two years to do the house. I did most of the work myself, and when I didn't, I say so. Had I worked on it full-time, I'd have been faster, but not much. There is no point in deluding oneself—doing up a house takes time. The photographs show the living room as it is now. It may not be everyone's idea of a beautiful room, but it works: When I am entertaining, a lot of people can form groups easily or talk comfortably in pairs. The room is also cozy for solitary occupancy. The material on the walls muffles sound and the lighting is subdued, yet, being directional, it is easy to work or read by. The autumnal colors are warm in a cold climate, but the large windows give enough light so as not to make the dark colors oppressive in summer.

Several magazines have photographed the room on the assumption that its overall appearance is one of luxury and timelessness. I am flattered by this, as I begrudged the room both money and time. In the next few pages, I would like to make it clear both where I skimped and where I sometimes felt the need to use the best in order to help along the illusion of luxury.

I own three good things, all of which appear in the photographs of the living room: the low pair of Empire chairs, the large picture of a midshipman, and the mirrors, one in the alcove and one above the fireplace. (B) The photographs were taken before I planned this book; otherwise I would have removed these pieces and substituted more self-made objects so as to prove that even without a "good" piece, one can give a room a sense of opulence. I did the room ten years ago. Since then, many of the things I used have so risen in price that I would no longer be able to afford them. As well as describing what I did at the time, I will try to give some idea of what I would do now to create the same effect without paying inflated prices.

B

The first thing to do was to remove some walls. Easily said. None of the inside walls of the house were supporting ones, but this does not mean they didn't carry a certain load of the rooms above. I think one partition wall, especially on a middle floor, can be knocked through without risk of the house falling down. Nevertheless, when we knocked down the wall separating what used to be the living room and bedroom (see A), we put up a wooden beam above the opening for additional support. (I say "we" in this case as I had help to make the opening. It doesn't take much professional knowledge to take down a partition wall, but it does take a certain amount of brute strength and the very boring carrying of bags of rubble.)

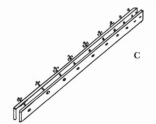

C

The beam we used at the top of the opening consisted of two $12'' \times 3''$ joists (small parallel planks for supporting floors and ceilings), $1'$ longer than the room is wide. We bolted them together with nuts and bolts (C) and embedded each end $6''$ into the brick walls on either side. To further support the beam, we placed two $4'' \times 4''$ uprights (pieces of wood) on each side of the opening, one against the wall and fixed to it, the next $4''$ away from it. (D)

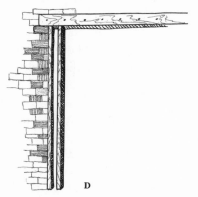

D

The gaps between the wood, as well as the wood, we covered with plasterboard. Over plasterboard comes plaster. Plastering, though enjoyable, is more difficult than it looks. I needed further help to plaster the rough edges of the opening.

The walls that formed the kitchen and bath (A) were paper ($2'' \times 1''$ uprights covered—literally—with cardboard). They came down like a house of cards.

The walls down, I was left with a strangely shaped room. (E) The opening where the kitchen used to be worried me. It was too small to be a room in its own right and would form a cul-de-sac if part of the living room.

I have always secretly yearned for a split-level room, but don't know how anyone except an agile zombie with servants could live in one. A room with more than one level could not have clutter: Anything—a newspaper, a wastebasket, a book—would spoil the visual symmetry. Then there would be the difficulty of getting the vacuum cleaner over the obstacles, the complication of handing a tray down into the "conversation pit," not to mention the insurmountable problem of climbing into it with tray in hand.

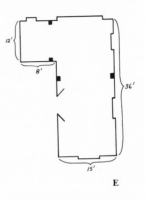

E

Apart from that, and the fact that whatever furniture I own would be useless in it, I have often thought it might not be a very expensive enterprise. The levels could be built out of bricks—or at least if one lived on the *ground* floor, the levels could be built out of bricks. The more prosperous and/or elevated could use bricks and boards. (F) The various levels could be covered with either thin (to walk on) or thick (to sit on) foam rubber. Then the whole undulating mass would have to be expertly carpeted, for which a definite talent would be necessary. Being foolhardy, I would try covering it myself, but in a material, some sort of thick one—denim or canvas—which, compared to carpeting, would be cheaper and easier to sew. Certainly any expert would tell me it wouldn't last, but I could always throw a rug over the parts that were walked on a lot. (For carpets, see Chapter 21.) Things meant to last a lifetime have always depressed me. They're so final, so binding. Better to spend less in the first place and furnish with fantasy than spend a lifetime stuck with the same boring investment.

F

Here, in what was to become my living room, was the chance to change a level without creating an obstacle course. My helper and I built (in what used to be the kitchen) a platform 18″ off the ground.

This was done by first constructing a frame out of timber. We put down and nailed to the floor pieces of 3″ × 2″ against and around the three walls and across the front. Onto these, every 16″, we nailed 12″ uprights of the same 3″ × 2″. On top of the uprights we laid three more 3″ × 2″ lengthwise. Rather like a playpen. Next, my helper produced some surprising steel objects called joist hangers (brackets) (G), which he wedged into the back wall every 16″. He did this by scraping

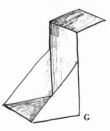

G

out a bit of mortar between the bricks and pushing in the joist hanger. Into each joist hanger he then slotted a 4" × 2" timber joist (or beam) and nailed its other end onto the wood on top of the front upright. (H) To do this, he used two nails driven at an angle (toenails). (I) On top of the joists we put chipboard flooring. (Chipboard, also called particle board, comes in 8' × 4' sheets and is 3/4" thick. It is the cheapest flooring material.)

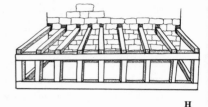

H

In a shop specializing in wood remnants, I had found a rather beaten-up wooden mahogany railing. It may well have once been an altar rail. We cut it in half and placed the two halves along the front edge of the platform, leaving a gap between them. Below the gap we built a central step (a box made out of plywood) and left storage space left and right of it, which I liberally dotted with moldings, sticking them on with wood glue and fastening them with finishing nails. (J) (See page 21 for how to attach molding.) I painted the step and the storage units to match the mahogany of the rail, using the technique described in Chapter 16. Usually the stereo deck is kept in one of the storage units and records in the other, but when the room was photographed, it was thought that books were better-looking. Eventually a friend of mine called the alcove the "czar's carriage," and I will call it that from now on (photograph 1).

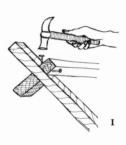

I

When various old pipes and partitions had been removed from the room, what was left of the cornice was a mess. I made one of my rare financial investments in the house and had a plaster cornice made (photograph 5). They can still be made to order and they do much to enhance a room, but the price has soared. Were I to be doing the room today, I would settle for making up a wooden cornice, as I did in the California bedroom on page 197 (photographs 40 and 41) or in the libraries in Chapter 44 (photographs 55–57).

J

The house, being Victorian, originally had a fireplace in every room. Now it was full of chimney-breasts (the area around and above the chimney that juts out and holds the flue) and some ugly mantelpieces. One mantelpiece in the living room (see photograph 5) was good enough to keep, although badly stained. Furious hours with peroxide and steel wool made it clean, if not beautiful—and marble, at least, it was. The second mantelpiece was wood, obscured by many coats of shiny

white paint. I was sorely tempted to have two working fireplaces in what was now one room. If at all possible, I would
never eliminate a fireplace; it gives the central point to a room,
toward which all seating can be turned—rather like an audience toward the stage. And what could be more luxurious than
two blazing fires? The answer is the time you save by tending
only one. Also, I needed the wall space. So out came the
wooden mantelpiece. (But it was soon to be rehoused on top
of a door.)

Of course, an open fire with logs is the most attractive, but
with ever-increasing heating prices, coal should not be ignored:
It exudes more heat and is cheaper. Any number of stoves—
wood or coal-burning—are now on the market and can be
attached to existing flues. In the barn (photograph 52), the
fireplace smoked and emitted depressingly little heat. Eventually I obtained a new type of fireplace to fit into the old one.
It is iron, burns coal or wood, has a narrow pipe that fits into
the flue so that no hot air escapes, and the heat convects back
out into the room through a narrow slit above the fire. (K)

K

If I was to have the grand living room I craved, I did not
want to enter it by a door two feet wide. I wanted tall, elegant
double doors. So my helper and I attacked the door opening
until, after the very satisfactory sensation of swinging a hammer at the walls, we had an 8′ × 4′ hole. Plain doors of that
size can be bought ready-made at a lumberyard. I also bought
two standard reeded columns at the lumberyard to build the
doorframe on the inside of the room. These we hammered left
and right of the door opening. Above the columns we put the
top of the scrapped wooden mantelpiece. (See photograph 3.)

To each of the two doors I attached four squares of heavy
molding. On the inside of the four squares, next to the heavy
molding, I placed yet another, thinner, half-round molding to
make the whole thing appear still heavier. (L) (For how to miter
—or, anyway, my amateur technique of how to miter—see
page 140.) Then I painted the door to look like mahogany. (See
Chapter 16 for how.) The moldings I gilded, but quietly, so
that it seems to have happened long ago. (For gilding, see page
65.) I now had a door (see photograph 3) that at first sight
could easily have come out of a palace—or at least out of a play
about a palace. I needed something to authenticate it a bit
more. So I splurged on a grand lock for my grand door. It is

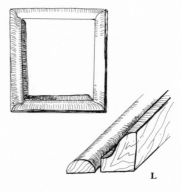

L

French, eighteenth century, and I found it in the Portobello Road (a London antique market). The lock for the door cost more than the door, but it does much to give the whole thing an imposing look.

The second door to the room I removed completely. I also took away the doorframe on the inside of the room. On the outside—in other words on the stair landing—I left the doorframe and squared it off at the base with a scrapped piece of framing from the other side. I slapped a sheet of plywood over the opening on the inside of the room. From the outside I nailed pieces of batten (bits of wood) to the recess of the frame. (M) Onto the bits I slotted some hardboard shelves I had cut to the size of the recess at the local hardware store. The depth of the recess is about the same as the width of a small hardbound book and slightly larger than a paperback. Eventually I painted the shelves to look like maple wood. (See Chapter 16 for method.) Now, on the stairs, there is a perfectly decent bookcase made out of an obsolete doorway. (N) When I covered the walls of the living room with material, the plywood back of the bookcase was covered up and became part of the wall.

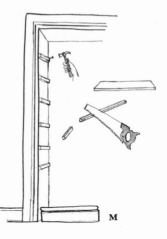

M

I had long thought two thin, tall bookcases standing next to each other would make any room look extremely smart. (O) In my living room they could fill the spaces left and right of the now unused chimney. To have them built as freestanding units would have been expensive, and I didn't then know a carpenter expert enough. So I went in for some visual cheating.

I was also economizing on the heating system and had off-peak storage radiators installed on both sides of the chimney —huge, monstrous objects. This spoiled my plan of having the bookcases there go down to the ground, which would have been more elegant. In fact, I was able to do this only with the ones left and right of the window (photograph 2), and there, of course, there wasn't enough room for two at a time. So I had to compromise.

N

For each recess on either side of the chimney-breast, I had a rather amateur carpenter build a box out of chipboard big enough to conceal the heater and leave enough space for air circulation. For the front of the cupboard, the carpenter made two doorlike frames, on the inside of which I hammered brass mesh, bought by the yard from building suppliers. It is expen-

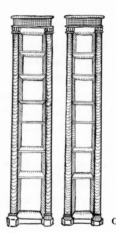

O

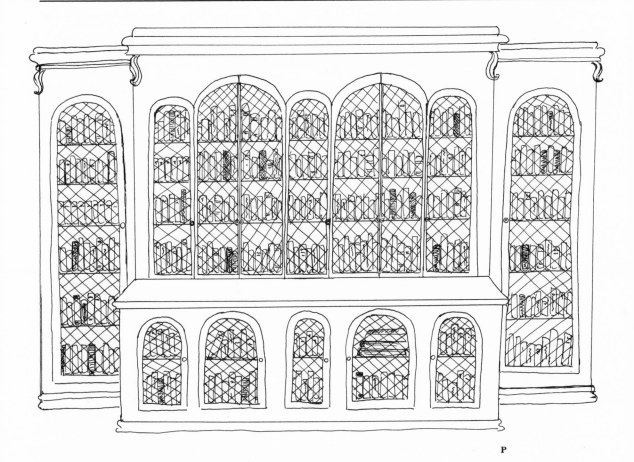

P

sive, but as Henry James said, "I find I can stand a great deal of gold," and some of it, at least, should not be painted on.

Mesh with which to hide radiators can also be bought in a cheaper metal. I have seen ordinary chicken wire used as netting for cupboard doors in the magnificent library of a French castle. (P) It also does nicely to hide a radiator, especially if dulled down with a bit of paint. Garden trellis, bought by the yard or made and painted (see page 267 and photograph 57), makes attractive doors for radiator covers, kitchen cupboards, bookcase doors—anything that is to remain hidden or enclosed.

For the shelves that were to go on top of the cupboards in my living room, a carpenter built two extremely rough structures, also out of chipboard: four shelves between three vertical boards. The boards and the shelves are the same depth as the chimney-breast (covered by the large painting in photograph 5). They are as wide as the space between the chimney-breast and what was left of the center wall. These shelves sit on top of the cupboards, and the cupboards jut out 10″ in front of the shelves.

Then I did my share of the carpentry. I bought three sheets of thinnish plywood 1/2″ thick. The plywood comes in 8′ × 4′ and 6′ × 4′ sheets. I drew the shapes I wanted on the plywood, cut them out with a portable jig saw and hammered the shapes against the shelving. (Q) I should have screwed them in properly, but as always, too keen to get the effect, I skipped a few steps, calming my guilt with the excuse that the material with which I would eventually cover the walls would also cover my not very tidy carpentry.

Q

TWO

I find almost every house beautiful. But I am quite pleased that I have never had, or been asked to arrange, a really perfect house. By this I mean a classically beautiful house, with correct proportions, the right paneling, doors and windows of the period, perfect floors and ceilings. The duty and respect such a house would demand! Never could its symmetry be vandalized by a funny or improvised piece of furniture, nor its lines ruined by some raffish bit of drapery. In a house of perfect furniture and perfect objects, each thing would clamor for and deserve recognition. Out would go the pleasure of treating a room as a whole.

I was certainly able to treat my living room as a whole, and did so. It's a brown velvet box, the carpet the same color as the walls, the woodwork stippled to look like mahogany—as close to the color of the walls as I was able to achieve. The czar's carriage (photograph 1) is, I hope, a surprise flurry within the brown box—an addition to loll about in, a tented and colored relief from all the browns.

I am a great believer in material-covered walls. It is less messy work than painting and in the long run cheaper, as it lasts longer. I usually buy dress materials for walls, for the sake of economy and because the choice is greater. If the material is light-colored, it can be taken down, washed and restapled every five years or so; even a painted wall usually needs redoing after that length of time. Dark materials on walls—like the living room brown—have a limitless life, demanding only an occasional going-over with the long tube attachment that most vacuum cleaners have. Material-covered walls seem warmer— the tea-cozy principle, I suppose. Also, they do something nice to sound, soften it within the room and help keep it out. Architectural effects can be achieved with material (see batik living room, photograph 15): Strange proportions can be camouflaged (see blue denim room, photograph 16, and orange room, photograph 54); two rooms made to seem one by the use of the same material; or one room turned into two by a curtain and different materials, as in the case of the czar's carriage within the London living room.

Lately a friend of mine had a well-known decorator make an estimate of how much it would cost to have her walls covered in material. It was $2,000 for the work alone. Admittedly this would have given employment to many costly workmen. First, a carpenter would have been sent to batten the walls. (Battens are strips of wood that get nailed along the top and bottom of the walls, down the corners and around all openings.) Second, a seamstress would have sewn together the padding (to go between the wall and the material) and the material to the exact measurements of the room. Third, a different person, armed with a staple gun, would have come to stretch the material from batten to batten. If the walls happened to be uneven, as seems to be the case in all old houses, the whole envelope for the room would have to be taken down, returned to the seamstress, remeasured, resewn and refitted.

I have covered, unaided, at least fifty rooms in material. The average-sized room takes me two days of hard work, no more. The professional might, but the amateur does not, notice the difference between my walls and the $2,000 walls. I work with an electric staple gun (not a necessity, but it does speed things up and is not at all demanding on the hand muscles), a normal staple gun, a pair of scissors, and some material glue. I also use a portable sewing machine, with which to seam the material, thread, a normal needle and a curved one. (A) (If there is no sewing machine available, the seams can be glued. This is not as satisfactory as sewing them, since it takes a hawk's eye to glue the seams straight and an all-too-gentle touch when stretching the material. But it can be done.) I eventually hide the staples by gluing over them a store-bought border or a strip made out of the same material as the wall covering. (See page 21 for how to make it.)

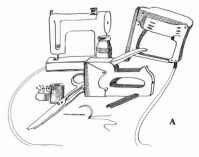

A

I do none of the more complicated things a professional decorator considers necessary to achieve a properly covered wall. I do not batten. I find battens in most cases unnecessary. That marvelous invention, the staple gun, shoots quite readily into any except the most stubborn surface. I do not use curtain interlining for the padding, which must be seamed and costs more. I buy polyester or cotton padding, sometimes called batting or wadding. It is thicker than interlining and wider— it can be bought up to 80″ wide. I do not seam this, but staple it in overlapping pieces straight onto the wall.

When I began work on my living room, the local department store was having its annual sale. In the dress-material department lay a huge roll of cotton velveteen, a horrible mustard yellow. At $3 a yard it was cheap even ten years ago. I sent it straight from the department store to the dyer's to be matched to a swatch of the brown carpet I had found the same day, at the same sale. Most dyers are quite excellent these days in achieving exact replicas of color. So am I, on a lucky day. If, however, I manage to mix a dye the color I really like, I tend to, frugally, want to use up all of it. In go clothes, cushion covers, almost anything I find. To describe the result as color coordination is an understatement.

I had 40 yards of the yellow—now brown—velveteen and presumed it to be enough. I was wrong. I needed 60 yards. I hunted far and wide for more of the same hideous yellow velveteen, but sale goods seem to come into existence for sales only. They appear on the first day of a sale, only to disappear forever on the last. I eventually bought an extra 20 yards of a much thicker pale-green velveteen, and it was cleverly dyed as brown as the rest. The slight difference of texture added to the shaded look of aging, which I like in houses anyway.

To cover the living room walls, I first stapled the previously mentioned padding as underlay. I did this by climbing an aluminum ladder—never a pleasure for me, but just bearable if the ladder is tall enough so that the upper part of one's body does not tremble unsupported in midair. I stapled the wadding straight off the roll to just under the cornice. (B) I dismounted the untrusted ladder and cut off the wadding just above the baseboard. I took the next bit up again, and so on. As the padding was wide, this procedure didn't take very long. I stapled only the top and the bottom and simply let the sides overlap by an inch or so.

Then I seamed the material. I seamed together only enough to cover an uninterrupted expanse of wall. In photograph 3, for example, I seamed together three lengths to reach from the corner of the room to the door.

I could have sewn four lengths together and cut out a space for the door, but I have found through trial and error and many crooked walls that the smaller the piece, the easier to stretch it properly. So for the narrow spaces above windows and doors, I cut a separate piece of material and glue it or sew it with a curved needle (page 33) to the larger piece of material next to it. (The material covering the wall in photograph 3 is sewn to the narrow strip above the door.) I always end the material in a corner, even if I have enough to reach further. You get a better stretch on the material that way. Also, to be truthful, I find sewing many long, straight seams on the machine the most boring part of the whole process.

To put up the material, I again mounted the ladder and stapled the material on top of the underlay, directly into the plaster. (Or whatever else the wall may be. Cement is tricky, an iron girder naturally impossible, stone, surprisingly, quite often workable.) Where there is no hope with the staple gun, one can always ad-lib with glue, either by gluing the material itself or gluing up a batten and stapling the material into that.

I shot in a staple every 6" or so. I didn't pull the material between the staples to stretch it, but just kept smoothing it along. Once the material was up, I moved to the outer edges and stapled those into place. At this stage I tried to make the

B

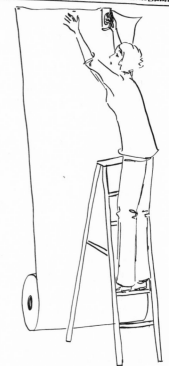

material taut. I used the hand stapler to staple straight into the corner. (The nose of my electric stapler does not fit flush into corners, but the hand stapler does.) Only when the three sides of my material were stapled did I give it a really good pull downward to take out any creases and stapled the bottom edge just above the baseboard.

One of my frequent trips to furniture markets and thrift shops yielded four columns. Most probably they had once stood in a church, or so the remnants of rather ecclesiastical Gothic stenciling led me to believe. I first thought of building a bed out of them—a huge fourposter with crimson hangings. (c) But the crimson hangings were slow in finding their way to the markets. The columns stood in the garage, where their gilding and stenciling further deteriorated in the damp.

C

So when I had removed the central stud wall in the living room and was obliged, for structural reasons, to support the opening with joists—thereby still having a divided ceiling—I made it appear that the columns were the supports (photograph 5). Apart from the illusion of framing and supporting the opening, the columns also hide the staples with which the velvet is attached to the wall. I put two columns on each side because I had four and because a single one looked a trifle thin anyway. To restore them to some of their past glory, I repainted them. (For how, see page 64.)

To cover the sliver of wall above the columns with brown velvet, I ran a length of material from one side of the room to the other. I stapled first the padding and then the velvet to just under the cornice on one side, pulled them both like a sling to the other side and stapled them there, under the cornice. I used the material lengthwise to save material as well as sewing and measuring time. This makes the nap run the wrong way, but it is barely noticeable: The eye tends to rest on the columns and ignore the slightly different shading of the material above them.

To stretch the velvet on the wall with the four bookshelves (two are visible in photograph 5), I seamed together four lengths, stapled them just under the cornice and let them hang, completely obscuring the bookshelves. Then, feeling for the openings in the plywood, I stapled along them. Once the stapling was finished, I cut the openings. (D)

To both hide the staples and cover the ragged edge of the

D

material, I used picture-frame molding, a narrow molding for around the bookshelves and a wider molding for around the top of the room, directly under the cornice (photographs 3, 4 and 5). The advantage of picture-frame molding over some other molding is its shape. It has a rebate—in other words, it goes around the corner rather than lying flat. (E) It can be acquired from a kind-hearted framer who will sell it, if he is well disposed, by lengths—already gilded or silvered, or of walnut, maple or any other finished or polished wood. It can also be bought in raw wood at a lumberyard. It can then be painted, grained (for how, see Chapter 16) or gilded (page 65). I attach all moldings with wood glue and finishing nails. A finishing nail has no head. When attaching a piece of molding, I first glue it on and then hammer it in, using quite a few of the thin finishing nails. I don't hit the nails all the way in, but leave them partially sticking out. When the glue has set, I pull out some of the nails and hit the rest right in. They leave tiny holes in the wood. This can be filled in with wood putty in a shade that matches whatever wood the molding is made of. If I have made a slight mess of mitering (page 140), that, too, can be amended with putty pressed into the join.

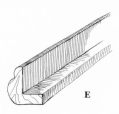

E

To hide staples when I am not using molding or some store-bought piece of tape, braid or fringe, I use strips of the same material, which I sew. For the living room I took long strips of brown velvet 2″ wide (pieced out of leftovers), sewed the edges together, wrong side out, and then used a safety pin to thread one end through the center of each tube so it turned right side out. These tubes I then glued on top of the staples in the corners of the room and above the baseboard. I make the same sort of tubes, only narrower, to hide staples on upholstery. These I iron, to make them as flat, and eventually as inconspicuous, as possible. To make ruffles to surround curtains or cushions, I start out with the same sort of strip. (See pages 162 and 194–95.)

After the walls were covered, I curtained one set of windows (photographs 2 and 3) and the entrance to the czar's carriage (photograph 1). The window has nothing more than twice two lengths of the same velvet seamed together and gathered. I stapled the gathers onto a piece of wood behind the cornice above the window. To the inner edges of the curtains I sewed a leopardskin–like border. The sofa cushions below the curtains

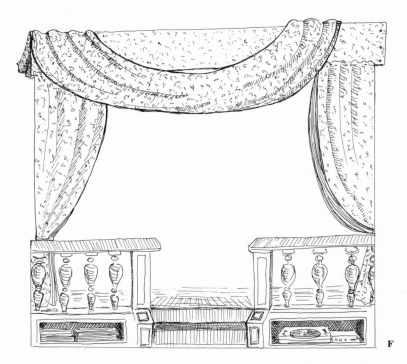

F

came later, to match the border. They are not, I hasten to add, real leopard.

I looped the window material back, using the arms of the wall lights to serve as tiebacks.

I made the same sort of curtains to form a separation between the brown room and the stripes of the czar's carriage (photograph 1). But this time I lined the velvet curtains with the striped material to make the czar's carriage look like a separate tent within the brown living room.

The curtains for the czar's carriage do not meet, as the window curtains do, but only frame the opening. For the top of the opening I made a valance. I nailed up a board covered in brown velvet. I took a long and narrow piece of velvet and pulled that over the board, from the back to the front, draped it across the front and stapled it to the back. Then I stapled the lined curtains to the front of the board and pulled the draped narrow piece of velvet down to hide the staples. (F)

I looped back the curtains on both sides. (A ribbon, stapled to the wall and tied, works sufficiently to loop back a curtain.) On the inside of the czar's carriage, across the velvet-covered board, I stapled more drapery out of the striped material to conceal the wrong side of the velvet drape.

I don't know why tents seem so romantic—at least, they seem so to me. Perhaps it is the impermanence they imply, or the images they conjure up—gypsies, the desert, seraglios, Arabs "silently stealing away." Perhaps it is more basic: A tented room such as the czar's carriage is the easiest way of achieving the greatest effect.

A tented ceiling like the one in the blue-and-white dining room, however, is the devil to get right (photograph 14, description on pages 94–96), and the Bedouin-tent ceiling (photograph 54, description on page 260) was also quite difficult on account of the curious architecture of the room. But just to cover a ceiling, especially a low one, by seaming lengths of material together and stapling them on without even padding underneath is easy. (See photograph 34 of pink bathroom ceiling.) And to fit strips of material between exposed beams and staple them on is so easy it's a downright pleasure. (See barn bathroom, photograph 44.)

The czar's carriage is not only an example of a simple tented ceiling, but also an example of the quickest form of wall covering. Once again, even the cheapest dress material will do for this; the more like a flimsy rag, the easier to work with, although, of course, since it is gathered, a greater quantity is needed.

The material in the czar's carriage has, by now, a history. I bought it in 1964 in one of the many wonderful wholesale stores which I still frequent in downtown New York and which are prepared to sell to a passer-by if the quantity you want is large enough. All that has changed is the price. In 1964 I bought 100 yards of the striped cotton for 20 cents a yard. Fifteen years later, in the same part of town, I paid $1 a yard for the material with which I covered the walls of a New York studio (photograph 50). My English sources are not as cheap. The Indian fabric for the tropical studio (photographs 47 and 48) was double the price. In England I have had the most luck with the summer sales at John Lewis (a London department store). Of course, if I don't buy enough, I'm done for.

The brown, cream and burgundy stripe in the czar's carriage was clearly destined for male pajamas. Instead, the 100 yards

G

made the move with me to England. I first lived there in a rented apartment where the stripes tented, curtained, wall-covered and upholstered my living room. (G) Five years later, when I moved, I split the 100 yards: One part went for the walls and ceiling of the czar's carriage, as well as covering the three mattresses within the carriage. Another part covered the walls and made the hangings of a fourposter bed for a friend. Yet another lot covered a client's bathroom walls, and still I had enough left to make tablecloths and napkins.

To do the walls of the czar's carriage, I first stapled up my padding, as in the rest of the room. The quantity of material needed to cover a flat expanse of wall is easy to figure out. You need the height of the room in material as many times as it will take to cover the room—how many times depends on the width of the material. (I allow an extra 2″ per panel for seams and/or stapling.) For gathered or pleated walls, I use approximately double the amount of material I would use for flat walls. In the czar's carriage, I stapled the material over the padding in pleats that I neither measured nor counted out. I didn't bother to seam the material, but always slipped the new bit under the fold of the last pleat. (H)

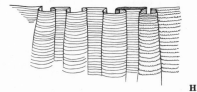

H

A neater way of getting the same effect (and what with the frequent travels of my material, the one I should have used) is to attach the material to curtain rods. The rods should be placed around the room as close to the ceiling, and as close to the floor, as possible. The material is cut 6″ longer than the length between the rods, and a 3″ tubular pocket is sewn at each end. The rods are then threaded through the tube and the material pushed into gathers. (I) Should you move, rods and material can move as well. If the next room is bigger, you'll need fewer gathers and longer rods, of course. If smaller, the material can be more thickly gathered. Only if the ceilings are higher are things difficult—unless one puts the rods lower down and makes a tent upward from them.

When a door or window is in the way, the material can be tied back. (The door must open to the outside for this to work.) On a window the looped-back material can act as a curtain. (See window of czar's carriage, photograph 1.) Looping back material in the same way over some plain shelves (bought ready-made) avoids building expensive bookcases. (See photograph 41, description on page 198.) A mirror treated similarly

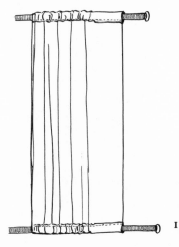

I

need not have a frame and can therefore be the cheap kind that is normally hung inside a cupboard door. (J)

To make a ceiling like the one in the czar's carriage, I first mark a circle at the center of the ceiling. I have my own system of measuring to find the center. (There are certain things I am cursed with losing: scissors, hammers and measuring tapes. All are vital to me. The lost pair of scissors is a disaster, especially if the material doesn't tear straight, but I'm willing to use any heavy object for a hammer and any old piece of string to measure.) To find the center of the ceiling, I staple a length of string into one corner, stretch it to the opposite corner and cut it there. Then I pull it down, double it and mark the middle. I then staple the string up again, and the mark gives me the center of the ceiling.

(It is no good measuring a 5′ piece of string off of a tape measure and using the same bit of string over and over again, relying on it to stay exactly 5′. String seems to grow with use. I carry the string length to whatever I want to have the same length, and compare. I avoid numbers.)

Should the plaster at the center of the ceiling refuse to hold or take staples, I have to attach a bit of wood to it. The piece of wood can be attached by screwing it into the ceiling joists (see page 198 for how to find where joists are) or by gluing it with a strong wood or ceramic adhesive. The wood need not

J

be circular, which is usually more complicated to find; an ordinary piece of board will do, as the material will cover it.

I take a length of material, scrunch up one end of it and staple this to the circle (or the board) at the center of the ceiling. Then I draw the material to the edge of the ceiling and staple it in a few irregular pleats. (K) More pleats will be necessary where the material is on the straight, and fewer where it is on the bias. (The bias makes its own pleats when stretched.) I staple the second scrunched-up length next to the first and draw that to the outside edge. I do this repeatedly until the ceiling is covered.

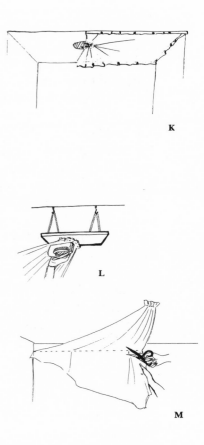

K

L

M

If the ceiling is too high, it can be lowered by lowering the board at its center. I staple a few strong strings onto the board (the strings are as long as the length by which I want to lower the ceiling) and attach them to the ceiling, either screwing them to the ceiling joists or suspending them from hooks. (L) If the ceiling is too low, attaching the ceiling material only a few inches down the wall will give the illusion that the tent has an apex. (In the czar's carriage, I came down 3″. See photograph 1.)

Once the material is drawn from the center to the side and attached there, it will leave an uneven remnant. (M) If one is clever about it, the uneven bits can be cut off and reused.

The center staples should be hidden by some form of rosette or knot. In the czar's carriage and in the blue-and-white tent (photographs 1 and 14), as well as in the canopy of the pink gingham bed (photograph 33), the knot is made out of woolen cords or fringe in the same colors as the materials (pages 219–20). The ceiling of the blue batik bedroom (photograph 38), as well as most other sunbursts inside the canopies, has a *chou* out of the same material as the sunburst (page 193).

The shutters for the second set of windows in the brown living room (photograph 4) are made out of 1″ thick plywood. (See pages 206–7 for how to make small shutters.) The two narrow windows are each covered by two panels; four panels cover the wider central window. I measured the space inside of the window frame exactly, subtracted 1″ from each panel for hinges and covering, and had the panels cut. When the plywood panels were cut, I covered them on both sides in the same material as the walls. I did this by first stapling a strip of padding to each side of the board. I didn't take the same piece of padding right around the edge; the padding would have changed the dimensions and made the board too wide. But I used only one piece of brown velvet to wrap around each section of shutter. (N) I stapled the material on three sides. These staples (at least on the long side) are hidden by hinges. It is usually not necessary to cover the staples at the top and bottom of the shutters: they seldom show. If, however, I think they might show, I cover them with a dab of oil paint in the same color as the material.

I used brass piano hinges to attach the shutters to the wall and to each other. (O) They are extremely fiddly to put on, but strong once attached and very good-looking. They come in brass or chrome, can be obtained from any better hardware shop and are much less expensive than they look.

When the shutters are open, they blend into the wall (photograph 5); closed, they enhance the jewel-box feel of the room (photograph 4). The window frame, which can be seen only when the shutters are closed, appears to be mahogany. In fact, I painted it. (For how, see chapter 16.) Huge brass hooks fasten the shutters at night—not to keep them closed, as they fit flush, but to be used as pulls for opening them. Also, because they look good.

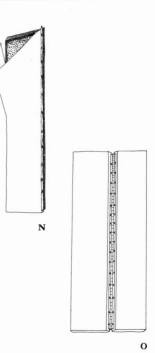

N

O

Three

I had some time between first seeing my new house and signing the final contract. I spent it rummaging through junk shops. In contrast to those fortunate people who can never find anything suitable, I think everything I see is ideal. Or worse, that it can be made ideal. This mad optimism made me believe, for example, that an understandably greatly reduced eleven-foot sofa covered in red, orange and yellow nasturtiums or some such bloblike equivalent would be perfect for the new house. The cushions were of chopped foam, a really nasty consistency, but the overall shape was all right, and if I got the house, the length would be perfect. If I didn't get the house, I could always make two sofas out of it. Therein lies my madness. To make two sofas out of one isn't that easy: I've tried; the insides tend to spill out.

I must confess that before I even owned the house, I had already bought for the living room: the really hideous 11′ sofa, three horsehair mattresses ($5 each at a country auction— impossible to resist such a bargain!), one Victorian chaise longue with a missing leg and covered in shredded red plush, one three-seater "conversation" with its springs dropping out and one rather formal Queen Anne sofa. I can't help thinking it remarkable that eventually all these, plus a few diverse chairs and yet another sofa, managed to fit into the finished room, but in it they all are.

When searching for a piece of furniture to rehabilitate, looking for shape is better than looking for color or for quality. Once you have found a shape that is pleasing, you should give slight consideration to the neighboring pieces. It's a mistake, for instance, to buy a huge overstuffed armchair to stand next to a small eighteenth-century sofa. (A)

Color and even quality can be changed. If cushions have foam, substitute feathers. If a chair is too tall, part of the legs can be sawed off; if too low, casters can be added; or if you do not want to slide around on it, four empty thread spools glued on to the legs work admirably well. (They must, of course, be stained or painted to match the chair.) If the legs are ugly, they can have material glued on them, or they can be hidden by a frill or pleats of the same material in which the chair is covered (pages 42–43).

Reupholstering furniture is easier than you might expect and saves almost as much in irritation as it does in money. I don't pretend that the amateur, especially the impatient one, can do as well as the best upholsterer. But certainly the amateur can do as well as the little man around the corner who is "half the price." (And who takes four months, puts foam rubber inside the cushion instead of feathers, loses one chair completely and puts the material inside out on the other two. This happened to me. I now sew my own.)

I find it easier to upholster (close-cover) than to make loose covers. When upholstering, I can pull the material to fit the shape, take tucks in it if I have failed, hold it all down with staples and glue something (gimp, braid or string) over the staples. A loose cover needs to really fit, without the advantage of being anchored to the piece of furniture. The only time I don't mind making a slipcover is when the chair or sofa already has a well-fitting slipcover and all I need to do is sew a thin covering of new material over it. I don't even mind making a new cover from scratch if I can tear apart the seams of the old, well-fitting one and cut the new slipcover according to the pattern of the old.

To know how much material to buy to cover a chair or a sofa, I usually drape a piece of string over the largest part of it, measure the length of the string, and double it. Not perfect, but quick. I hate measuring. Apart from never having the right measuring device, my mathematics are appalling. As I seldom buy material that costs more than a couple of dollars a yard, even if there is some left over, I don't feel like a spendthrift, and it always comes in useful anyway. A cushion, a stool, a cardboard box or just a loose-leaf binder is inevitably waiting to be covered with leftover material.

It is simpler to reupholster a sofa or chair if the old covering is left on. If the piece of furniture has been well-upholstered originally, it will most probably have piping at the seams.

Chairs without piping look rather poor and it's quite difficult to put new piping on (not to mention covering it, which has to be done with a strip of material cut on the bias—see page 44). Even if the piping is in an unacceptable color or the material on it is dropping off, it is invaluable to the amateur upholsterer. Whatever material is used for the new covering can be anchored to the piping.

One way to do this is to sew the new material to the piping on both sides by stitching under the piping and leaving it exposed. (B) If the old piping is quite the wrong color for the new material but still in good condition, it can be painted with the mixture I seem to use for most things: turpentine-thinned oil paint (pages 32–33). Another way is to cover the old piping by bringing the new material up to and slightly over it, wrapping it and sewing the material together under the piping. (C) A third way is to cover the existing piping in an almost orthodox manner: Cut a strip of material on the bias (page 44), cover the piping with it and then bring the upholstering material up to it on both sides, as in the first method. (D)

If chair cushions are meager, they can be puffed up with extra feathers. This is a messy job. I buy cheap bed pillows or feathers by the pound, isolate myself in the smallest room available (preferably a bathroom, since it's easier to pick up the escaped feathers there) and prepare to keep my breathing to a minimum. I rip open the seam to make a hole in the bed pillow large enough for my hand to get through, make an equal-sized hole in the cushion to be revitalized, and push handfuls of feathers from the one into the other.

For square sofa cushions I also buy bed pillows—the cheapest variety of feather pillow available (I haunt "white sales" for them)—and shake all the feathers to one side. I sew the empty edge on the machine and only then cut off the excess. (E)

I have a horror of the ready-made scatter cushion, a little postage stamp usually covered in fake Thai silk, costing the earth and filled with some disquieting lumpy substance. But I have a great weakness for cushions in general. They are a quick and easy way of achieving comfort, building up proportion, harmonizing colors or introducing new ones. They can also turn an old mattress—or a new bench—into a smart sofa. (See photographs 1, 2, 6, 12, 13, 14, 16, 18, 28, 47, 53, 54. For more cushion ideas, see pages 35–36 and 194–95.)

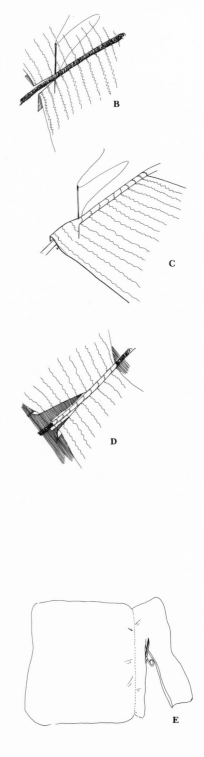

I bought the living room sofa (on the right in photograph 5) at a village auction. It had a good Chippendale-like shape, slightly formal (which I felt I needed for that part of the room), upright (a help to all the aged and less aged friends suffering from back trouble), with simple, inoffensive legs. It was covered in a particularly ugly, tattered, dirty green brocade, and its seat cushion had become lamentably thin and lumpy. Originally, however, the covering had been well done, so the valued piping was there, and the cushion, though thin, was made of feathers.

My equipment for covering the sofa was: 8 yards of cotton material 48" wide, two inexpensive (but feather) bed pillows, a spool of heavy-duty thread (any color), a straight needle, an upholsterer's curved needle (they can be bought at a needle shop, a Woolworth's or an upholsterer's), scissors, a few pins and the inevitable staple gun. And, to disguise the old piping, a tube of oil paint and some turpentine.

I covered the sofa in five hours. First, I cut away the tatters of the old, peeling green brocade. I did this to avoid bulges under my somewhat-too-thin new covering, a brown-and-cream cotton. The brocade was badly torn only on the arms, so I was able to retain all of the old piping. I painted the piping that outlined the arms and the cushion with burnt umber—

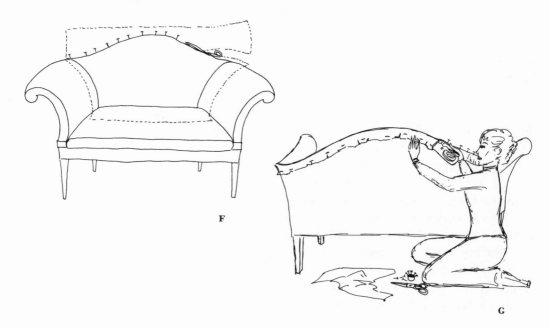

F

G

about 1/2″ squeezed out of the paint tube onto a plate, thinned with a thimbleful of turpentine and applied with a small watercolor brush. I had to give it two coats. Had I applied the first coat too thickly, it would have taken weeks to dry and turned hard.

When the paint dried, I pinned the material to the sofa and cut it to shape right there. First I cut a piece for the inside back, leaving enough (3″ or so) extra to tuck in between the back and the seat. (F) The top bit of the material I turned over the backrest and stapled to the back side of the wooden frame. (G) Once it was anchored, I drew it tightly over the inside back and sewed it into the crease between the inside back and the seat. I also sewed it into the creases between the inside back and the arms. I used the curved needle and the heavy-duty thread. (The joy of a curved needle is that when you make a stitch, the needle comes out again automatically. This makes it possible to sew cloth where only one side is reachable. [H]) I repeated the same procedure with the arms: first pinning, then cutting, while leaving ample material to tuck into the creases. I stapled the material to the frame under the curve of the arm, drew it over the armrest, sewed it to the piping on one side (folding 1/2″ of the material under) and sewed the other two sides into the creases, using the curved needle. On the outside of the armrest, I stapled the material under the curve of the arm, pulled it down, attached it to the piping on one side, stapled it to the wooden frame on the other side and at the bottom. Once the two armrests were covered, I sewed curved strips of material cut to shape between the piping on the front of the sofa arms. Along the base I ran another strip of material, stapled one edge to the wood and covered the staples by gluing on a border. Then, with large stitches, I attached the other edge to the seat under the cushion.

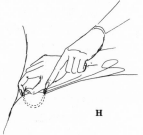

H

I puffed up the cushion with the help of some feathers from the two new bed pillows and then reupholstered it using three pieces of material, one each for the top and the bottom and a long band for the sides, leaving the piping exposed. Finally, to cover the outside back of the couch as well as to hide the various rows of staples, I used the curved needle to sew on the material 1/2″ past the staples along the top and the left and right side, and stapled it on at the base. (I)

I

Four

I had planned to put my desk under the window between the two bookcases (photograph 2). Once I put it there, with a chair in front of it (a desk without a chair seems to me as incongruous as rooms called "libraries" that have three rows of leather-bound, unread books in two matched cabinets), the desk chair looked wrong. It was turning its back on the rest of the seating. So I abolished the desk—not with much despair, as it was only a few boards on two trestles covered with some false suede. (See pages 149–50 for how to construct and use trestles, page 150 for covered tables.) When I removed the desk, however, I missed the brown of the suede and thought how well a brown suede sofa would pull everything together. The sofa had to be exactly 6′ long—that was the space I had —comfortable, deep and cheap. After many weeks of looking, all I had were cards from unhelpful, if hopeful, salesmen who seemed certain I would eventually buy their exorbitantly priced, "very popular" but to me totally unpalatable sofas. I decided to settle for a bed.

Since the shortest standard bed is 6′ 3″ long, I couldn't just go out and buy one. (I have found fantastic variations in the price of box springs and mattresses depending on what section of town I am shopping in. Perhaps, as salesmen try to tell you, all is lost for the back that lies on a bed costing less, and the one costing more builds straight-backed Adonises, but I doubt it. Mercifully, this difficult choice doesn't have to be made if the bed is to be turned into a sofa. No salesman has yet been heard to issue warnings about the jeopardy of sitting on an inexpensive sofa.)

There are places that make mattresses to measure. Generally, the least expensive made-to-order mattress will cost more than the least expensive ready-made one but a lot less than the expensive ready-made one. The only thing to remember when ordering is not to explain your intention too exactly. Make them believe the 4′ × 4′ mattress is for a fat midget. If you explain that it is to make a sofa, you will be told it is unsuitable for that; a sofa is something different and they make only beds.

Once when I ordered a 12' mattress for a very long and deep sofa I was making (the barn sofa, photograph 52), the men delivering the mattress asked if they could see the gentleman who was going to sleep on it. I was sorry I didn't have a Goliath folded up in the closet to show them.

For my recess under the window, I ordered a 6' long bed, 4' wide. When it arrived, I sawed off half of each of its legs; beds are higher than sofas. Compared with the enormous prices I had been quoted for suede sofas in the shops, I felt I had already saved a great deal of money with my mattress, and decided to cover it in real suede.

Fortunately, the mattress came with thick piping around the edge. (I think all mattresses do.) So, comforted by the thought that my job would be that much easier, I took on the task of covering the mattress. At a leather wholesaler's, I bought five skins. I seamed the two largest skins together on the machine. (Suede or any fine-quality leather sews perfectly well on an ordinary machine; all that may be needed is a different needle.) I sewed the seamed skins straight onto the mattress by hand, using a special three-cornered needle designed for sewing leather (it can be bought in department stores or upholstery shops) and working it in and out behind the piping. The stitching didn't need to be neat since it didn't show.

When the top of the mattress was covered, I made a strip out of the smaller, uneven bits cut off from the sides of the skin, fitting them together like a jigsaw puzzle to save leather. I seamed some pieces on the machine and some by hand, without worrying if little flaps of leather were left loose. I then sewed the strip to the edge of the mattress, but this time over and around the piping.

I covered the box spring in brown velvet left over from the walls and curtains. As the velvet is more or less the same color as the suede, it is hardly noticeable that I was too stingy to use the real thing. I used a curved needle (page 33) to sew the top edge of the material to the box spring (page 172). I hemmed the bottom edge and let it hang. (A)

A

I made two large suede-covered cushions for the back of the sofa and a bolster for each side (see photograph 2). Each cushion is filled with feathers from three bed pillows. The correct way of making a cushion that size would have been to first make a cover out of cambric. (Cambric is a waxed, down-proofed material.) This cover would have had three separate spaces inside it. It should look rather like a house with outside walls, a floor, a ceiling and two parallel inside walls. (B) A bag of feathers (or the contents of a pillow) would fill each of the compartments. This method ensures that all the feathers inside a large cushion don't creep to one side and leave the rest of the cushion an empty sack.

I made my cushion by sewing the three bed pillows together. I first had to square them off; otherwise my finished cushion would have looked like what it was: three bed pillows sewn together. To square off a bed pillow, I bend all its four corners inward and sew them down. The ear should be 4″ long on the bend. (C) After doing this to all three pillows—and continually hitting them into some form of square shape—I mark lines 2″ left and right from the seams. I line up my cushions, standing up, A, B and C. I then sew the marked line on the right side of pillow A to the line on the left side of pillow B, and the right-side line of pillow B to the left-side line of pillow C. I end up with more or less the same structure as a professional would to make a large feather cushion. (D) Except, of course, that the outer edges are not properly squared off. I find, however, that if the cover for the cushion is well-made, the sides will mold themselves to it.

I sewed the suede covers for the cushions on the machine with a heavy-duty needle—two rectangular pieces of leather with a 5″ strip between them (this includes 1/2″ seam allowance on both sides). The bolsters I filled with feathers and covered in suede as well. (For bolsters, see pages 117–18.)

The third sofa in my living room (in addition to the suede and the Chippendale ones) was the nasturtium-covered 11′ long thing. It filled the wall, but also seemed to fill the room. It was as ugly as it was big. In the dress fabric section of a department store, I found some brown flannel which, since it wasn't very good quality, would have made a rather stiff man's suit. But it makes an excellent and sturdy cover for a sofa.

Both the back and seat cushions had thin piping on them —nasturtium-covered. I felt the piping had to be covered in flannel to make it thicker. Painting such thin piping would not have helped it. I cut flannel strips on the bias (page 44), and for weeks, whenever I was watching television or talking to friends, a cushion was with me. First I covered the piping on

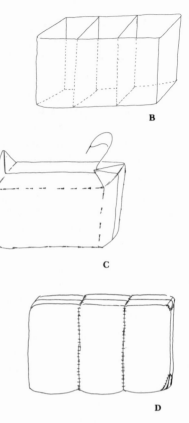

B

C

D

the cushion, using large stitches; then, also using large stitches, I covered the cushion itself on the top and bottom; then the side panels between the piping, with still larger stitches. By the time the material was on the top, bottom and sides, the cushion had been sewn so often in large stitches along the same line, it was as well sewn as if it had been sewn once in small, neat stitches. (E)

I covered the entire backrest by pinning on lengths of material the wrong side out. (F) I took the cover off, sewed it on the machine, turned it the right side out, slipped it back on and anchored it in large stitches with a curved needle to the bottom of the inside backrest and with staples to the back. Then I ran a strip of brown flannel around the base of the sofa, attaching it to the seat with the curved needle and thread, and to the wooden part of the base with staples (pages 33, 35 and 172). In a small trimmings shop, I bought the widest cotton fringe I could find (3″ wide), dyed it to match the brown flannel and glued it over the staples to hide them.

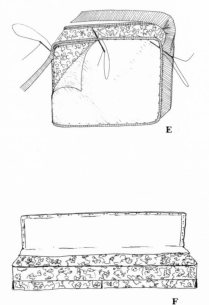

E

F

The fringe was an unusual extravagance for me: I usually make my fringes (pages 221–22) or find some old remnant to reuse. The nasturtium-covered sofa didn't have fringe for me to dye or reuse, only a kick pleat. Normally, I can find in an old box or paper bag some bit of trimming that can be adapted. But this sofa outdistanced any length of fringe I could hope to unearth from within my stores.

I blame my hoarding instincts on being a "displaced person." In fact, when we were called D.P.'s, I was a displaced child. I yearned for a cupboard of odds and ends to dress up in, such as existed in the home we had to leave. Now I have the dressing-up cupboard I wanted, but I use it to dress up furniture. If, in a rummage sale or at an auction, some cheap, tattered curtains appear, they may have fringes that have remained whole. I have bought curtains for their fringes, collapsed sofas for their horsehair or feathers, smashed tables for their legs, and packed them all away for some future use. For the joy of hoarding, two things are necessary: storage space and a phenomenal memory. As I have sufficient of neither, I have been reduced to dozens of easily accessible department store dress boxes, which I cover in material and keep under every bed, sofa or piece of furniture to which I have been able to staple fringes that hide what's underneath.

It's nice to be able to sit next to a fireplace. The 11′ sofa had to go against the window (photographs 4 and 5), for if I had placed it closer to the fireplace, there'd have been a 3′ corridor between it and the window. Ugly and space-consuming. Had I put a small sofa on the right side of the fire, jutting out, it would have blocked and reduced the size of the room. I tried it with the Chippendale-style sofa; it looked awful. An armchair didn't look too bad, but turned to the fire, it made the space between it and the columns useless. Placed against the wall, the armchair wouldn't profit from the fire. The Victorian chaise longue (seen in photograph 5) was the answer. It fills the empty corner by the columns, and when I sit on it, I have the impression of sitting by the fire—at least my feet do. When there are a lot of people in the room, a person sitting at the foot of the chaise can talk to the person—or persons—on the "conversation."

When I bought the chaise longue it had a few holes in the upholstery and one missing leg. I replaced the leg easily with one I had removed, and saved, from an old box spring and mattress that I had turned into a sofa. (The leg was the screw-in kind.) Even though the shape of the leg wasn't drastically different, the color was. So I painted all the wood that was showing (it was scratched anyway), including the new leg. Then I stippled it to look like mahogany. (See Chapter 16 for method.)

Into the holes in the upholstery I stuffed some balls of padding. I then recovered the chaise longue with some lining material, stapling it to the wood. I did this primarily to hold in the padding. I reupholstered the chaise longue in the same color (brown) but not in the same material as the 11′ sofa. This time I used linen, again from the dress material section of a department store.

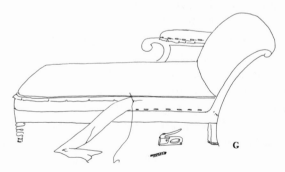

G

The seat of the chaise had the ever-welcome piping left. I sewed the seat material around it and another long strip of material under it. Then I stapled the long strip into the wood. I sewed a covering for the armrest and stapled that, all around, into the wood. (G)

To cover the backrest of the chaise longue, I stapled the material first into the wood at the base of the back, then to the wooden sides, across the top and to the front sides. Then I sewed it, with a curved needle, into the crease between the inside back and the seat. (H) I covered the top back staples by gluing on a band of the same material (see page 21 for how to make it); the bottom staples (as well as all the other staples that were showing) I covered with rows of brass-headed tacks. To do this, I first measured across a tack head and added a tiny fraction. Then I marked equidistant dots (separated from each other by the length of a tack head plus a fraction) where the material met the wood, all around the chaise. Then I hammered a tack into each dot. It took hours, but it wasn't difficult and the result looks professional. (I once tried to upholster directly with tacks, which I believe is the correct way, skipping the stapling stage. The results were disastrous. Little pleats and bumps formed, and the tack heads looked like a musical score.)

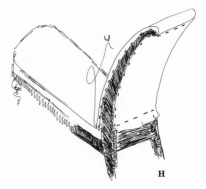

H

I finished off the chaise longue by making a bolster (see pages 117–18 for how to make them) and draping a paisley shawl at the foot of it. The chaise longue gave the room a nineteenth-century feel, and the paisley shawl furthered it.

I covered an invalid's chair (photograph 48) in very much the same way as the chaise longue, but I didn't use tacks. To cover the staples, I glued on thin bands of a border, the border taken from the batik that I had used to cover the chair itself.

A piece of furniture that only a decade or two ago would have evoked cries of disgust and now produces shouts of delight is that strangely named and shaped nineteenth-century seating arrangement called the "conversation." It is also called the *"indiscret,"* the "flirtation," the "vis-à-vis," the "confidente," the S-shaped "canapé" or the "tête-à-tête," depending on the amount of people it will seat and the nationality of the person talking about it. One stands in the center of the brown-velvet living room—it's probably an *"indiscret,"* as it seats three (photograph 4). Another, different one, on the left of the California living room (photograph 6), is an S-shaped "canapé"

I

—and perhaps a "flirtation." The one I found for my living room was in a pretty deplorable state but had the advantage of being small. The large circular ones—often with a palm sitting in the center (I)—were made primarily for hotels. That was, I suppose, why they were unfashionable for so long. "So like a bad hotel," I remember hearing. For me it would be a dream come true to live in such a hotel. And indeed even the Plaza Hotel in New York until recently used to sport one of those objects—rather akin to a huge feathered beret—in its front hall.

When I bought my three-seater conversation, it had a definite lean and the springs were dropping out. As I had to dismantle it in order to repair it, I realized it would be possible to make a simplified modern version out of wood and foam rubber. First, I would cut a three-leaf clover out of plywood. Then I would buy some 3″ doweling, cut it into six 5″ lengths for the legs and attach them to the bottom of the "clover" with glue and screws. (J) The top of the wood I would cover with 3″ foam rubber, cut to the outside shape of the clover, but leaving a central triangle bare. (K) I would then staple lining material under the wood, stretch it over the foam rubber and pull, so that the cushioned part would look curved. I would attach the lining, via more staples, into the center triangle, creasing it and taking darts. (L) Into the uncovered center of the wooden seat I would drill a hole 3″ in diameter. I would cut four equal triangles, each the size of the foam-rubber trian-

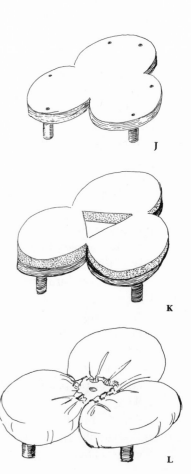

J

K

L

gle, out of plywood, glue three together, then glue them to the fourth to form a pyramid. I would attach a 3″ piece of doweling to the bottom triangle with glue. I would wrap the pyramid in thin foam rubber and staple it on. When the pyramid and the seat itself were covered in whatever material they were to be covered in, I would slot the pyramid into the middle of the seat. (M) I would hide the rather meager-looking legs by stapling on a skirt and some fringe around the edge.

I treated my conversation in more or less the same way. The doweling had broken off—hence the lean. I stuck on a new piece of doweling, and the backrest straightened up. The springs that were dropping out needed to be tied back up. This is an unpleasant job and one I avoid if I possibly can. Not that it is so difficult, but it takes time, is dusty and the springs are often rusty.

Springs are tied with string, usually four strings to a spring, although the especially well-made ones have eight strings. With time, some strings tear. This causes the spring to hang in a lopsided fashion, the seat to become crooked and an ominous bulge to appear at the bottom of whatever piece of sprung furniture has suffered the accident. The first thing to do is to remove the dust cover (the piece of brown canvaslike material covering the bottom of an upholstered chair or sofa). If I find the spring itself is broken, I'm afraid I behave like a surgeon who sees no hope for the patient. I close the chair back up and send it to an upholsterer. If it is only the strings that have torn, however—and this is more usual—they can be tied up again.

My way, I hasten to add, is most certainly not the correct way, but it is the fastest way to make an obviously sick chair look a little healthier. I turn the chair upside down. I tie up the strings that have torn by knotting a new piece of string to the old, praying the old one is not totally rotten. I tie down the springs until they are all an even height. Then I hammer tacks into the four sides of the chair frame and run a network of strings across, looping them into the top of the springs. (N) Over the springs I weave chair webbing (O), and over that I staple on a new dust cover or any other strong material I have lying about.

The conversation has a buttoned backrest, and a very strangely shaped buttoned backrest at that. The conventional

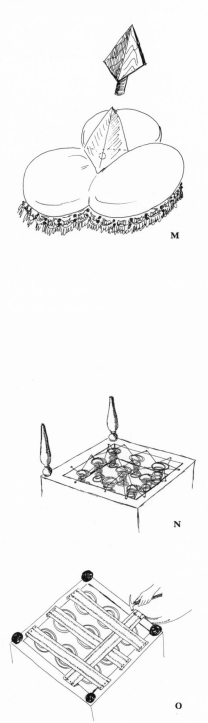

M

N

O

way to cover it would be first to remove the old buttons and have them professionally recovered. Then the new material would be put on in three sections, each section cut and sewn to shape, and stitched to the upholstery with a curved needle, the stitches hidden with braid or piping. Then the buttons would be sewn back on, using a very long upholstery needle (available from upholstery shops) and sewing right through the upholstery. I can't say I covered mine correctly, but I did it faster. Although I did cut the material into three sections, I didn't remove the buttons. I simply held each section up over the old covering and marked with a pencil where each button was. Then I cut a small slit (the size of a tight buttonhole) for each button and pushed the original buttons through the slits in the material.

I stapled the sections of material to whatever wood I could reach on the backrest along the spine and at the base. (P) I covered the staples by gluing on, with a suitable material glue, a strip of the same material, sewn on the machine. (I make the strips for furniture the same way as I do those to cover staples on the wall. See page 21.)

The now exposed buttons were a rather dirty orange. They certainly didn't match the brown-and-yellow paisley cotton with which I was covering the "conversation." I took a paint-brush, reached for my box of oil paints and painted the buttons in burnt umber thinned with turpentine in the same way as I paint piping (pages 32–33).

I upholstered the three seats of the conversation in the way I have already described, utilizing the existing piping and sta-pling the material onto the wooden base. To hide both the staples and the rather ugly legs, I used a collection of fringes. There are a few things in decoration—and fringes are one of them—that, if one is to use at all, one might as well use to excess. The first fringe I stapled around the conversation was some I had left over from the large brown sofa. I bleached out the brown and then soaked it in some strong tea to yellow it. (See pages 195–96 for how I bleach material.) The second fringe, stapled on top of the first, consists of brown tassels made by me. (For how, see pages 220–21.) I pulled the whole thing together by gluing a separate border along the top edge. (Q)

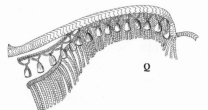

I decided to hide the legs not only because they were ugly but because there were already quite enough legs on display in

R

S

the room. I find that a thing to watch out for when arranging a room with a lot of seating space is either too many legs or too many skirts. Arrange some diverse chairs next to a few small tables, and in no time the room looks as though there's nothing in it but malformed legs. (R) At the risk of saying the obvious, it is better to alternate legs with skirts. (S)

A way of leading the eye away from a particularly incongruous set of legs without weighing them down with fringes or a skirt is to cover the legs in the same material with which the chair is covered. If the legs are straight, this can be done quite quickly with a staple gun. If they are curved, the material can be glued on. The round legs on the bed in photograph 40 have just a piece of material tied around them in the fashion of the Christmas present one is too lazy to wrap properly. (T)

T

I reupholstered the two Louis XVI–style armchairs (photograph 3) in a Provençale cotton. It was an extremely thin cotton. Twelve years ago, when I covered them, Provençale prints were not as popular as they have become. They were more reasonably priced but did not come in as many varied qualities—for upholstery, clothes, napkins, quilted or plain, and so on—as they do now. My twelve-year-old chairs are just now beginning to show slight signs of wear on the arms. Considering how many human arms rubbed against them over all those years, I think they have lasted well.

The chairs were my first "serious" upholstery job. I bought them at an auction. They were comparatively cheap, made out of light, unpolished fruitwood and covered in a salmon-colored embossed velvet almost, but not quite, the color of the wood and clashing with it. They were not tempting to the eye.

Around the backrest, the arms and the base, they had silk braid. I pulled it off. This exposed the many little tacks holding the material to the chair. There was no way I was going to pull them out. With what? And how long would it take? The staple gun had recently come into my life. I cut the Provençale cotton the same size as the inside back of the chair and stapled it on, just past the little nails. I repeated this on the arms and at the base of the chair. The material that I had stapled along the base I sewed to the existing material on the seat under the cushion, using a curved needle. (u) The cushion was nice and plump. I didn't remove the old cover, but sewed the new cotton covering straight over and around the piping (page 31) and to the old velvet.

U

I felt rather guilty that it was so easy, as if I was trespassing in the realms of upholstery carrying a staple gun. I knew that really well-upholstered chairs have double piping, so I tried that. The time it took was penance enough. I have devised shortcuts since then.

I buy 1/4" piping cord in a department store or anyplace that sells sewing supplies. I have used ordinary twine when I couldn't get hold of any cord, but cord is better.

The material to cover the cord has to be cut on the bias. Folding a square of material into a triangle forms the bias. For single piping, I make strips about 1" wide; for double piping, about 2" wide. If I have a ruler handy, I use it. I don't bother to draw lines, which I probably should, but cut the material along the ruler. (v) Then I seam the strips together, the angled ends just overlapping. (w)

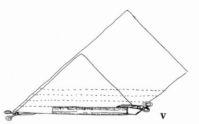

V

Piping should be sewn on the machine with a piping foot. I don't have one and don't know how to use one. It works quite well on an ordinary machine and even better by hand. Stitching a strip of material around some cording is just the sort of work that can be done with the hands while concentrating on something else.

W

For double piping—as used on the armchairs—I first cut two pieces of cord the length of the circumference of the upholstered backrest of the chair. (Or the circumference of whatever I am going to surround with the double piping.) Then I cut, on the bias, strips of material that, when joined together, are just the same length as the cord plus 1". I fold the strip down the center and iron it. This gives me a center line. I open the

strip up and lay the first cord next to the center line, slightly
to the left of it, on the wrong side of the material. I fold the
left side of the material over the cord and let it overlap the
center line by about 1/4". I pin it and sew it along the center
line. (I prefer doing this by hand, but it may be on account of
my having given up on the piping foot!) To the right of my
stitches I lay a second cord and cover it with the right-hand bit
of material, with 1/4" overlap. I attach it the same way as the
first, with stitches down the center line. (x)

On a chair that is double-piped by an expert, there is no join
visible in the double piping. God knows how it's done. On my
own chair I have no difficulty finding where the piping joins,
but I have to look quite carefully. Mercifully, I have never met
anyone who examines double piping when they enter a room.
Perhaps professional upholsterers do when visiting one another.

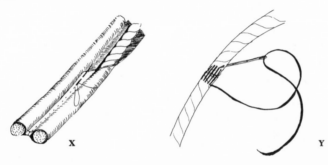

X   Y

When my two pieces of piping cord are covered, I sew the
ends of the cords together—not overlapping them, but making
them just meet. I do this by sewing the cords with long, looped
stitches. (y) A dab of glue works almost as well, but it takes
time to set. Once the piping is joined, it forms a circle (one
hopes of the right size). I fold one of the end flaps of material
over the other, turning it 1/4" under. (z) Then I sew it. The
visibility of the seam depends on the neatness of the sewing.

Once the circle is complete, it gets glued over the staples.
This again takes quite a while and requires patient holding
until the piping has stuck. I have attached piping quite successfully by stapling it down along the center line, avoiding, if
possible, the staples underneath. Then I spread glue over the
top staples and hold the two rows of piping together until they
stick to each other and hide the staples.

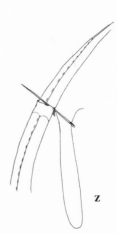

Z

As much as I may object to doing it, I couldn't avoid making some slipcovers. I made the one for the couch in the green kitchen (photograph 23), and I made the blue denim one for the batik living room (photograph 15). The blue one was a new sofa—uncovered, with foam-rubber seat cushions and no back cushions—but it was the only inexpensive large sofa I could find in a hurry. (I got rid of the foam-rubber cushions—only to use them later, heavily disguised. See page 217.)

To make the slipcover, I first laid lengths of material over the sofa, the wrong side out. (A) Then I cut the lengths into pieces to fit the exact shape of the sofa, adding 1/2″ for seams. The only places I allowed for extra material—about 5″—was at the bottom for hemming and on the inside back and sides for tucking in.

I pinned the pieces together as I cut them (B), then took the slipcover off the sofa and sewed the pieces together on the machine. I left the back panel open on both sides, to make the slipcover easy to pull on and off. A strip of Velcro on both sides holds it closed. (C)

For the six sofa cushions, I first made covers out of cambric —plain ones for the three back cushions, with internal separations for the seat cushions—and stuffed them with feathers bought by the pound. (See pages 35–36 for how to make cushions.) The denim cushion covers I piped (pages 44–45). I cut two equal pieces of material for the top and bottom of each

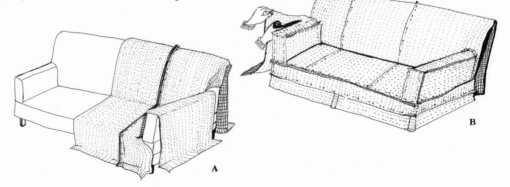

A

B

cushion, and a long side strip to surround it. I made double the length of the side strip in matching piping. (D) I pinned it all together, wrong side out, with the two rows of piping facing inside. I then sewed all around the cushion cover on the top side. On the bottom side I sewed three quarters of the way around and put a zipper in the last quarter. (E)

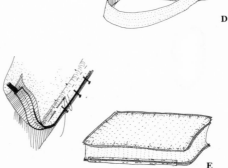

D

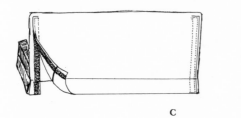

C

E

On one wall of my brown living room, I have a montage of pictures and objects (photograph 3). If I had a Vermeer, I wouldn't crowd it. As I don't, I have a collection of memories, works by friends or things that please or entertain me. There is no limit to the things that can be hung on a wall. If attractively grouped together, they will look a thousand times better than a mediocre oil painting hanging in isolated prominence. Once I painted a quick outline in oils to fit a rather nice empty frame. The frame carries the not very good sketch. (See top left-hand corner of photograph 3) If I find a cheap, ugly picture in a passable frame, it is sometimes worth buying the horror for the frame. If the frame is badly gilded, an irregular coating of a metallic paint, Liquid Leaf, may save it. If it's an ugly color, rubbing in some oil paint, straight out of a tube, can help.

I also framed an enlarged, out-of-focus photograph (second from left and second from top). It is nothing if not Impressionistic. Below it I have a collage rolling pin by a Czech artist named Kolach, hence "collage by Kolach"—the joke is feeble, but the rolling pin is charming. It consists of black-and-white photographs torn out of glossy magazines, glued over a rolling pin and then lacquered. If making a collage in this manner, it is important to tear the pictures. Cutting them out with scissors gives a hard and thick edge, whereas torn bits of paper overlap one another more smoothly. The same process can be used to cover boxes or screens or simply to make a collage picture. Driftwood can look lovely on a wall, either among pictures or by itself. A picture with an irregular shape among more conventionally framed pictures can do wonders to cheer things up. (See angled picture in photograph 3.)

With a lot of pictures on a wall, some are quite likely to hang crookedly in time. This is less likely to happen if each picture hangs on two nails or picture hooks instead of one.

If I hang an object among my pictures (my wall montage includes an articulated wooden hand, probably once an artist's or glovemaker's prop, and a couple of small carvings), I fasten it to the wall with gilt picture wire. I don't use the wire as it comes, but unwind the many strands and use only one. The single strand, which is practically invisible, I wind around the object and then hook onto two or three small nails.

There is a convention for grouping things on a wall, one that I seem to have followed on three sides of the wall pictured in photograph 3 and forgotten on the fourth side. It is: If you form straight lines—in other words a square, rectangle or triangle—with the outside of the pictures, you can go haywire on the inside. (A)

A series of something or a made-up collection of something (prints, drawings, book illustrations, children's paintings, even photographs) looks quite attractive suspended from the same ribbon, webbing or cord, particularly in a room with a nineteenth-century flavor. I have also used strips of striped material in this way, or borders from some tattered old shawl. I don't hang the pictures directly onto the border, since it would entail both waste (the pictures would hide most of it) and a lot of fiddly counting to get the distances right. I hang the pictures in a vertical line, then staple material to the lower back edge

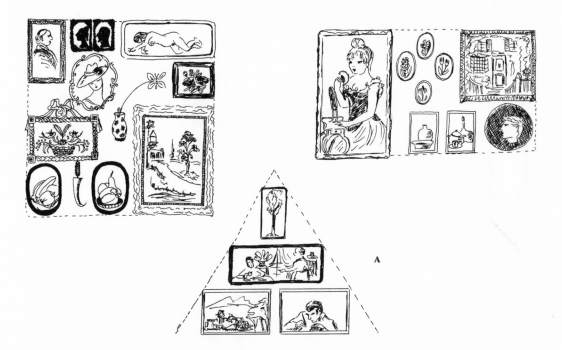

A

B

C

of one picture and tuck it in behind the top back edge of the next. (B) For the top, I make a rosette (page 222) or a three-sided ribbon out of the same band of material. To make a three-sided ribbon, I sew a third loop to a conventional-looking bow (C) and nail or staple that to the top picture or to the wall. On the last picture of a series I leave a tab hanging out. Such a series can just be seen hanging on the stairs of the California house (photograph 9). In the California living room, I joined the two papier-mâché and mother-of-pearl trays over the fire-place with two pieces of black velvet ribbon (photograph 6). I hung the trays separately (they already had a ring attached to them) and scotch-taped the two ribbons onto the trays, from one tray to the other.

Plates hung on a wall in this way—seemingly suspended from a ribbon—are extremely decorative. (See Chapter 21, figure A.) But usually I hang the ribbon first and then hang the plates over the ribbon. (For how to hang plates, see page 90.) To group my blue-and-white china in the red dining/television room (photograph 10), I started with the soup tureen and tried to balance the rest of the china in more or less of a circle around it. (See page 90 for description.)

For a more eighteenth-century look, I hang a picture on some scrunched-up material. (D) I take a square of material, about the size of a head scarf, cut off one of the corners, make a rosette or a ribbon out of it, scrunch up the rest and tuck the other narrowing end behind the picture. Or I use two pieces of material for a double ribbon. I don't necessarily suspend the picture from the material, but hang it on a hook and use the material only for decoration. (See page 49.) (If the picture looks like, or is, an eighteenth-century picture, then of course all the better!)

All these nice amusements look rather strange with modern —above all abstract—pictures. These demand uncluttered walls from which to put their message across.

D

Seven

I was more than flattered when a friend, a well-known writer, asked me to come to California to do his house. I arrived with nothing—no knowledge of California, no addresses of suppliers—and knowing nothing about the already purchased house in the Hollywood hills. The house turned out to be in the Spanish style, the style I learned to appreciate the most of all the many, varied flights of architectural fantasy rampant in California. This particular one, however, must have been conceived by an architect with a loathing for symmetry. It's no pleasure to find a slit of a door next to a huge arch, next to a square window, next to a lengthwise rectangular window. And not a molding or architrave framing anything. Just as well. This way the interior could make no claim to a classical style I would have to follow.

If I try to think of the ideal house for California, I think of the outside coming in. White walls framing huge windows, the windows pictures of color. Bright skies and bright vegetation entering a calm room, ruling it. White furniture—little of it —and huge plants. (The smog that would creep in to blacken the white furniture I will ignore for the moment.)

Alas, I had a low ceiling, no view and dark rooms to work with—and besides, I hadn't been invited all that distance to help arrange a Spanish hacienda or a beige-and-white oasis.

What made the house dark was the sumptuous greenery outside, the heaviness of it. I felt the house called for a toned-down look of the mid-nineteenth century, with an Oriental influence. Drapery, but not too much. Plants and fringes, but not too many. Regency furniture bordering on early Victorian. Opulent colors; perhaps less opulent clutter. A lot of black and red.

There was no furniture in the house. Some borrowed cots were the only blemish on the empty floors. The house, as well as the owners, were giving me the freedom to embark in which-ever direction I pleased. I was free to choose whatever I found. I was delighted, but I was also terrified.

I find nothing more daunting than being asked to create a backdrop for someone whose work I admire. Writers' tastes are historically or literarily influenced, seldom visually. So when we discussed the house, I suggested, "Perhaps the dining room could be out of Turgenev, almost a set for *A Month in the Country*. Reds and dark wicker, with perhaps a glint of gold that the samovar might have given in the twilight of a Russian evening." The bedroom: "What about something reminiscent of Princess Caroline Murat's, in the watercolor by the Comte de Clarac? Light voiles and mahogany Empire furnishings." And the library: "Could it not be like the one belonging to Lord Macaulay at the Albany in London?" I produced an illustration, torn from a magazine, of a reproduction of an oil painting in which even Macaulay—not to mention the room—was obscured by vast piles of books. As for the living room, low, huge and dark: "Should it perhaps echo the somber lushness of a Venetian *palazzo*, when Venice was the gateway to the East and traders brought back every imaginable style and object?"

Those were the ideas I tried. They were accepted—whether out of kindness or persuasion, who's to know? I am pleased with the result: It looks as I first imagined it, which always comes as a surprise. What is more important, it pleases the owner.

The first thing I did on my arrival was to scan the local yellow pages for auction houses. I eliminated those names that were familiar or that I was told were in smart neighborhoods. Nowadays only people who are overconfident in their knowledge of the art market dare to walk into an unknown antique shop, especially in an unknown city, and pay the prices asked. Anybody with any sense would rather trust the price paid at an auction. It means, however, that too many enthusiastic auction addicts can push the price up unrealistically by outbidding each other. This happens when many people are in pursuit of the same "tasteful piece of furniture in good condition." I prefer the auctions where a few furious dealers rake over junk in "bad" condition, or where whole households, including rusty pots and pans, old-fashioned kitchen appliances and old trunks, come and go. There the possibilities still exist. There, if one is lucky, a sow's ear may be hiding out of which to make a silk purse.

I was not kept to a strict budget for the California house; nevertheless, I know where such talent as I might have lies. It is certainly not in going from one smart decorating shop to another and wasting hours "making contacts" there. A terrible sort of exchange of credentials takes place: "Yes, we know that decorator, no, we wouldn't work with that one, in Paris they are making the shades this way, so-and-so is now also making sheets, have you seen the new light fixtures from Italy?" In exchange for this boring and, at least for me, hard work (and if my credentials are right), I'll be sold something expensive and perhaps be given a few addresses. I have no talent for these maneuvers and begrudge the time. I can put it to better—and far more satisfying—use by trying to face-lift a bit of junk into something original.

The particular auction house I found was everything I could ask for. Of the four I phoned, it was the only one to have an auction that afternoon. It had no such things as catalogs, previous viewings or estimates; not even an eagle-eyed auctioneer landing the inadvertent nose-scratcher with an unwanted purchase. Just a friendly seller, wandering between his wares, sometimes ignoring a bid—presumably to hang on to the item for the following week's sale or for his own use. At the end of the day, my host and I returned the proud owners of: the two living room armchairs (photographs 7, 8 and 9), at this stage covered in spotted and torn red plush; the bench with the curved sides just visible through the living room arch in the same photographs; the two small columns now used as tables in front of the banquettes—one can just be seen on the left of photograph 6; and the child's chair and the folding camp chair, also in photograph 6. Quite a few other objects that we bought are dispersed around the house: the wicker, some of which is in the music/guest room (photograph 53); the mahogany sideboard that became the dining room sideboard (photograph 19); and the earthenware pots—turned blue—in the supper room (photograph 18).

Needless to say, I was back again the following week. As we had easily been the most prolific buyers the week before, we were now greeted enthusiastically by the owner. "Last week," he said, "we had a lot of junk, but this week it's a really good sale." There they stood, dozens of reproduction mahogany dining room tables with matching chairs and modern living room suites in "good condition." We left, sadly, but with our purse intact.

The first room to come under attack was the living room. It is a large room (15' × 30'), the ceiling far too low for that size of a room, all openings (six of them) of different height and width. And despite the multitude of windows, doors and arches, the room was dark. The beams of the ceiling were painted in a thick brown paint (which was in no way reminiscent of wood), as was the frame of the unexpectedly wonderful curved window (see photograph 6). The curved window became my guide. I would copy its curves wherever I could; I would base the room on it. I needed a carpenter—not as easily found as said. I didn't know one in California. The few inquiries I made revealed that a month would pass before anyone was free—and surely yet another before I could persuade any of them to accept my shortcuts. I had only one month. I did something that at first might make the title of this book seem inappropriate: I flew over a carpenter from England.

After laborious calculations, I decided my flamboyant plan would, in fact, be financially advantageous to my client. The comparatively low cost of stand-by air travel from London to the United States, coupled with the desire of a brilliant carpenter I knew (and who knew my ways) to see California, made it less of a mad idea than it might seem. In exchange for a ticket, board and lodging in the grand but misproportioned house, Mr. Lewis instructed each morning in the art of carpentry. Each afternoon and late into the night, I and two charming students who were looking for pocket money frantically tried to put into practice what we had been taught in the morning. Our aim was to give proportion to those six different-sized openings leading into the living room.

The first step was to take away the heavy window frame from the window, mount it on the opposite wall at the same height, build some shelves within it and a cupboard under it (photograph 9). The cupboard stores the television set (on wheels), musical equipment and unsightly bottles. (A)

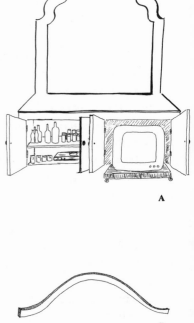

A

B

The frame with the shelves and cupboard was pretty much the same height as the arch next to it. The three French windows on the next wall, however, were much shorter and looked squat near the tall, curled arches. I had to try to give them the illusion of height. Using an electric jig saw, we cut, out of 3/4″ plywood, three curved pieces 2″ wide. (B) The curve was about the same as the curve on top of the arched window (and on top of the window frame), minus the leaps at either end. We sanded down the edges of the three curved pieces with an electric sanding machine. We did the same to six long, straight pieces of 2″ × 1″ wood. The curved pieces were then nailed up above the short French windows at the same distance from the ceiling as the other arches. The long, straight pieces of wood support the curved ones and reach the floor. The gap between the curved pieces of plywood and the tops of the doors is covered by white shades (photograph 6. See pages 190–91 for how the shades were made).

On the wall opposite the three French windows and next to the fireplace there was, surprisingly, yet another French window (photograph 8). The photograph illustrates the incongruity of heights that was such a worry to me when I first saw the room. I didn't want another white shade next to the rather bizarre white fireplace to disrupt and unbalance the wall even more. How I wished that French window away—it led nowhere—yet the room needed every bit of light there was. I decided to camouflage the problem with a screen.

We found a Chinese screen at an auction—unfortunately, too short a one. When photograph 8 was taken, I hadn't yet raised it to the height of the French window it now hides. To raise the screen, I made a matching but shorter frame out of pieces of 2″ × 2″ wood. In fact, I made it the shape of another little screen, hinged. I stapled some canvas onto it—not the expensive kind from an art shop, but the inexpensive sort from a fabric shop. I then painted the canvas with three coats of flat black paint. There was no point in trying to emulate the nineteenth-century paper of the large screen, nor the design on it, so I treated the small, new screen as if it were different and divided by a chair rail. I did paint the edges of the new, supplementary screen to match the style of the wispy border on the original one, but I didn't try to paint a central design, not wanting to detract from the Chinese screen. (c) Then I glued the two screens together. The unbalanced French window is now hidden by the screen from most points in the room, although it still lets in some light (photograph 9). And the finished room looks as if all the doors and windows are more or less the same height.

Left and right of the large curved window we built corner banquettes (photograph 6). We built skeletons out of 2″ × 1″ battens and screwed them to the sides of the wall. More 2″ × 1″ battens marked where the backrests would come. (D) We covered the seats and the bases in chipboard—all, that is, but the corner base panels, which we left open to place stereo speakers into. This way the speakers were hidden but the sound was not impaired. There is a removable chipboard panel in the seat of the banquettes, should it be necessary to reach the speakers, and so as to use the banquettes for additional storage. (E) Later, when I covered the banquettes (see page 74), I stapled the canvas covering in front of the speakers, minus any wadding or foam.

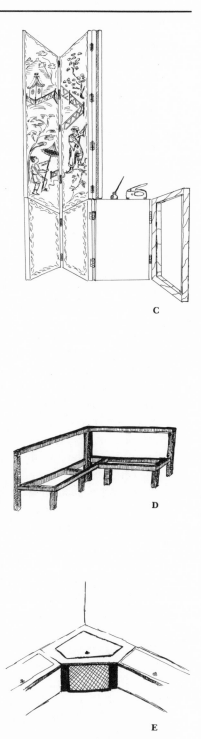

C

D

E

Eight

Before any more work could take place, a few decisions on lighting had to be made. Lights. How important they are! And how I hate them. They are the most difficult things to get right. The choice of lighting depends on how much there is to spend, where the existing wiring and plugs are placed, and the sort of activities the lights should light. But it doesn't stop there. There are so many different lighting possibilities—most of them visually incompatible with one another—that I'm hard put to make a choice.

I make constant trials and errors with indirect lighting—uplighters, downlighters, spotlights, lighting tracks. No matter how strategically I try to place spotlights, I end up with the same results: an occasional blinding glare where I cross the path of what I thought was a discreetly placed spotlight, with the rest of the room in semidarkness.

Over the years I have found my *modus vivendi* with lights. I never have a center light—it makes everyone and everything hideous. Of course I'd love to have huge chandeliers aglow with candles; of course I'd love to live in Versailles. But in the meantime I don't want to live with two spotlights hanging in the center of any ceiling I've had anything to do with. Nor do I want an eyeball light or downlighter harshly glaring at me from the ceiling—except perhaps in a kitchen. (I like downlighters over kitchen counters. A good strong pool of light over the chopping board is a help. Over the balding heads of friends, it's not.)

If there already is a naked bulb in the middle of a bathroom ceiling and I don't want to incur the cost of moving it, I cover it with a round, inexpensive basket lampshade. First, however, I darken the lampshade with some burnt umber (same process as described on page 76) and then lacquer it with a shiny lacquer. This gives it a nineteenth-century appearance (anyway, an old appearance) rather than the "easiest and cheapest" look.

In the California living room I made a small compromise and included a few spotlights. They are the weakest directional spotlights available (20 watts). I put them on the ceiling (photographs 6 and 8) in place of a few of the rather surprising knobs (to be seen in the same photos), which we shaved off. These particular spotlights have the bulb so deeply set into the shade that they cause very little glare. But then neither do they give much light. They quite pleasantly pick out objects, light up pictures and make pools of shimmer on the red walls. I used the same weak directional spotlights to light the pots in the supper room (photograph 18), as well as the pots and china in the blue-and-white-striped tent (photograph 14).

I don't mind uplighters (the bucket kind, standing on the floor), providing they are out of the way. They seem to me possible only in a large, sparse room where they can stand behind some piece of furniture (a freestanding sofa or a table, for example), illuminating a plant or statue. If not, they blind, are stumbled over or are used as a wastepaper bin, with unpleasant results.

The ideal bedside lamp seems to me to be the metal one with the hinged arm. It used to be called (and probably still is) the Billy Baldwin light, after its designer. You can pull it over your book when reading and push it out of the way when less light is necessary. There are models in brass or chrome, without lampshades (the shades can be bought separately—for the most part I use dark-brown or black lacquered paper ones), with shades—harmless beige linen ones, or with their own metal shades (see photograph 54). The ones with metal shades give less light, but take up less space. I find these lamps so useful that I also put them next to sofas or anywhere else a person with a book, newspaper, pen or needle may wander to. In the California living room I placed them above the banquettes (photograph 6) as well as in the bedrooms pictured in photographs 41 and 42. They are above the sofa bed in the tropical studio (see photograph 47). I used the same lamps in my own living room left and right of the suede sofa, where they double as tiebacks for the curtains (photograph 3) and for which I made the shades myself.

In the late fifties, when I was arranging my first apartment, I searched for large Chinese-looking vases to make into lamps. (See London living room and New York studio, photographs 5 and 49.) Once found, they would remain, month after month, unwired. Once wired, the long wait for the shade began. The nice plain parchment shades seemed to have vanished from the market, and the pleated silk ones were beyond my means. Eventually I learned to make my own. I buy wire frames obtainable from large department stores and do-it-yourself shops, and cover them.

When I find the right skeleton for a lampshade, I wind some off-white or pale-pink seam binding around it, securing the first and last end with a few stitches. That way I hide the wires and have something to attach my lining to. (A) For the lining I use a piece of pink silk. Pink creates a warm and flattering light. I try to make the lining fit by cutting it into four pieces and seaming the pieces together. I put this inside the wire frame —seams facing the outside—and attach it to the beribboned wires. (B) As it's inevitable (at least for me) that it doesn't fit perfectly, I take a nip and tuck against and around the armature until the silk is taut.

For the outside of the lampshade I buy off-white silk chiffon. I cut a strip 2″ more than the height and twice the circumference of the lower edge of the shade. Then I pleat the chiffon straight onto the shade, sewing it at the top and at the bottom. When it is finished, I cut two narrow strips of chiffon on the bias (page 44). One is to hide my untidy stitching on the top of the shade, the other on the bottom. I sew them on as neatly as possible, turning the frayed edges under (C)—and the shade is finished. (See photographs 2, 3, 35 and 49.) It all takes a long time. That, plus the fact that department stores are now

A

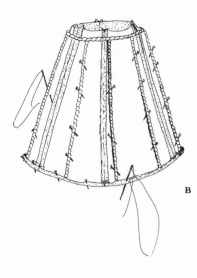

B

C

flooded with the Chinese jar-shaped lamps I'd spent years looking for, has turned me off lampshades whenever an alternative form of light is possible.

In the California dining room and in the bookcase of the living room, I used shadow lights (under the tray in photograph 9 and under the picture in photograph 19). I had never seen anything like them before I spied them at an auction. They are a perfectly ordinary strip light hidden by a frame that is ornate on three sides and flat on the fourth. The two shadow lights that came up at auction were gilded. I have since made my own, gilded some (page 65) and painted others to match whatever they are standing on.

To make one, I buy an ordinary 9" strip light. I make a box for it 4" longer, wider and higher than the light. To make the box, I use a piece of ornate molding for the front and plywood for the rest. It would look better if the ornate molding was (as it is in the originals) on three sides, but to glue some plywood together is easier than mitering molding. When the box is painted overall, it is hardly noticeable that some bits don't quite match up. I drill a hole through the back panel for the wire to pass through and screw the strip-light fixture to the "floor" panel. (D)

A shadow light must stand on a high shelf under a picture or whatever else it is meant to illuminate. If it stands below eye level, one sees only the ugly strip light. I am not sure they weren't designed to hang upside down, attached to the wall. Personally, I wouldn't like them that way at all; if that sort of light is wanted, an inoffensive picture light, either in brass or painted to match the wall, looks better. (See lights over the hatches in photographs 10 and 28.)

In the California dining room (photograph 19), I used one of the shadow lights to light the Dutch still life. The other light in the room comes from a brass overhead Edwardian chandelier—a contradiction of my principles, but I couldn't resist it. It was just what I wanted for the Chekhovian (or what I hoped was Chekhovian) atmosphere of the room. When the photograph was taken, it was, alas, not yet hung properly. The chandelier is now on a pulley, for which the original handle is just visible in the photograph. This way it can be pulled down low over the table when the table is used for writing or card playing.

D

The chandelier is on a dimmer. Any lights that are being newly wired, provided they are in a room that is going to be used for entertaining, should be put on a dimmer. There is nothing more depressing than trying to work or read without enough light. On the other hand, people look, think and speak better in subdued lighting. The dimmer makes both alternatives possible.

If the lighting is already installed and dimmers for it would cost too much, I put lower voltage bulbs in the existing lights and attach a dimmer to the plug of one lamp with a strong bulb in it.

Electrical sockets, light switches and dimmers can be bought in brass or chrome. It is these small details that do a lot to smarten a room. They also cost a lot. They cost to buy, they cost to install. If plastic switches are already there, they might as well stay. You can always disguise them. In the rooms in which I would like to use brass switches, I paint the plastic switches with brass Liquid Leaf, or with pewter Liquid Leaf where I would use chrome. If the sockets or switches are on a wall that I am stippling in a color, I stipple the color right over them. They must always, however, be well protected with a good lacquer: Treasure Sealer does nicely (it's available in art-supply stores and made by the people who make Liquid Leaf —see page 65) as does polyurethane; otherwise the color wears off rapidly.

If I am arranging a one-room living space and have practically nothing to spend on lighting, the choice, oddly enough, is easy. I try to find a large tin canister (the kind used for gasoline, vegetable oil or lacquer). In a Woolworth's, I buy a do-it-yourself light-bulb holder (the kind with a cork works well) and a cheap lampshade holder. I buy the cheapest white-paper lampshade that I can find, in a shape that I can stand. If I can't find one, I make it, but then I stick to a drum-shaped frame, which is much easier to cover in paper, and I use white poster paper. (E)

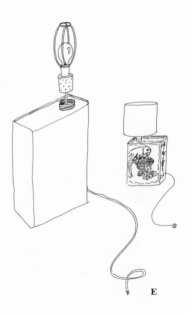

I give the paper lampshade—whether bought or made—a wash of yellow-ocher artist's oil paint, greatly thinned with turpentine. When the paper is a greasy-looking beige (still wet), I dip my fingers into fresh turpentine and flick them at the paper. This gives a splattered effect, very much like parchment. (See page 105 for more on same technique.)

E

The canister needs a hole through which to thread the electric wire. A nail hammered into the side of the canister close to the base achieves this. With luck the cork light-fitting can be crammed into the original opening in the tin; if not, a new one can be made with a can opener. I decorate canisters to look like toleware. (See Chapter 9 for how.)

Nine

Any inexpensive metal object, such as a wastebasket, bread bin or box, can be made into something smart by japanning. Japan is the method used to lacquer and color metalware. It was practiced extensively in the eighteenth and nineteenth centuries in Europe and from the middle of the eighteenth century in the United States. Toled, or japanned, trays were often decorated with chinoiserie or with bright flower designs on a black, dark-green or dark-red background. American toleware was usually decorated with Pennsylvania Dutch designs. (A)

To japan tin, I use japan paint, if I can get it. It is a quick-drying varnish with little or no oil in it that comes in cans or tubes and can be found at rather specialized artist's suppliers. Failing there, I use blackboard paint (a flat paint obtainable from specialized paint shops) or a water-soluble acrylic (from any art supplier). If, for example, I'm painting a tray or a lamp to use in a formal room, I paint the background black and decorate it in gold, silver or pewter. I use Liquid Leaf (a metallic paint), painting it on with a fine paintbrush. Some simple chinoiserie design copied from a plate is always effective.

The design that I painted on the bedside column in the yellow gingham bedroom (photograph 31, Chapter 28) I copied from a blue-and-white plate. A few feathery strokes in gold for the bamboo, a fragment of a trellised pagoda and a bit of

A

a cherry tree (the blooms livened up with a touch of pink oil paint) is a fast and effortless decoration for any lamp, tray or column. (B)

For the same yellow gingham bedroom, I painted two ordinary terra-cotta flowerpots in a flat black acrylic paint and decorated them with a gold rim and a quick flower design, painted on with Liquid Leaf. (C) I also used terra-cotta flowerpots as decoration in the first away-from-home room I ever had. I painted them with Greek figures, using black magic markers (see Chapter 40, figure A).

For a more rustic room, where I don't want to use gold or something as delicate as a chinoiserie design, I use a colorful flower or fruit design. I have made quite good flour, sugar, tea and coffee jars using old coffee tins painted to look like tole. I gave them a dark-green background, an ornamental cream plaque with the contents written on it, and the rest I decorated with fruit and flowers. (D)

For anyone not wishing to spend time on a freehand painting, a stenciled design works quite well. To do a first-class job, one ought to, I suppose, get the proper equipment. As stenciled walls, floors, furniture and tinware are becoming more in vogue, supplies for the work become more numerous—but it becomes less clear which to use and where to find them. A stencil can be made out of thin tin, wax stencil paper or, if it needs to be transparent (to follow a pattern around a ceiling for example), clear vinyl. All have to be cut with a utility knife. There is also a wide range of expensive stenciling brushes on the market.

When I stencil I make a dive for the kitchen drawer, where I hope to find some waxed sandwich paper. This I fold and cut out according to the paper-doll principle. (E) I scotch-tape the stencil around a canister, on the wall or on anything else that I might be painting. As I almost always have a very worn-out smallish paintbrush around, I take a pair of scissors to it and cut its worn bristles straight. This, for me, is a more than adequate stencil brush, and it looks just like one of the expensive ones made exclusively for stenciling.

Let us say I want to stencil a leaf-and-flower design to form a cornice around a room. I either copy and simplify a design from a book, a piece of chintz or wallpaper, or else design something myself. If I want to use two colors, I make two

B

C

D

E

separate strips out of waxed paper, one with the flowers, the other with the leaves. I don't make the paper strip any longer than about 2' (I scotch-tape the waxed paper together); otherwise it gets crumpled or torn and is clumsy to put up and take down. A short strip has to be moved more often and also replaced more often (as it gets wet with paint), but it is still easier to manage than a long strip.

I attach it to the wall with masking tape if I have some, Scotch tape if I don't. (Masking tape is less likely than Scotch tape to pull the paint off the wall.) First I tape up the flower motif—red tulips, for example. I use japan paint if I can get it, acrylic if I can't. Then I thin the japan paint with turpentine, acrylic with water; in either case not too much—for stenciling to work well the paint cannot be too runny! I first paint the tulips red, moving the stencil right around the room. As the paintbrush has flat bristles, I don't paint the paint on in the conventional sense, but hold the paintbrush at a right angle to the wall and more or less push it on. When the tulips are dry (usually the first tulips are dry by the time I have finished a wall), I tape up the leaf stencil over the tulips and paint the leaves green.

The result can be a rather flat-looking design. One or two things can be done to it freehand to give it a bit of life. The flowers can be outlined, either completely or only on one side to make them appear shadowed. (For this I use the original color with a small amount of black added to it.) Lines can also be drawn inside the flowers to give them depth (in pink, for instance—using the original red color with some white added). The same can be done to liven up the leaves. (F)

Another attractive use of a stencil is to flower a wall or a floor

F

at random. If I were doing a whole room with a single flower, I might try and get a stiff material out of which to cut the stencil. (A plastic divider out of a loose-leaf folder did nicely for my last one.) I would stencil the tulips on the wall as if they were scattered. Rather like gardening books tell you to plant bulbs: Throw out a handful of them and plant them where they land. I try to achieve this scattered effect on the wall; the imagination, however, has to do the throwing. As for the floor, there is nothing to stop the romantic perfectionist from scattering around a bunch of real flowers, petals or leaves and marking where they land.

To paint the decoration on the black sideboard of the California dining room (photograph 19), I made a paper pattern. I drew a ribbon-work design onto a piece of paper and cut it out. (G) I traced it first onto one side of the drawers of the sideboard, then I turned my pattern over and traced the other side. I painted the ribbon work plus the other lines and trim on the sideboard using Liquid Leaf.

G

I have used the same sort of paper pattern to paint material and walls with ribbon work, using magic markers or oil paint (page 238). A good tool to help with a ribbon-work design is the French curve (H), a useful object that can be bought in art-supply shops. It works as a guide in drawing any number of curved shapes. When the shapes are there, they can be varied by drawing within and around them freehand.

H

The columns in the brown living room (photograph 5) were stenciled. To repair them, I first regilded them, carefully applying Liquid Leaf paint around the already existing stenciled design. The design itself simply needed a bit of touching up here and there with India ink. From time to time, when the ink ran out on the paintbrush I was using, I went right on painting in the hope that the ever-fading markings would seem the result of time.

This taught me how to make new tin look old. If I am painting a tray or a biscuit tin in the hope of making it look like an antique, I first give it a dark background. (Car sprays are the quickest way—see pages 97–98). Then I paint it freehand or stencil it, but I paint the same way as I repaired the stenciling on the columns: When the paint on the paintbrush runs out, I don't immediately refill the paintbrush. In other words, I *don't* paint some of the design. I hope it looks worn off.

Liquid Leaf is an excellent product. A metallic paint, it comes in little bottles of different shades: copper, light gold, Renaissance, classic, pewter, brass, Florentine, white fire. There is also an external gold (to touch up an outdoor carriage lantern, I imagine). Treasure Gold, another metallic paint, is made by the same company. It comes in small pots (again in different shades) and gets rubbed on with a finger instead of painted on. By using two or even three varying shades (of either kind) on top of one another it is possible to achieve shadings reminiscent of aged gold leaf. I have used this method to doll up countless picture frames and mirror frames. I used it to gild the picture framing around the bookcases, the ceiling and door moldings in the brown living room (photographs 1–5) and to gild the mirror framing, the shutters and the barbecue frame in the blue-and-white tented dining room (photographs 13 and 14). I first painted all these moldings thoroughly with the copper Liquid Leaf and then, when it was dry, streakily with classic Liquid Leaf. This way the reddish tinge of the copper shows through one of the brighter golds. The gilding—both Liquid Leaf and Treasure Gold—is sealed with a coating of Treasure Sealer, a clear lacquer made by the same company. All are available at art-supply stores.

One of the many uses to which I have put Liquid Leaf is to paint leather with it. When I had the leather tooling (indented pattern) made for the desk in the California library (description on page 264), I decided that there must be a cheaper way of achieving the same effect. I have since painted a small pattern in Liquid Leaf around the edges of a piece of new leather, which I glued on over a tabletop where some old leather had worn away. Admittedly the leather isn't tooled (indented), but one can't have everything. I carefully sealed the gold I had painted with Treasure Sealer, painting it on only over the pattern.

Liquid Leaf painted onto a leather trunk (page 119) or any other flat leather object could be sealed in the same way, carefully painting the sealer over and just beyond the paint. (1) It is only when painting on something flexible, such as a leather or suede cushion, that I am not sure the gold could be sealed to adhere permanently. Not sealing it could, of course, be an advantage: It might look timeworn rapidly.

I have always admired Cordova leather, which is embossed,

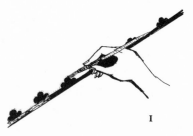

1

painted and gilded. (Wall hangings were being made out of it in Cordova by the tenth century, screens and chairs by the sixteenth century.) I have tried to make a screen that looks like an old Cordova screen. To make it, I covered a wooden frame (see page 55) in an imitation leather. The "leather" is a dark-brown plastic, but it looks realistic enough. I stapled it to the framework and glued on a strip of the "leather" to hide the staples. I bought some dull large tacks (from a specialized brass-fittings shop) and hit them in, every 6" or so, to make the screen look more authentic.

J

Then I painted it, following the design on a photograph of a seventeenth-century Spanish screen. (J) I used oil paints and copper Liquid Leaf to give it a subdued tone. I made my own stencil for the flowers (for how see pages 62–64). For the curlicues I used a French curve. (See figure H.)

Ten

nce the spotlights were up and the wiring was ready, we had the brown ceiling of the California living room painted white. A wonderfully efficient team arrived with impressive machines and sprayed it in a flash. I was grateful I hadn't undertaken the task myself. I am disdainful of the gelatinous modern paint that doesn't drip, and out of false pride, I would have probably spent days with liquid paint running down my arm and dripping into my hair. When the ceiling was white, I set about painting the walls Venetian red.

I am often asked the name of the method I use to paint walls or simulate wood. Stippling? Distressing? Dragging? I really don't know. If I have mastered a technique, I've done it by simply messing about. This messing about is all I am able to describe.

For anything I am about to paint (false wood, false marble, or a stippled or dragged wall), I first give the surface to be painted a coat of white shiny oil paint (eggshell in the United Kingdom, enamel in the United States). If I am about to paint a wall that is already white or light-colored and the paint is still in good condition, the coat of shiny oil paint is unnecessary. It is slightly easier to work the new color onto an oil-based paint than onto a water-based one, but the difference is hardly worth the cost and time of repainting a room only to paint over it again in the next step.

For the next step I use artist's oil paints, which I buy in tubes from an art-supply shop. The suppliers usually have them in two or more qualities. I buy the cheapest, which is usually referred to as "student" or "practice" oil paint. I buy gum turpentine, much cheaper than refined turpentine, and various paintbrushes, but inevitably end up using only one—the largest rounded artist's brush I can find. Again I buy the least expensive, because I give it a short life. As I end up using the same brush to both lay on the paint and stipple—which breaks the hairs—I kill an average of three brushes per room. To preserve the brush longer, one can apply the oil paint and turpentine with an ordinary 2″ house-painter's brush and then stipple with the artist's brush. (Both can be seen on the book jacket.)

The walls of the California living room were already white. I attacked them armed with a house-painter's brush to lay on the paint, an artist's one with which to stipple, two yards of cheesecloth, two large tubes of Venetian red oil paint and a pint of gum turpentine. (Rubber gloves might have been useful; my hands looked as if I was trying out stage effects for the role of Lady Macbeth.)

I first squeeze the Venetian red oil paint (about 4″ of it) onto a broken or unloved plate. I fill a cup or glass with turpentine, dip the paintbrush into it and then dab the wet brush against the paint—gingerly, so as not to pick up too much. Then I smear the brush with a circular motion against the wall. The paint will be rather runny and may drip downward sometimes. This doesn't matter as long as it isn't making puddles on the floor. I wait for the paint to set a bit (a minute or so) and then dab at the wall with the smaller, artist's paintbrush, giving it a mottled effect.

When the color on the wall is beginning to dry (about five

minutes after dabbing at it), I take a wad of cheesecloth (about half a yard) and rub the paint into the wall. I paint only a small surface at a time (about 2' square). Larger surfaces are tricky: Borders form where the dried paint and the new paint meet. Although the whole effect is one of unevenness—that is why, I think, it is called "distressing" a wall—it shouldn't look like a wall with damp patches. The unevenness must be even—a smudge here, a smudge there. If successful, the effect is rather like old leather. (See photographs 6–9.)

When I have the texture and color I want (or have settled for), I leave the walls to dry for at least forty-eight hours before I lacquer them. During this time the careless finger mark can cause unending damage: There is, in fact, no way of repairing it. No matter how much you stipple on top of it, once the paint has partially dried, an outline of the mark will remain.

I lacquer all painted surfaces—walls included—with either polyurethane (it exists in gloss, semi-flat or flat), yacht varnish, shellac or French polish. Shellac and French polish give about the same amount of sheen to a wall, rather like a highly waxed surface. (The California living room is shellacked, and the supper room, photograph 18, is French polished.) If I want a higher gloss, I use a shiny polyurethane or yacht varnish. Polyurethane is quicker—one or two coats are usually sufficient—but I can't help thinking it looks a bit like plastic, especially over a plain surface. So I use it only when I need it for maximum protection and if it is over a patterned or textured surface.

The real silkiness of a perfect lacquered wall needs long and patient labor, a very smooth wall to begin with and about eight coats of yacht varnish (which is made the old-fashioned way, with no plastic). Between coats the wall should be sanded. The result is a wall that glimmers and displays a depth of color like no other (but I must confess I have never yet reached coat number 8).

Walls that are to be dragged (with almost imperceptible lines) or ragged (texture created by a crumpled piece of material) should first be painted in an oil-based paint. Colors can be dragged onto a white background, onto a contrasting color, or onto a lighter tone of the same color—dark green onto light green, blue onto gray, red onto pink—anything that might please.

Let us say I want to drag pink on pink. I buy ordinary pink household paint in a shade that I like, and paint the walls. When they are dry, I make the dragging mixture: I mix something called "glazing coat" or "transparent glaze" (which can be bought in specialized paint stores) with half as much gum turpentine. I color the mixture by adding oil stains (also bought at a specialized paint store). In this case I would use a half a quart of turpentine and add red stain, enough to achieve a pink slightly darker than the one already on the walls. For dragging, I use two large 4″ paintbrushes, one to put the paint on, the other (a dry one) to drag the paint. A rag with which to wipe the dragging brush after each run is also necessary.

With one paintbrush I paint on the dragging mixture in a strip from ceiling to floor. (As with all these methods—not too wide a strip!) Then I get back up on my ladder and, starting at the top, drag the other, dry paintbrush downward. (A) The glazing coat makes the paint slightly tacky, which helps the dragging. If a mistake is made at this stage, the paint can be wiped off without harming the flat first coat. The only thing that is impossible to repair is a mistake that has been allowed to dry. There is nothing to do but start again, even if it means removing the dragging paint from an entire wall with turpentine. The dragging glaze will dry flat and needs no further sealer.

A

Panels or moldings—where there are none—can be painted on successfully by dragging. I use masking tape to form a square or rectangle or whatever shape of panel I want. Then I drag my paint—down for the vertical lines, across for the horizontal ones (the corners mitered). To make the panels look more sculptured, I darken the dragging paint slightly and paint a thin line on the inside L of the "molding." On the outside of the opposite angle, I paint a line with a slightly lightened dragging paint. If I were being exact about this—instead of just following this system all around the room—I would place the shadows in relation to the source of light, the light angles turned toward the window. This, however, would result in a problem somewhere along the way: two shadows next to each other. I cheat. When I reach a door or a corner, I switch shadows. (See left corner of room in figure B, next page.)

For ragging a wall, I use the same mixture as for dragging. The only difference is that I use a rag instead of the dry brush.

B

I begin with a crumpled piece of cloth—cotton, linen, an old dishtowel, anything—and roll it from the ceiling downward. (c)

Before discovering the existence of glazing coat, I dragged walls more or less successfully using different shades of household paint. But I made the first coat the darker one because it was easier to add white paint to the original color to lighten it for the second coat. To rag walls in household paint may be possible as well, but I've never tried. I have ragged walls with the same mixture I used to stipple the California living room: oil paint and gum turpentine.

Once the red paint was on the walls of the California living room and the doors and windows were on their way toward some symmetry, even the fireplace looked better (photographs 6 and 8). Its hugeness plus the ornateness of the supporting columns had terrified me when I first saw it. Now that there were a few other tall shapes in the room, and the shades on the French windows promised a balancing white expanse on the opposite wall (see photograph 6), the fireplace seemed less enormous. The red tiles on the hearth, which were far too red when the room was white, now blended successfully with the walls.

The curved window minus the surround that now frames the bookcase on the opposite wall was left with only a narrow

C

molding that holds the glass. I painted it black, using water-soluble flat black paint (in this case black acrylic, bought in a tube in an artist's supply shop). When the molding dried, I lacquered it with a couple of coats of shellac. I used the same method to paint the moldings around the French windows and the black part of the frame around the bookshelves. I painted the shelves and the edges of the frame in Venetian red, the same as the walls, and picked out the narrow moldings in gold (photographs 8 and 9).

In a bric-a-brac shop I found some rather wonderful Chinese carvings. (They later became window valances in the bedroom —photograph 42.) I also found some broken remnants of Chinese carvings. The latter we incorporated into the edging of the shelves (photograph 9). Where the remnants ran out, we constructed small panels, under Mr. Lewis's tutelage, and pinned to them tiny slivers of molding (page 21). (D) These I gilded with Liquid Leaf.

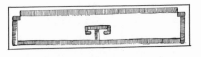

D

Eleven

To do the house in California, I made two separate one-month visits. During the first month we completed the woodwork and the painting. I spent the interval between the two California trips in New York, where I collected some more bits and pieces for shipment to Los Angeles: the S-shaped settee, the small Regency table, the nest of papier-mâché trays, the mirrored sconces and an Edwardian brass chandelier. (All can be seen in photographs 6, 8, 9 and 19). (I might, of course, have been able to find all of these things in Los Angeles as well, had I had more time to look and explore.) I also bought a few bolts of inexpensive material and a few lengths of a more expensive kind. With materials—as with furniture—I find it worthwhile to buy one really good piece and surround it with inexpensive pieces. For instance, one grand petit point cushion surrounded by cottons and canvas can look wonderful.

If I possibly can, I like buying all the materials in one day; spending days with a handful of swatches confuses me. I am confident of my "vision" of how a house should look. But I must follow that vision, not run around with a horrid piece of carpet and an inch of a curtain in search of another, varied, five inches that will harmonize. That way I only lose the "vision." I imagine the room and then try to find the things and match the colors that resemble my fantasy—fast. And I was able to do just that with the California house.

First, I bought four yards of a beautiful, dominant, rather expensive thick cotton material looking like a kilim carpet (see chairs in photographs 8 and 9). The orangy red in the material matched the living room walls. I matched the rest of the materials to it in style as well as in color. For the supper room (photograph 18), also already painted (Chapter 10), I bought, in the same place, four yards of a Moroccan-looking stripe, which became the window shade. The stripes are in blue, brown, beige and rust. Then I carried my spoils to a wholesaler specializing in dress fabrics—Indian cottons, batiks, plain cottons—and there I bought the materials for the rest of the house. I didn't do this because I wanted them to match exactly, but so that the transitions from one room to another wouldn't be too startling. By making all the colors in a house blend, there is very little waste: If I buy too much for one room I can use it in the next. This applies to furniture and paint as well as to material.

For the bedrooms I bought batiks. They, too, are based on the colors of the kilim material: an ocher-yellow-and-brown one for the walls of the master bedroom, a green-and-yellow one for the walls of the second bedroom (photographs 40–42) and a brown-and-black batik (the same pattern as the ocher-yellow-and-brown one) for the upstairs library (photograph 55). The dining room is separated from the supper room by only an open arch, so it was important that they, too, should harmonize. The supper room was well on its way to having a Moroccan flavor. For the dining room I wanted a nineteenth-century Russian arbor. For both, stripes would be appropriate. I found an enchanting striped Indian cotton, the stripe the same width as the Moroccan stripe. Alas, the colors were wrong. The red was too red—perfect for Russia, but clashing with the rust of Morocco. I turned the material around: The reverse side had a smudged pattern and softer colors. I bought the bolt and eventually put the material on the walls the wrong side out (photographs 19 and 20).

The blue batik with pink flowers—the only one with colors that don't match the kilim material—I used in the music room, which is not adjacent to any of the other rooms (photograph 53).

The prices of all those cottons ranged between $2 and $4 a yard. When I returned to California I bought cotton supplements in solid colors: the rust-colored canvas to combine with the kilim material for the two armchairs (photographs 7–9), the plain unbleached muslin out of which the shades for the living room were made, the voile for the hangings in the master bedroom (photograph 40) and the brown-and-green lining materials out of which I made the curtains and bed hangings in the second bedroom (photograph 42).

I wanted to cover the living room banquettes (photograph 6) in a beige canvas (the color once again taken from the kilim). But the need for a sofa in the living room—both to sit on and to see how and where it would best fit the room—became acute before the room was completed. We found an ideal one, ready-made in gray canvas. The gray looked good with the red walls, less good with the kilim. Above all, I had to discard my idea of beige banquettes, but I managed to buy a material that is an old friend. It comes from France. Because it's imported it's not cheap, but then neither is it very expensive. It is canvas and looks like awning material in an orange, gray and off-white stripe. There was a problem, however. The stripes didn't look good in combination with the kilim design I planned to use on the living room armchairs, although the rust color in both materials was the same. I realized that if I covered the armchairs in the fashion of a nineteenth-century carpet chair (A), using the kilim material only down the center (see photographs 8 and 9), I would achieve two things: The backs of the chairs would be covered in a plain color (photograph 7), so I would

A

use less of the expensive kilim material. The kilim and the stripe would be facing each other across the room and would therefore never be seen at the same time (see photographs 7 and 8).

So there I was, with all the bolts of material waiting to be stapled and sewn. I couldn't face it alone. My first month's work in California had been made a great deal easier by the presence of Mr. Lewis. Whatever mad thing I want to construct, he knows the easiest way to go about it. I am short on technical terms, but he understands, by now, what I'm hoping to build without my needing to use the right words. Yet the talented and clairvoyant are seldom well organized or have any sense of time. I am not much better. Such organizational capacity as our three-member team has rests in the hands of Fran. I called for help and Fran arrived. With cool-headed realism she quickly pointed out our inability to cover the walls, make the curtains and upholster all the furniture of a ten-room house within a month. My megalomania stretches to the point where I believed I could—and with Fran's help I more or less did. I gave in to her only marginally: We sent out the tattered red armchairs to be covered professionally in the rust canvas and kilim material. We also sent out the muslin shades for the living room and the striped shades for the supper room. The rest we did ourselves.

To complete the living room, we upholstered the banquettes. First, we wrapped thin (1/2″) foam rubber over the wooden structure. (See Chapter 7, figures D and E.) A layer of padding came over that, and then the material. All attached with staples (see Chapters 3 and 4), the staples hidden by a woolen cord. (See pages 219–20 for how to make it.) The padding makes the base look as fat and voluptuous as the cushions that go on top of it. (B) The backrest is covered in the same way as the base—a layer of thin foam, a layer of padding, then the material, then the cord. Both the loose seat cushions and the back cushions are filled with feathers (see page 31).

The S-shaped settee (photographs 6 and 8) I had purchased in New York had been badly painted a shiny black. I repainted the wood in black acrylic paint. I picked out the knobs on the uprights in Liquid Leaf, unevenly (page 64). Then I gave the woodwork a light coat of French polish, skimping on the polish so that it would not become too shiny. I tried to give the black

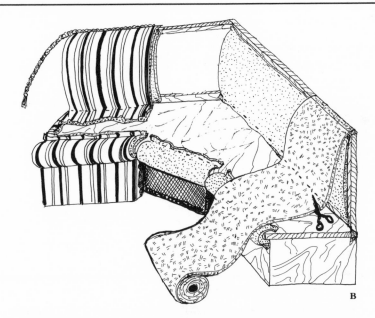

B

and gold the same tone as the black and gold of the japanned antique Regency book table standing between the two arm-chairs (see photographs 7–9). After painting the settee, I covered it. I used an old paisley shawl, one that I had found at the Pasadena swap meet (a marvelous antique and not-so-antique market). It had a few holes in it, but the border was in good condition. The settee had been covered in velvet. I anchored the delicate paisley to the sturdy velvet using a straight and a curved needle, thread and staples. The border of the shawl covers the S-shaped arm. It was just wide enough to also cover the existing piping on each side (page 31). In order to make the border (which was not cut on the bias) follow the S shape of the arm, I had to take occasional tucks in it. I first attached it to the piping on the outer curve, then made the tucks (sewing them by hand using a curved needle) and then sewed the border to the piping on the inside curve. (c) I cut another piece of border in half and used that for the lower strips on the arm, from under the piping down. Then I stapled what was left flapping onto the underside of the armrest. (D)

I covered the two seats with the center piece of the shawl. I cut notches for the supports of the armrest and stapled the material to the wood at the base. To hide the staples, I twisted up some wool in the colors of the paisley shawl and glued it over the staples (pages 219–20).

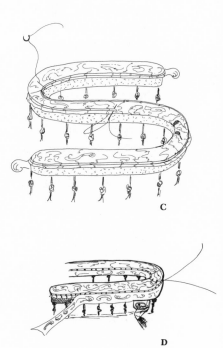

C

D

An even more tattered shawl, also from the Pasadena swap meet, went to cover the cushion in the middle of the gray couch and the seat of the traveling chair on the near right of the room (photograph 6). Another similar shawl, but without holes and from a smart antique shop, is draped over the side of the couch in case someone should want to take a nap. I love a beautiful piece of material just lying around. Yet I hate anything lying around to no purpose, no matter how lovely. At the end of a couch or chaise longue, there's an excuse (photographs 5 and 6).

The coffee table in the center of the red living room is a modern wicker table we bought in Los Angeles. When we bought it, it was unpainted. To make it fit the room better and to suggest that it might be old, I painted it in burnt sienna artist's oil paint. When it was dry, I lacquered it with polyurethane. When that was dry, I painted over the polyurethane with black oil paint, diluted with turpentine. The moment a section was painted, I wiped the black paint off again with a cloth. The only black that remained was the little that sank into the creases of the weave. This makes it look as if time dirtied the wicker. To make it look less like new dirt, I painted the table again, this time with a coat of French polish (pages 102–3).

I put the small columns we had bought at auction in front of the banquettes as low tables. They were very beaten-up mahogany. I needed another bit of gray in the room to echo the gray of the canvas sofa. So I painted the tops and bases of the columns to look like gray marble. (See pages 103–4 for how to do this.) The column part had had, at some time, material glued to it. As I was unable to remove it completely, it was hardly a possible surface for the smoothness of marble. I hid the bumps by gluing another covering over them. I chose black canvas. (E)

The three trays in diminishing sizes, matching but all slightly different, that I had bought in New York are Victorian papier mâché inlayed with mother-of-pearl. Their shape is very similar to the shape of the curved window and bookcase—but sideways. I hung one above the top shelf of the bookcase and the two others on the chimney breast (pages 49–50, and photographs 6, 8 and 9).

E

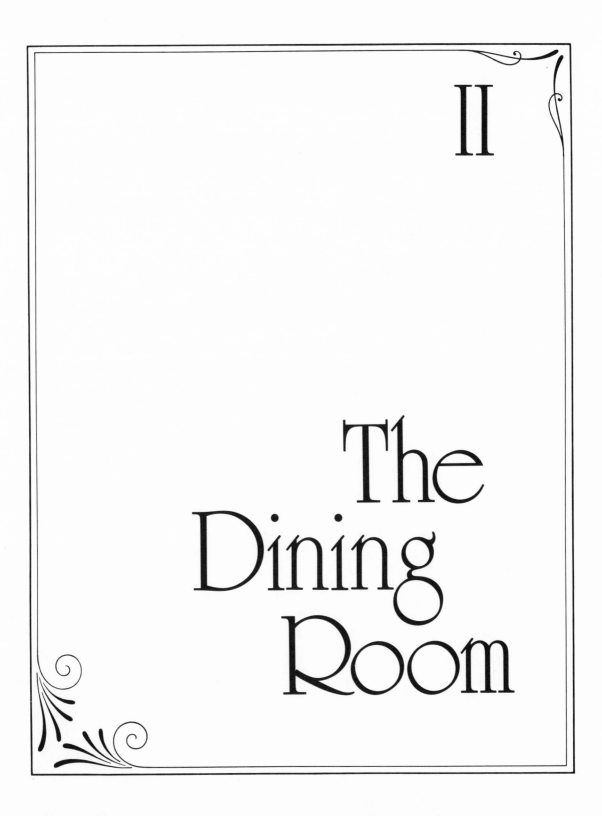

II

The
Dining
Room

The greatest waste of a room seems to me the conventional dining room. There it sits, mostly unoccupied, often austere—looking as if "the man who came to dinner" hadn't come. When he does come, the table (at least in my experience) is never the right size for the right occasion. The chairs —often uncomfortable—are either too many to hide when they're not being used or too few to seat guests when giving a dinner party. In eighteenth-century France, they thought dining rooms superfluous. No matter how exaggerated their supply of rooms, they dined in whichever room took their fancy. (Unless, of course, a grand banquet was taking place; then, presumably, the grand dining room was used.) A table, usually round and the right size for the number of diners and their fare, was set up most anywhere. That way, seasonal advantage could be taken of the warmth of a fire, a current of air or a spectacular view. Of course they had dozens of helpers to rush in and set up the whole performance and to dismantle it when the meal was over.

There is a fairy tale I remember. Actually, I have forgotten the story but remember one memorable line: *"Tischlein deck' dich!"* It means, more or less, "Little table, set yourself!" Apparently some character in the story had the power to wave a wand and there stood not only the table, beautifully set, but also an array of constantly changing covered dishes (spectacular china, naturally) disclosing delicacies undreamed of and— above all—not cooked by the wand-waver.

I have been pursuing that fantasy most of my life. The closest I have come to it, at least in plan, is as follows: a kitchen large enough to house a table for eight (miracle food for more is just impossible); a table with wheels; swing doors leading from the kitchen into the room the food will be eaten in— doors large enough to allow the table to pass through (swing doors open in both directions on account of a special hinge). The room, I imagine, would be a living room, a dining room/ library, a hall, an alcove in the hall or even a guest room.

In the kitchen the host or hostess places the first course in the center of the already laid table. The wine stands ready in carafes. The table is wheeled in among the guests—who are sitting in a group—and is placed in front of the sofa. Such chairs as are available are drawn up to encircle the rest of the table. With the first course over, the table gets pulled or pushed back into the kitchen, cleared, relaid with the main course and wheeled in again. This procedure is repeated with each course until the table goes back into the kitchen for good.

I see this fantasy extended further: a banquette built directly in line with the kitchen door and shaped to accommodate the table. The swing doors to the kitchen would be not just double, but split into quarters. (A) The lower doors are the height of the table, plus a wine bottle. The table is on some form of electrical rail. The hostess pushes a discreetly hidden button and the unaccompanied table—fully laid, with all the courses and with a built-in hot plate—appears through the doors. If the hostess is lucky enough to have a helper in the kitchen, the table could go back and forth with each course. Otherwise, the food has to be eaten in one go, and then table and debris can retreat.

A

Two of the dining rooms pictured I arranged for myself: the red dining room (photographs 10 and 11) and the blue-and-white tent (photographs 12–14). I designed both to accommodate my china, which is blue and white and which moved with me from one house to the next. Each I tried to make into not just a dining room, but also a room that is comfortable to be in while not eating.

The red dining room has two corner banquettes, left and right of a large stone fireplace. The right-hand banquette consists of two different boxes: One is the size of a double bed mattress, the other a narrow, single one. The boxes are made the same way as the other banquettes (described on page 55).

The house is in the country. For the occasional overflow of guests, the banquettes can revert to being mattresses. They are both covered in blue linen, sewed to and around the piping (see page 31). Under the mattresses there are liftable boards covering storage space. On the wall opposite the right-hand banquette there is a serving hatch (visible in photograph 10). Under it, out of the same clapboard as the wall, we built a low cupboard. It houses a television set, which can be watched from the banquettes. (For ideas on how to conceal TV sets, see pages 176–77.) On top of the cupboard is a hot plate, and food is placed onto it directly from the kitchen.

The banquette on the left of the fireplace is made in the same way as the right-hand one, but it is narrower and higher. Higher because the seat cushions on top of it are not as thick as the mattresses on the other banquette. The cushions are also covered in blue linen. (For how to make the cushions, see pages 35–36.) The banquette surrounds a small table, which is used for breakfast. (B, next page) Breakfast has to take place somewhere other than the large central dining room table, which I keep constantly set for dinner or lunch. I do this to save time. Also, the room looks better with a set table than with a bare one. I keep the table set for four, finding it quicker to add places (if we are unexpectedly more) than to begin laying the table from scratch. I like to overload a table. I find it pretty. But I don't much relish unloading it. This way all the unused things can remain and I just add clean plates as needed. If we are only two or three, I leave the extra places, or place, set. I justify my sloth by saying I prefer the look of a balanced table.

The dining room chairs, in the Louis XIV style, I collected

B

one at a time (photograph 11). All are slightly different heights,
but they have the same shape and more or less the same legs.
Despite ten years of keeping a watchful eye for more at a
reasonable price, I have only six. When I have extra people to
seat, I slot in kitchen chairs. They are tall, ladder-backed and
rush-seated. Two I've had for ages, four I added over time.
Although they are modern, they are not all the same. The older
ones are dark wood, the newer ones were a horrid pale-yellow
lacquered pine. I made them all an "oakish" color. (See Chapter 16 for how to do this.) (Eventually the two old armchairs
and two of the modern ones landed in my green kitchen—
photograph 21.) Being rustic, the kitchen chairs mix with the
seventeenth-century–style chairs quite well. The seventeenth-
century ones have very wide seats, and I would be unable to
fit twelve of them around the table, even if I had them. By
combining them with the kitchen chairs, which are narrower,
I can just manage to seat twelve people.

If there is a downright invasion of family and friends, I drag the kitchen table into the dining room. It is a good 3″ lower than the dining room table, so I push a thick book under each foot. I slide the end of the kitchen table, which is rectangular, *under* one end of the oval dining room table to avoid the little nipped-out triangles that would appear if the two tables were simply butted end to end. To make this possible the kitchen table must remain 1″ lower than the dining room table. This inch-high step shows. (Not to mention that my four books, none of them equally thick, make it a crooked step.) To hide it, I put a folded blanket over the lower table and then cover the whole unbalanced expanse with a tablecloth. (c)

For tablecloths I use mostly sheets—two pretty flowered double sheets are large enough to cover even my enlarged table. I lay the edge of one sheet on top of the edge of the other, which is no more noticeable than if they were sewn together. When they are not tablecloths, they revert to being sheets. I quite happily use a double sheet to cover a round table as well. Where it is too long, I tuck it under (pages 174–75).

If I make tablecloths—and I make quite a few (the ready-made tablecloth is both expensive and never large enough to reach the floor)—I make them out of unexpected materials: denims, canvas, muslin, awning material, lining material or some pretty, inexpensive patterned material. I make napkins to match. Sometimes I throw a piece of inexpensive cotton lace over a plain cloth to dress it up for a dinner. (See pages 113–14 for more on lace.)

A tablecloth in a solid color shows off china, silverware and glass better (see photographs 12 and 13). A table covered in a printed cloth looks better with plain china on it. Wood, of course, is the perfect background for china, and I stick to the bare wood table whenever I don't need to cover it for some reason or other, such as to enlarge the table, to seat more people than I have—or can fit in—place mats for, to give color to the table or simply to make it more festive, which I find a tablecloth does.

The denim tablecloth (photographs 12 and 13) is a strong blue. I like the color—it isn't a cold blue—and I use it a lot. (For instance, on the walls of the dining room in photograph 16.) It looks especially good with my blue-and-white china.

As I have yet to work out how to make a round tablecloth

C

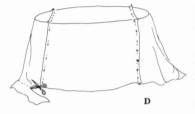

D

properly, I simply lay a length of material across the table, pin two other lengths to each side of it, cut off all the bits that hit the floor and then sew the three pieces together on the machine. (D) I hem the circle by hand.

I use the leftover pieces to make napkins. I cut squares and pull out the threads until I have an inch of fringe all around. (Faster than hemming.) For the fringe not to go on unraveling in the washing machine, it can be overstitched by hand. (This is only necessary if the napkins are to get a lot of wear and wash.)

Thirteen

I reupholstered the seventeenth-century Louis XIV–style chairs in a blue-and-white-checked cloth. I sewed together two pieces of material, wrong side out, turned them right side out, slipped them over the backrest of the chair and stapled them under the backrest. The material for the seat I cut to size, made darts for the two front corners, cut two holes for the struts of the backrest in the other corners and stapled it straight to the chair. (A) I would never close-cover (upholster) dining room chairs in this way if I were not making additional loose slipcovers to go on top. (Judging from how dirty my dining room chairs get, I can only imagine that my friends have difficulty differentiating between chair and napkin. As I make them out of similar material, perhaps it's excusable.)

A

To make the slipcovers for the chairs, I used the same checked cloth. This time, I made the cover for the backrest wider. To each side of it I sewed three sets of ribbons out of the same material. I left a 2″ gap between each of the two ribbons. When the cover is on, I use up the extra width by tying the ribbons into bows. French chairs of this period often had bows on the sides, although they were mostly decorative.

The slipcover for the seat is a square piece of material with two small squares cut away to accommodate the struts. To shape the two front corners, I sew darts. When the cover fits the shape of the seat, I sew elastic to it, four pieces of elastic, one on one side of each leg. Then I tie the elastic together under the chair. (B) At first I had tied on the cover with only ribbons, but people not only spill during meals, they wriggle. The cover used to end up all twisted and crushed. The tension of the elastic prevents this.

The advantage of having the permanent and the removable covering in the same material is that if the removable cover slips, there is something underneath. Also, when the cover is temporarily removed for washing, the chair looks the same.

For the kitchen chairs' grand outing into the dining room, they get blue-and-white-checked slip cushions (loose tie-on cushions). I made them out of thin foam rubber—only 1″ thick. (C)

They can also be made out of horsehair or coir fiber—which is the way they were made for hundreds of years—but they are more trouble, although they have a more authentic look and feel to them. If I make cushions out of horsehair or coir fiber (the modern equivalent of horsehair), I make them very flat; otherwise they rapidly become lumpy. I make a cambric cover with narrow separations (for more on method, see pages 35–36) and pack as much hair as possible into each separation. (D)

To make the kitchen chair slip cushions, I first cut the 1″ thick foam rubber in the same shape as the seat. (Foam rubber that is 1″ thick is easily cut with a pair of scissors. For thicker foam I use a bread knife.) Then I cut two pieces of the checked material 1″ wider and longer than the foam rubber. I cut a strip about 2″ wide and as long as the circumference of the foam rubber, plus 1″ for a turn-in. Using a sewing machine, I joined the two pieces of material to the strip (leaving one side open). I cut notches on the corners (E) and turned the slip cushion

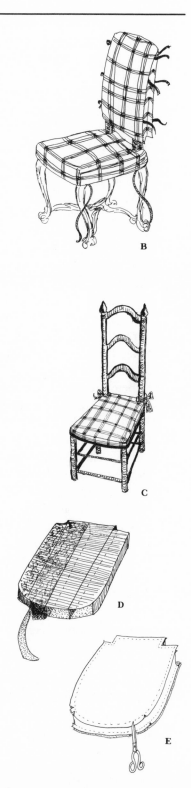

B

C

D

E

cover inside out. To the two back corners I sewed a double ribbon, made out of the same material, with which to tie the cushion to the backrest. Before putting the foam into the cushion cover, I wrapped it up in padding (as if wrapping a parcel) to disguise the obvious fact of it being foam rubber. When the cover was on, I closed it with a few stitches. The neater might prefer Velcro, a zipper or some snaps. To smarten the slip cushion, you can button or pipe it (see photographs 20, 53 and 56).

When I first began decorating the house in California, I bought the wicker furniture at auction in a bulk lot: three armchairs, a rocker, two tables, a lot of side chairs. Some were in better health than others. All the armchairs had extremely well made cushions. There were only two things wrong with them: they didn't fit the chairs they were on, and they were covered in the most profoundly awful flowered canvas. But they had piping and they were buttoned. Best of all, they fitted perfectly onto the four modern wicker armchairs we later bought for the California dining room (photographs 19 and 20).

Before covering the ugly flowered slip cushions, I painted their buttons and piping black. I used a black laundry marker; I had no black oil paint in the house, which is what I normally use for this (see pages 32–33), but the laundry marker worked just as well. I covered the cushions the same way as I covered the buttoned conversation in my own living room (photographs 4 and 5, description pages 41–42): material to size, small holes for buttons (I stitched around the holes in large stitches to keep the material from fraying), material buttoned to cushion and then sewn to the piping. The same on the reverse side, with a band of material covering the space between the piping. The material is darkish and heavily patterned, so I counted on its looking clean for some time.

Six of the auction's wicker side chairs were good enough to keep. Where they were unraveling I wound some string around them, and when I painted over the chairs, I painted straight over the string.

To repair wicker I used to buy split cane, soak the cane, cut away all the unraveled old stuff and begin afresh. It took too long. So I started wetting the old cane with a sponge, raveling it up again and gluing it together with wood glue. To hold the cane in place until it was glued, I had to clamp it somehow. I twisted string around it. Once I didn't apply the glue neatly enough and the string glued itself to the wicker. So I painted over it and it was hardly noticeable. Now, whenever I repair wicker, I glue what is left of it to the wood and neatly wrap the mend with string. (F) Then I paint the string the same color as the chair.

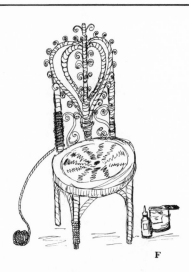

F

The furniture was green when we bought it. I painted it with burnt-umber oil paint, a dark color, so I was able to apply it right over the green. Later I lacquered all but the table tops with French polish. Those I lacquered with a polyurethane, which is more resistant to spills.

I put four of the repaired wicker side chairs in the California dining room, two in the music room (foreground of photograph 53, where the repaired wicker rocking chair, armchair and table can also be seen). I gave the side chairs a beige canvas covering, red piping and red buttons. As they would be used infrequently (only for large dinners), I risked the light color. Their covering and style made it possible to use them in any of the ground-floor rooms as needed.

G

Anyone who has ever hired little gold chairs (G) for a party must surely regret it. They are uncomfortable, rickety and very expensive. What is more, there are many occasions when it is impossible to get them because they are partying elsewhere. The many types of folding plastic ones for hire are simply too ugly to consider, and they add injury to insult by also being expensive. If the little gold chairs are for a once-, twice-, or thrice-in-a-lifetime event, then maybe it's worth it. But since entertaining at home—for business or otherwise—is so much nicer (and cheaper) than dining out, there are people who pay for the hire of gold chairs as often as once a month. It's a mistake.

If one entertains frequently, a collection of a dozen side chairs (more or less, according to need) is an excellent investment. I would never buy them all in one go in a department store or furniture shop. But then, I would never buy any furniture that way. Bit by bit I'd collect. Pieces of furniture are like friends, to be found one at a time over the years, not picked up a dozen at a time. Extra chairs, to be used only occasionally, must be stored. Folding ones, which can be stacked in a cupboard, are useful but often uncomfortable or ugly. Bamboo

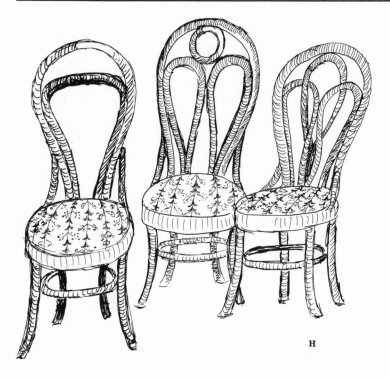

H

ones, which look better, collapse. Director chairs—the best-looking and most comfortable folding chairs—take up too much space around a table. So the best way of storing chairs that will be used for dining only sometimes is to use them for something else the rest of the time.

My own chairs-in-reserve are made of bentwood. They vary in shape. (H) I never paid more than $5 a chair; usually they were cheaper. Those that had cane seats in bad condition and those that had no seats left at all got the same treatment: First I hammered a piece of plywood, cut to size, over the seat. Over the plywood I stapled a piece of foam rubber and over that some material. (I) I painted the wood of all the chairs black, with an occasional gold trim. This gives them some uniformity when they are dining room chairs. The rest of the time, one stands in front of a dressing table, another in a bathroom, two in the front hall and so on until it was necessary to shut away only the last two in a closet. All of them are covered to match the rooms they are in, but I have made extra matching slip cushions to place over their covering for when all twelve chairs become special party chairs.

I

Fourteen

f I could afford to do so, I would dearly love to have a
Meissen or Sèvres china service to feed an army. Endless
matching dishes of varying shapes and sizes—sweetmeat
dishes, vegetable dishes with beautiful china lids, all sizes of
platters to serve up a quail or an ox. But I have no such service,
and if I did, I wouldn't use it for fear of breaking it. Nor would
my table be big enough to display it in its full glory.

Ten years ago I started collecting blue-and-white china. Surprisingly, my collecting hasn't been greatly impaired by infla-
tion, nor by the fashion for blue-and-white china. This is because, with time, I have learned to settle for lesser quality. My
base of antique china is good enough that a modern onion
pattern or willow pattern (A) is easily upgraded by the better
pieces. None of them, or only a few of them, match. In blue-
and-white china there are many variations in tone, both in the
blue and in the white. So keeping to the same tone helps when
building up a dinner service. It is also wise to try for plates of
the same size. A setting with a huge dinner plate next to a
setting with a small one ruins the symmetry of the table and
might give offense to a guest. But I find great satisfaction in
each plate being slightly different. The cracked or chipped
plates I hang on the wall.

I comb antique markets and junk shops for my blue-and-
white china. The only time a really attractive Delft tulipière or
some grand Worcester covered dish will reach and stay at the
markets I frequent (at a price I'll consider) is if it has a piece
missing. These cripples I buy especially to put on the wall,
placing them so that they turn their healthy side toward the
audience. In my dining room/television room (photographs 10
and 11), I painted the walls in red. It is the red of Pennsylvania
Dutch barns, and the blue-and-white china stands out against
it extremely well. Who's to know that one of the Delft covered
vases lacks the back half of its lid, or that the Minton tureen
above the serving hatch (photograph 10) has a chunk missing?

If I am going to hang a broken plate on the wall, I often
retouch it with white enamel paint in the places where I have

A

glued it or where it is chipped. I mix a small amount of gray or blue artist's oil paint into the enamel to get the right shade of white. The design I repair with blue oil paint and a dab of picture varnish to make it shine.

I hang the plates with wire plate hangers if I can find them in the shops; they have a spring and adapt to a range of sizes. Or if it seems too complicated to go shopping, I make my own. I use garden wire, making a circle and attaching more hooks to hold the plate than the commercial plate hanger has, to make up for the lack of tension. (B)

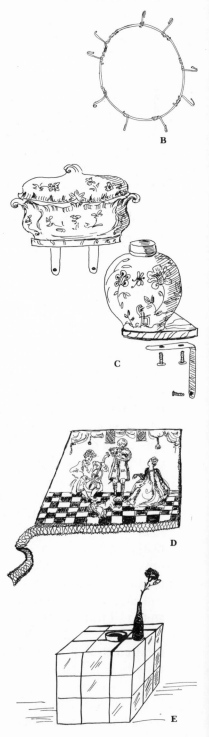

To mount the tureens and vases on the wall, I cut a stand from a piece of wood 1/2″ thick. I make it the same size and shape as the base of the china piece in the front and sides, but flush to the wall at the back. I attach it with brackets to the wall and paint the whole thing to match the wall. (c)

I use Delft tiles as coasters (see table in photographs 10 and 11). I had originally hoped to collect enough to cover a whole table with them, but they rose in price so much that I gave up. I got up to a dozen, which is quite enough to use as coasters for the wineglasses on the dinner table. To hide the unglazed edges and to dress up the tile a bit, I glued blue borders (gimp) around them. (D) For place mats I use smoked mirror tiles (again, photographs 10 and 11). I buy them in any do-it-yourself shop and glue green felt on their backs to avoid scratching the table. (You can buy the felt ready-made, with a sticky back.) The mirrors usually have smooth edges. If they seem sharp, a ribbon, border or strip of material glued around the edge (as with the Delft tiles) can be the answer. The napkin can match the border. I use rectangular 12″ × 18″ mirror tiles (more commodious), or square ones (12″ × 12″) if I need to fit more people around the table.

I have also used mirror tiles for covering tables. Tea chests covered in them make excellent occasional tables, (E) and a few boards nailed together and covered in mirror tiles make a coffee table reminiscent of the twenties. I have boxed in baths with tiles, covered walls with them and made screens (page 110 and Chapter 17, figure K). (The little bits of sticky felt that are sold with mirror tiles as adhesives are not strong enough. If they need to be relied on to stay firm in steam and not crash off the wall unexpectedly, an extra dab of ceramic adhesive will make them secure.) A box made by gluing five square pieces of plywood together and covered with five square mirror tiles makes a perfect stand for an ornament.

I was asked by a magazine to arrange an ideal dinner table. I could borrow the linen, china, glass and silverware from anywhere I chose. The effect was to be as splendid as I could achieve, the cost no object. I made the rounds of the grandest shops, and my belief that the expensive is not necessarily the most beautiful was once again confirmed. But it is a great pleasure, of course, to be able to combine the very grand with the ordinary: to place a vermeil (silver gilt) seventeenth-century saltcellar next to a modern gilded-metal pepper mill on the principle that both have pleasing shapes, rather than to give one prominence over the other because of value.

I arranged the table for the photograph in my own dining room (see photograph 12). Although the finished product is all aglow with real gold, the inexpensive things dominate the table: the denim tablecloth and napkins, the background of the blue-and-white-striped sheeting, and some of the blue-and-white china.

The blue-and-white pots for the soup are varied: The lids do not match the pots but originally belonged on some other pieces that had broken. The plates under the soup pots are all different from one another and from the pots. The tiny blue-and-white plates holding the butter I found, one at a time, at various markets: They originally belonged to dolls' tea sets. The serving plates, candlesticks, saltcellars, and knives and forks in the photograph are gold. Borrowed gold. When I give a dinner I often put a modern gold-luster plate·(the oven-to-table variety) under the blue-and-white arrangement, and the effect is more or less the same. The loss of the assurance gold might give is made up by the insurance that need not be paid.

The table arrangement in photograph 13 is my own dinner setting. Nothing borrowed, nothing gold. I don't think the two tables look very different. My saltcellars and pepper mills are brass, from Italy, my knives and forks are brass, from Thailand. For candleholders I use glass snowballs from Sweden with a "night light" candle in them (see photograph 14). They give the best light, and as they are low, they don't visually dissect a guest's view of the person opposite.

The pink glass borrowed for the magazine display (photograph 12) is modern and quite expensive. I find that pink glass mixed among the blue-and-white china gives just enough additional glow to take the slight chill off the blue and white. Just as the red of the cushions does (photographs 12, 13, 14) or the red carpet in the blue batik room (photograph 15). Of course, a bright bunch of anemones or some other flower, or a bowl of cherries (see photograph 13) does the trick as well.

With patience and perseverance I have found Victorian pink glass quite cheaply, but only a glass or two at a time and none of them identical. I mix the ones I have with clear glass (photograph 13). As with the china (and the dining room chairs) I find slight variations pleasing to the eye. Symmetry is one thing, mass production quite another.

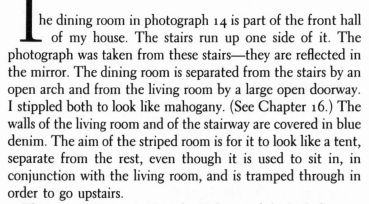

Fifteen

The dining room in photograph 14 is part of the front hall of my house. The stairs run up one side of it. The photograph was taken from these stairs—they are reflected in the mirror. The dining room is separated from the stairs by an open arch and from the living room by a large open doorway. I stippled both to look like mahogany. (See Chapter 16.) The walls of the living room and of the stairway are covered in blue denim. The aim of the striped room is for it to look like a tent, separate from the rest, even though it is used to sit in, in conjunction with the living room, and is tramped through in order to go upstairs.

There is a painting in Paris by Delacroix (of which figure A is a very amateurish copy) that has always seemed to me the most tempting of interiors. It is one of the paintings Delacroix did that represents the bedroom of the Comte Charles de Mornay. The stripes are blue and white, the hanging behind the bed is crimson. I am not alone in being strongly influenced by Delacroix paintings and drawings. The decorators Bob Denning and Vincent Fourcade—who have greatly helped and

A

influenced me—put into their decoration a definite Delacroix flair. If I could afford to do so, I would deliver myself into their hands and live happily in the surroundings they create. As things are, I can only try to achieve interiors of similar splendor, if not of equally perfect execution. Where they free their clients from the work and worry and present them with palaces completed by trained artisans, I would like to show how to create a palace by improvisation and hard work.

I had never found the right blue-and-white stripe to make a Delacroix room until I found the blue-and-white-striped sheeting that now covers the walls and ceiling of my dining room (photographs 12–14). I had often flirted with a wonderful striped French material, but it costs an arm and a leg. It is used a lot by a lady of genius, Madeleine Castaing—a Paris decorator and the owner of the most tempting shop I know. (Madeleine Castaing has been playing about combining wicker, paisley shawls, Victorian settees, Regency and Biedermeier furniture with remarkable talent for the past three decades—long before anyone else.)

Ticking, although I like it, never has a strong enough stripe. Sometimes I find pajama materials in an attractive blue-and-white stripe, but those I have found lately had a nasty consistency—flannelet. The typical Empire-style striped material that can be bought in upholstery shops costs a lot and is usually drab in color and shiny (silk, or worse, rayon) in texture.

The striped sheeting in my dining room is cotton, bright, inexpensive—just what I wanted. I found it in a department store. It comes by the yard and is 90" wide—3 yards of it, hemmed, make a sheet for a double bed. At $4 a yard, it costs $12 a sheet (not counting the hemming labor), which seems quite reasonable. Because of its size it is also the fastest material to put on walls and ceilings. A lot of seaming is avoided. I stapled it on the walls and on the ceiling (see Chapter 2 for how this is done), and covered the banquette (page 74) and cushions with it. (See pages 194–95 for how to make cushions with ruffles.)

On account of the width of the material, I became ambitious. I tried to cover the ceiling in a more complicated way than I usually do. I tried to form a flat sunburst, employing the stripes as pleats. It was a challenge. The room wasn't square, which made it harder. I should have sat down and pinned the material on the floor first, or at least limited myself to treating

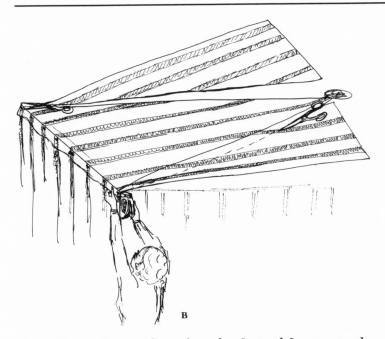

B

the ceiling as four wedges of a cake. Instead I got onto the
ladder immediately and made eight wedges, straight onto the
ceiling. It took hours of irritation and still the wedges aren't
exactly equal, but no one notices—or at least they are too polite
to say so.

I first marked the middle of the ceiling. (See page 26 for how
to do this.) Then I chose a stripe that was central to a length
of material and stapled one end of the stripe into the middle
of the top of a wall, the other end of it into the middle of the
ceiling. Then I stapled the wide side of the wedge, left and
right of the first staple, flat to the top of the wall. I cut away
the two angled pieces that were left dangling from the wedge.
(B) I sewed those together and the seam gave me the central
stripe for the next wedge. (C) I stapled it on the opposite side.
I did the same to form the two other wedges. Because the room
was rectangular, I was now left with four uneven corner wedges
to fill in. I did the same as before: I took a central stripe, stapled
it into the corner and ran it to the ceiling center. The complica-
tions started when the one side of the wedge had a different
bias than the other. I had to pull and push to keep strange
lumps from forming.

I tried to match the blue stripes where they met, but as they
are varied in size and in tone, this was practically impossible.

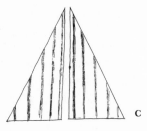

C

When I had it looking almost right, I folded the bias edges of a top wedge under and stitched them here and there to the material underneath, using a curved needle. (D)

When I finished I realized I might have achieved almost the same effect by stretching the striped material flat across the ceiling (as in the gingham bathroom, for instance—photograph 34), making separate blue ribbons out of more stripes, and stretching them from the center of the ceiling to the various points around the walls to mark the wedges. It would have been not quite as nice but a great deal faster.

To hide the staples in the center of the ceiling, I made a circle out of a woolen cord, coiled up, and glued it on carefully with material glue. I could have also used a rosette made up out of the different shades of blue stripes. (See page 222.)

The red-covered Victorian swivel chairs and red cushions are there to "heat up" the cool of the blue and white (and to follow the color combination in the Delacroix picture). The banquette is made like the other banquettes I've already described, except that the front is curved (see photograph 14). The curve is out of thin plywood, bent. The seat cushions are stuffed with horsehair (see page 85 for method), the blue-and-white-striped cushions with feathers. (For how I make cushions and slipcovers, see pages 35–36, 85–86, 118 and 194–95.)

A long time ago, at an auction, I bought two eagle console tables. They are copies of ones designed by William Kent. They were passably well gilded, and as I have a weakness for furniture in animal shapes, I bought them. Gilded eagles aren't quite as charming as a monkey holding a tray (E) or a smiling camel turned into a table (the latter visible in photograph 5). They looked too grand and imposing no matter where I placed them. Also, they had the sort of fleshy-pink marble tops I don't much like. So I built one eagle into a sideboard and made the dining room table out of the other. (Both can be seen in photograph 14.)

The sideboard is in the left corner. The eagle console was too low, so I put a few wooden blocks under it to raise it to counter height. I left the marble top on it (for additional height) and placed a large triangular piece of plywood on top of the marble. Mr. Lewis, the carpenter, built a triangular set of curved shelves to go above the sideboard and two curved sides to hold the shelves. They, too, are made of plywood.

The measuring for the two sides was trickier than might appear. There is a boxed-in pipe in the true corner of the room. If the sides of the shelves were to fit flush with the wall on each side (without a gap) they had to be slightly different. To work this problem out on paper seemed impossible. From newspaper, I drew and cut out a shape that pleased me. (Newspaper, because of its size and availability, is remarkably handy for making paper patterns—see page 265.) Mr. Lewis then followed the paper shape and cut it out of plywood with his portable jig saw. This was the side to go into the corner. (F) By holding it in the other direction, across the boxed-in pipe, I was able to see how much wider the right side would have to be than the left for the completed shelves not to look out of proportion. Mr. Lewis cut the second side, screwed the two sides together and attached the curved shelves within the sides. He used plywood, which is slightly more expensive than chipboard, because it is stronger and he could securely screw the shelves to the sides without the aid of brackets.

Where plywood has been cut something horrid appears. That's why all shelves made out of it have to be faced with a strip of some other wood. To face the shelf unit, I bought some very narrow, but fancy, molding. I had hoped, as it was so narrow, that I would be able to bend it around the curve. I was wrong. It snapped merrily. So, to soften it, I threw it in a bathtub full of water and soaked it for a couple of days. This softened it well enough for the curved bits around the front of the shelves, but still didn't make the molding sufficiently pliable to curve around the sides. I had to take the kitchen knife to the rest of it. I made a lot of little slits halfway through the molding to help it follow the side curves. I attached the bent molding with glue, holding them in place with thin nails until the glue dried. (G) Later, I removed the nails (page 21).

The corner shelf displays my blue-and-white china. On the sideboard I have a hot plate. When I give a dinner, my guests usually help themselves. The hot food, in blue-and-white covered dishes, goes on the hot plate. On the two "reachable" shelves above the hot plate, more blue-and-white dishes can hold the cold food. I painted the shelves a dark burgundy red to offset the blue and white of the china.

To avoid the tedium of priming and undercoating wood before painting it, I have made, for my needs, a useful discov-

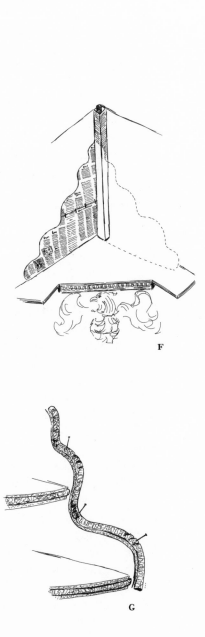

F

G

ery: car sprays. They come in a multitude of colors and form an extremely durable undercoat. I buy the small spray cans. They are quite expensive, but save on time. On the few occasions I need larger quantities, I buy the paint by the gallon and use a sprayer that I borrow from a garage. I used car sprays as the base coat for the corner shelf, the sideboard and the lid of the dinner table in the tented dining room. I also used them to undercoat the kitchen cabinets in the converted barn (description on page 152, photographs 26 and 27), and to make the swimming pool surround less stridently blue (page 271 and photograph 58). The shelves and the sideboard I sprayed blotchily, alternating two different colors, so that it looks like soldiers' camouflage, though in this case in very uncamouflaging colors—red and dark brown. Over that I streakily painted burnt sienna and alizarin-crimson artist's oil paint. The blotchy base and the uneven top coat quickly gave an effect that would have otherwise required centuries of use to achieve (or at least weeks of hard work). I picked out the molding in Liquid Leaf (page 65). Since the molding is narrower than the plywood edge, it still left part of the rough edges showing. I painted these in a darker shade of Liquid Leaf.

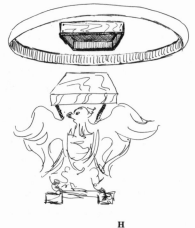

H

To make the table (photograph 14), I went to my favorite junk shop, where I found a solid, round tabletop. Its legs had long since disappeared. I carted it home. Minus its marble top, the eagle console ended in a square block of wood. Mr. Lewis attached a square of wood made out of some 2″ × 2″ on the underside of the tabletop. (H) This square fits over the block on top of the eagle. The lid is further secured to the block with screws.

The tabletop had been painted once—a very long time ago. What was left was peeling. I should have stripped it, but that is a task I shy away from. I don't know what I dislike about it more—the mess when the paint peels off or the fear of what is in the stripper to make the paint peel. I simply sanded the top and then sprayed it with car spray—this time in a pale yellow—as a base for my *faux bois* (false wood). Then I painted the table lid to look as if it was made out of a light fruitwood. (See Chapter 16 for how to simulate wood.)

The table is 4′ 2″ across and just manages to comfortably seat six. If I had the space in which to hide them, I would have lids of varying sizes to put on top of the table to enlarge it. I would have a 5′ lid for eight people and a 6′ lid for ten to twelve. Anything larger wouldn't balance on top of the eagle —even the 6′ one might need a couple of snap-on legs to give it extra support. The lids could be of plywood, the smaller hinged in the middle, the larger hinged to fold in two places. (A good hiding place for the lids is under a bed.)

If the lid is to be cut at home out of a sheet of plywood by an amateur, the easiest way to draw a circle or a half circle is to tie one end of a length of string to a pencil, the other end to a nail. Hit the nail into the center of the sheet of wood, and run around it with the pencil on the taut string. (I) (The string must, of course, be half the length of the diameter of the desired table.)

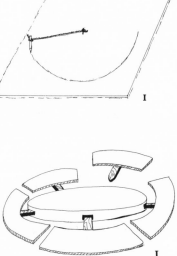

I have also used this system to paint some form of decoration onto round tabletops. I admire light fruitwood tables *(bois clair)*. They often have a circular inlay of a darker wood, usually ebony, around the edge. This is quite easy to paint on, provided the guidelines have been drawn.

Because I had no space in which to hide a large table lid (whereas I had a lot of space under the banquette to fit in small additions), I devised a more complicated system for enlarging my dining room table. I have five segments, 1′ deep, made out of 1/2″ plywood, to surround the table. Each segment has a 2″ × 1″ piece of wood screwed to the underside of it, project-ing about 9″. The tabletop has five slots in its rim. The seg-ments get attached to the table by sliding the 2″ × 1″ pieces into the slots. (J) They are further secured by a clasp under the table that snaps to join one segment to the next.

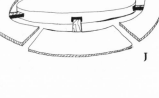

I cover the enlarged table with a cloth, since the enlarge-ments are not neat enough for the table to be left bare. The unenlarged tabletop, however, is uncovered most of the time. I have little wooden plaques glued to pieces of 2″ × 1″ that I plug into the table's rim to hide the slots. (K) They are painted to match the tabletop.

The curve of the banquette follows the curve of the enlarged table. It is easy to eat off a smaller table when sitting on the banquette, but it would be impossible to fit in a table that was larger than the curve of the banquette.

There are other things to remember about banquettes. Though they are much nicer to look at than a row of chairs— and in my view more comfortable—it is impossible to serve people sitting on a banquette. If, as is mostly the case in my house, guests go to the sideboard to help themselves, they have to remember in which order they came out, to slot themselves back in. So I have limited myself to ten: four on the banquette, six in chairs. By having only four on the banquette, there are only two people who may suffer claustrophobia or who are dependant on the whim of their neighbors. If possible, I have the first course on the table when people sit down, preferably cold and in covered dishes so that it hasn't been too obviously exposed. Then the guests serve themselves to the main course. The dessert I again put in the center of the table. On those occasions when I do have someone to serve, the two people in the center of the banquette are again dependent on their neighbors to fill their plates for them, since the person serving cannot reach across. Oddly enough, I find that a certain amount of confusion in the management of a dinner party heightens the spirits of the guests—providing, of course, they have enough good food and wine.

Sixteen

The system I use to paint imitation wood is very much like the one I use to paint walls. (See Chapter 10). I start out with a white or light-colored shiny base. I most often have a white base because I invariably have a can of white paint around. A shiny paint is better to work on than a flat paint because the color flows better. If the surface is already a light-colored flat paint, there is no point in repainting it, although the color will slip around a bit less freely. In fact, the ideal base for the lightwood colors is a shiny pale yellow; for mahogany or dark oak, a shiny light brown.

The basecoat must be completely dry before you begin to simulate wood. To simulate it, I work with artist's oil paints and turpentine. For all the different woods I use a varying mixture of the same colors: yellow ocher, burnt sienna, raw umber, Vandyke brown, with the rare addition of black and white.

For all maple woods I use a mixture of yellow ocher, burnt umber and raw umber. Maples vary from pale yellow to reddish brown, so I change the proportion of my paints accordingly. I apply the oil paint in the same way as described on pages 67–68. When I use two or three different oil paints, I don't mix them, but dab my brush at them alternately. The eye must be the guide to where more of one paint and less of another is necessary. Parts of the surface I am painting will be darker and parts lighter, depending on how much of each color I had on the paintbrush. This is exactly what I want as long as the differences are not too extreme. No piece of wood is exactly the same color all along. Commercial stains seem so obviously stains because of their uniformity.

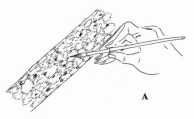

A

When simulating bird's-eye maple—the kind often used on picture frames (see book jacket)—I first smear on the paint well diluted with turpentine and then stipple it (dab at it) with a paintbrush. Bird's-eye maple has little dark dots in the grain. To make these, I wait an hour or so, until the stippled paint has partially dried. Then I tap on the marks with a thin brush (A), on which I have Vandyke brown, only slightly thinned with turpentine. The dots will look rather hard, so I make a ball of cheesecloth (or, if that isn't readily available, some soft rag) and dab it ever so gently against the dots. If the paint has become too dry or if I dab too hard, a smudge will appear. This should be avoided, if possible. Only when simulating burr maple (a wood with swirls in the grain) can the careless smudge be an asset. A passable replica of burr maple can be achieved by pressing a finger (making a fingerprint) onto the freshly stippled wet paint.

The dining room tabletop in the blue-and-white tent is "maple" and so are the cupboards under the stairs reflected in the mirror (photograph 14). The New York studio (photographs 49 and 50) is full of "bird's-eye maple." On the ceiling, doors and window frames of the dining room in California (photographs 19–20), I tried for "walnut."

If I am trying to simulate a wood with an obvious grain (such as pine, walnut or other fruitwoods), I follow the same principle as with the dots for bird's-eye maple: I draw lines with a fine watercolor brush (or just some hairs plucked from any brush), and dab the cheesecloth against them to smudge them. I always try to look at the wood that I want to copy while I'm painting. When, for example, I want to simulate mahogany, I need to look at a piece of mahogany. It is a close-grained wood without obvious markings, so the effect can be achieved by simply stippling with a paintbrush. I use burnt umber and raw umber for the brown varieties. For red mahogany I add some burnt sienna. In the London living room (photographs 1–5), I painted "mahogany" on the steps of the czar's carriage, the door, window frame, bookshelves and cupboards that hide the heaters.

For pine, which has a straight grain, I have had some quite good results by dragging a paintbrush hardened through neglect across the half-dry paint, having first stippled with raw umber, yellow ocher and a touch of white. I also add a bit of white to Vandyke brown to simulate weathered oak. Burnt umber and Vandyke brown with a little yellow ocher made the color of the "oak" cupboards in the converted barn (page 257).

I have devised a pale color to go with bamboo—a cross between the color of parchment and lightwood. (See photographs 17, 47 and 48.) To mix it, I use yellow ocher with just a dab of Vandyke brown (to dirty up the brightness) and a lot of turpentine. I wash the paint on rather than stipple it, and if I want the spotty-parchment look, I splash it with more turpentine. When I want it to really look like bamboo, I paint on raw-umber knuckles (see stairs, photograph 17, and bamboo chair, photograph 54) or just an occasional smudged raw-umber line.

Once the paint for whichever wood I'm trying to simulate is dry, I seal it. For surfaces that will come into contact with water or alcohol (tabletops, kitchen counters or the wood surrounding washbasins and baths), I use a semi-flat polyurethane. For surfaces that are safe from water spills, I use French polish. It gives a more realistic shine, more like polished and waxed wood, than the polyurethane does. The confusion with French polish arises from the fact that it seems to have different names not only from country to country but also within each country. I have bought it as "French polish," "wood polish," "brush polish" or "padding lacquer." But the mixture always consists of shellac processed and refined with alcohol. It also has wax added to it, which gives it a dark, syruplike color. Its advantage over pure shellac is its coloring and the fact that it doesn't crack if used on wood that might shrink or expand.

The professional applies French polish with a pad of cotton wool inside a wrapping of cheesecloth. A small amount of French polish is poured onto the pad and the pad is rubbed in a circular motion, over and over again, against the surface. I think this gives an even, very smooth, high-gloss surface, rather like that on a grand piano. I am afraid I take the less complicated route, with more rustic results.

To apply the French polish, I use a 2″ house-painter's brush. If it loses hairs, they must be picked off immediately, before the polish hardens. The paintbrush must be cleaned in methylated spirits. I would like to be able to say that I give two coats of French polish to the work, but usually it gets one and "waits" for the second coat. After the second coat, perfectionists might sand with a very fine sandpaper and rub furniture wax into the wood. That way it is more likely to acquire the patina of age. (I did this in the libraries, photographs 55, 56 and 57, and to some of the new wood in the converted barn, with quite good results.)

Although French polish looks better than polyurethane, it scratches and stains easily. Polyurethane is strong and makes a surface watertight. As with French polish, I put it on with a house-painter's brush, but in this case the brush can be cleaned in gum turpentine. The more patience the more coats, and the more coats the better—especially if each dry coat is also rubbed down with fine sandpaper before the next one is put on.

For imitation marble I use very much the same technique as I do for imitation wood. I first choose the dominant color existing in the marble I am trying to imitate, and paint the surface with it evenly. This initial basecoat has to dry thoroughly. Next I color the surface in darker and lighter tones. It is important that these effects are completed before they begin to dry; otherwise the flowing look of marble cannot be achieved. If doing larger surfaces (like a whole bathroom), it is important to do only a patch at a time. Finally, if the marble I am imitating has veins, I paint those on.

To turn the tops and bases of the small column-tables in the California living room (just visible in front of the banquettes in photograph 6; see also Chapter 11, figure E) into gray marble, I first gave them a coat of pale-gray shiny enamel paint. Onto the gray undercoat I streakily painted the next shade. I used an ordinary 2″ house-painter's brush and a mixture of artist's oil paints out of tubes—gray, a bit of black, a touch of blue—and thinned with turpentine. Then I dabbed at the streaky paint with a wad of cheesecloth. Cheesecloth comes in various qualities: The larger the holes the cheesecloth has, the coarser the markings. If a really rough-looking pattern in the "marble" is wanted, scrunched-up newspaper dabbed against the wet paint is best. Next, the pattern made by the newspaper must be smoothed out with a dry soft brush. I use a house-painter's brush, but with natural bristles.

The next stages depend very much on what sort of marble one wishes to simulate. For the gray marble I use the original wet brush and dab on the same mix of paints as above (less diluted) in semicircular arches. (B) Then I smooth it with the dry paintbrush. (C) Next, I paint the veins. I do this with a small watercolor brush, using the same mix of colors, lightened by both additional white and some glazing coat (page 69). If I don't have any glazing coat handy, I thin down the paint with turpentine and add a drop of cooking oil. I paint on the veins with a shaky hand, turning the paintbrush as I go. (D) Followed, once again, by the dry brush to smooth things out. If I want especially thin veins, I pluck a hair or two out of the large bristle brush and use them. A feather dragged and turned over the wet paint is also often used to make veins; they look slightly different from painted ones but not so much better as to warrant the struggle to find a feather.

All the veins in marble meet. In a slab of marble, they continue around the edge. To make imitation marble look more authentic, it helps to follow the same principle.

Gray marble often has some black specks. I make these by first diluting black artist's oil paint with some glazing coat or turpentine, dipping a small watercolor brush into it and then flicking the brush over the paint as if I were trying to dry the brush or shake down a thermometer. If the paint is still sufficiently wet, this will make interesting speckles, which must, however, once more be smoothed out with a dry brush.

The New York bathroom (see Chapter 39, figure E), which I marbleized to look like Siena marble, had white tiles. I left them white instead of painting them a pale-salmon color. I did this primarily out of laziness, but tiles are also a very pleasant surface to marbleize (as are bathroom fixtures or kitchen appliances): The paint flows better on enamel or china than on a painted surface. Siena marble sometimes has some white (or almost white) blobs in it (or so I wished to believe to avoid undercoating the whole bathroom).

I painted about a yard square in raw sienna, streakily. Then came the cheesecloth stage, then the smoothing stage and so on, as with the gray marble. One difference, however: The marble I was trying to copy had markings on it like little pebbles. These were lighter in color than the rest of the marble. They can be achieved—and are great fun to do—by dipping your fingers into turpentine and flicking them at the wall. If the paint on the wall is the right consistency—not too wet and not too dry—the drops of turpentine will form small uneven circles. Then I smoothed the circles with a dry brush and painted the veins in burnt sienna.

Splattering with turpentine to create a pattern works more easily if flicking the turpentine down onto a flat surface. On a vertical surface (walls), the turpentine drops tend to run downward unless the paint on the wall is exactly the right consistency and the drops fine enough.

I managed to get the tortoise-shell–like effect of the supper room in the house in California (photograph 18) by allowing the drips of turpentine to run down. First I undercoated the vaulted room in a pale-orange enamel paint. When it was dry, I stippled the wall, a patch at a time, in burnt umber. Then I flicked the turpentine at it and let it work the patterns as it pleased, without any additional help from me. When the whole room was dry, I coated it in French polish.

Marbling is really trial and error, smudging about, not being afraid of a mess—something, sometimes, comes out of it. And if it doesn't, it's important not to feel defeated, and to have the courage to take the paint off and start again. Once pleased—or at least not appalled—with your marbling technique, it is possible to marble rooms, floors, mantelpieces, doorframes, baseboards, tabletops, picture frames, bottles or jam jars, or to make a modern cement garden ornament into a seventeenth-century porphyry urn. (E)

The mantelpiece surrounding the fireplace visible in photograph 25 is green "marble." I painted it first white, then with

E

a mixture of green oil paints, and dabbed at it with a crumpled wad of newspaper. The green lamp in photograph 49 was very pink when it was given to me. I stippled it green and black and then shellacked it. The hidden pink gives it a nice luminosity. The bottle next to it is an ordinary wine bottle. I tried to make it look like onyx. I first gave it a coat of white enamel paint and then splattered it with oil paints that I allowed to drip.

Seventeen

Large mirrors, which do so much to add zest as well as size to rooms, grow continuously more expensive. Occasionally, however, rather cheap unframed mirrors can be found in a department or hardware store. These mirrors can be framed with unpainted picture-frame molding, which can be colored or covered as one might wish. Any mirror that is already framed in an unpleasing way can, of course, also be recolored or covered.

A way of making a grand frame for a mirror with little expense and minimal technical skill is: First of all, hang an ordinary, unframed, store-bought mirror (the kind meant for inside a cupboard door—but not too narrow). Put it up according to the accompanying instructions, with either mirror corners or mirror screws. Then surround the mirror with four ordinary boards (cut and bought at a lumber yard), placing them as close to the sides of the mirror as the fixing will allow. (A) How wide the boards are—that is, how wide the mirror frame will be—is a matter of taste. Hammer or screw the boards into the wall, then cover them with material.

Renaissance mirror frames were quite often covered in this way. Old velvet or brocade looks best, or a tattered bit of silk. (A modern remnant can be aged for this purpose. For how, see pages 195–96.) Leather can be used or even imitation leather, which can be painted with Liquid Leaf (page 65) to look like

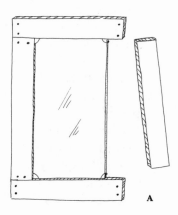

A

tooling or with oil paint to simulate Cordoba leather (see Chapter 9, figure 1). The material to cover the wood should be the same width as the wood plus 1/2″. Having avoided the tedium of mitering the wood, you must miter the material (sew it to form angles at the corners). The easiest way to do this, I find, is to lay it out on the floor or table and pin it, cut it and then sew it by hand. (B)

Then the material gets stapled to the wood on the outer edge, into the side of the wood, and on the inner edge, to the top of the wood. (C) The staples have to be hidden by molding. In the best frame I made, I covered the wood in a dark-red velvet. I hid the outer staples with a half-round molding painted black. The half-round was 1″ wide, the board was 1″ thick. This meant the board ended in a curve. The second half-round (the same size and also painted black) covered the staples and the join—or gap—between the mirror and the wood. The two sets of half-rounds had to be mitered (page 140). Where I didn't succeed too well, I filled in the gap with plastic wood putty.

If there is a discrepancy between the thickness of the wood (plus the half-round) and the mirror, another flat molding or a wood slat may be necessary. It can either be slotted underneath the half-round (D) or lie next to it, depending on which is needed or which looks better. This molding looks best painted gold or silver.

In the blue-and-white-striped dining room (photograph 14), I desperately needed space. Short of moving house, a mirror was the best way of achieving this.

I own quite a nice Chinese Chippendale–type gilt mirror. I hung it up, in the conventional way, above the fireplace. I might just as well have hung up a mirrored postage stamp for the depth and enlargement it gave the room. So Mr. Lewis and I mirrored the entire chimney-breast.

In a department store sale I bought six mirrors in varying sizes: two 18″ × 60″, two 24″ × 48″, and two 18″ × 30″. We glued them to the wall using a strong adhesive especially designed for affixing mirrors. But because of the weight of the mirrors, the adhesive would not have been sufficient, and we had to build them upward, starting at floor level, resting one on top of the other, with wooden slats between them for support (the slats 3/8″ wide). We glued the two 18″ × 30″

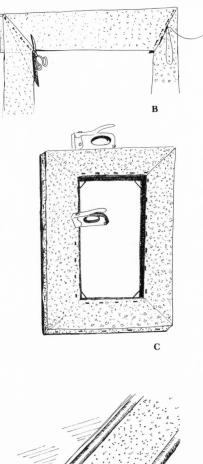

mirrors vertically, left and right of the fireplace. On top of
them Mr. Lewis screwed a wooden slat (60″ long) into the
chimney-breast. The next mirror, a 60″ × 18″ one, is glued
horizontally to the chimney-breast and rests on the wooden slat
beneath it. On top of the horizontal mirror, another slat supports the next two 24″ × 48″ mirrors, which are glued vertically. Again, on top of them, a slat of wood 60″ long across the
chimney-breast, and on top of that, the last mirror, placed
horizontally. (E) Over the central gap I hung the Chippendale
mirror, so saving on the cost of an extra mirror.

We covered the slats of wood used to support the mirrors
with molding, which I first painted with Liquid Leaf (page 65).
The molding—5/8″ wide—was slightly wider than the
wooden slats. By nailing it on top of the slats, it not only
covered them but overlapped where the slat met the mirror and
so served as a further safeguard in holding the mirrors. On the
corners of the chimney-breast, I used picture-frame molding,
treated in the same way.

If I had used the fireplace in the striped hall/dining tent as
a fireplace, I or a guest would have been cooked during dinner.
I decided I'd rather cook the food in it. Out of the lower half
of the existing opening we made a cupboard. We glued two 12″
× 18″ mirror tiles to plywood doors. The top of the cupboard
is made out of some iron bars, set into the brickwork of the old
fireplace. On top of the bars we placed a double layer of an
asbestos-substitute fireproof board, which formed a platform
for a barbecue. The opening for the barbecue is narrower than
the original fireplace opening. Its walls are out of wood, but also
lined with a double layer of fireproof board. (F)

The barbecue opening is framed with a rectangle of picture-
frame molding, which I gilded with Treasure Gold (page 65).
I use an ordinary hibachi barbecue inside the opening. Not
only do I find it excellent to cook on (indoors or out), but the
glowing coals look warm and welcoming, even before the food
has been put on them. In the mirrored cupboard under the
barbecue, I store the charcoal and all my barbecue equipment.
When I am cooking and feeding guests, I always take one of
the two red swivel chairs for myself. That way I can look after
the fire without appearing to neglect my guests.

Two bronze candleholders (sconces) in the shape of mer-
maids are attached to the dining room mirror (photograph 14).

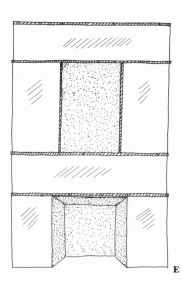

E

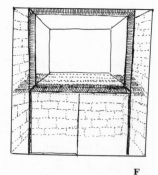

F

G

As they are quite heavy, this would be impossible if it wasn't for the strip of wood beneath the molding, through which the sconces are screwed into the wall.

China and glass display beautifully in front of mirrors. Small shelves, fitted onto the wooden strips before they went on the chimney-breast, would have enabled me to have the same arrangement against the mirror of the tented dining room as I made in the red dining room (photograph 10). (G) Plates, unfortunately, cannot be mounted this way against a mirror, nor can busts or anything that doesn't look as good in the back as in the front (my tureens, for instance, which are chipped). Plates can be hung, like the sconces, flat against a mirrored wall —which is also attractive, but not as dramatic as the reflection of a perfect piece of china.

A picture or a clock hung against a mirror or a mirrored wall can be very effective. It looks best suspended on a ribbon or a cord. As the ribbon or cord is unlikely to be strong enough to hold it, a picture wire can be hidden behind the ribbon. If the wall is covered in mirrored tiles (pages 90–91), either a whole tile or a chip of a tile could be removed, a nail to hold the picture hammered into the wall, and the ribbon suspended over the mirror only for effect. A clock hung in this way is usually some grand eighteenth-century one. If short of those, a kitchen clock, some Liquid Leaf (page 65) and perhaps some extra material puffed around it looks just as good. (H)

The window in the blue-and-white-striped hall/dining room is long and narrow—an awkward shape. I mirrored the shutters. Now, when open, they give the illusion of a wider window and also reflect what light there is (photographs 13 and 14). When closed, they are the same blue-and-white stripe as the rest of the room (photograph 12). The shutters are made out of plywood. They are attached to the wall and to each other with brass piano hinges in the same way as the shutters in the brown living room (see page 28 and photographs 4 and 5). The plywood is faced with a strip of wood. The strip is 1/4" wider than the plywood. (I) It protrudes and forms a frame around the plywood shutter for the mirror to fit into. Because of the singular shape of the shutters, the mirror had to be cut to size. The mirror is glued to the shutter with mirror adhesive. Where the framing and the mirror meet is concealed by a half-round molding. I gilded the molding with Liquid Leaf. It is pinned to the plywood with finishing nails through the narrow gap between the framing and the mirror, as well as glued over both. (J)

Mirrored screens—much in fashion in the twenties—do wonders for a room and can be made in the same way as the shutters. They can be made more cheaply by using mirrored tiles (see pages 90–91). Even though the wooden strips may not be necessary to ensure that the tiles are held safely, I like the look of a screen with a quantity of small mirrors framed in molding. (K)

The two blue pots in the corners above the banquette (one can be seen in photograph 14) adds—I hope—an Oriental mood to the tented dining room. They stand on top of two brackets that are much too small for them. I wanted to use the brackets (which I already had) because they have eagles on them and I thought they'd fit in with the rest of the aviary (the eagle in the sideboard and the one supporting the table). The pots are heavy and people sit under them. It is extremely

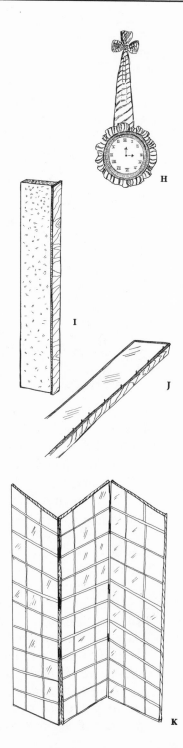

important that they remain in place. Mr. Lewis made a triangle out of three 2″ × 2″ pieces of wood and screwed it into the corner. (L) He then screwed a triangular shelf made out of 2″ plywood to the 2″ × 2″ supports. He attached the bracket to the front edge of the plywood shelf. Where the triangular corner shelf extends beyond the brackets I glued on some ornamentation. (M) (The "ornamentation" is little pieces of plaster that I picked off a rather ugly broken picture frame.) I gilded the shelf part and the ornamentation. What was visible of the 2″ × 2″s below the shelf I covered with a strip of striped material, stapled on. The wood now disappears among the rest of the stripes.

The shelves that support the figures in the czar's carriage (one is visible in photograph 1) are attached the same way as the shelves for the pots, except that they have no additional brackets. The shelves are out of 3/4″ plywood and painted imitation marble (pages 103–6). I cut a horizontal slit in the pajama-stripe material, out of which the shelves protrude, and stapled the material under the shelf to hide the triangle of 2″ × 2″ that supports it. The figures—a gentleman and a lady (only the gentleman can be seen in the photo)—were in a dark metal when I found them. A generous application of Liquid Leaf made them much grander-looking, especially when I also picked out the stripes in their turbans in red paint and more paint turned their jewels into rubies and emeralds.

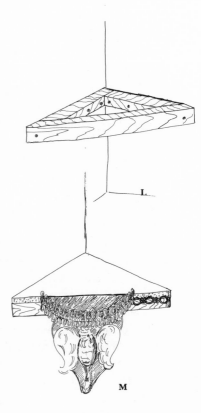

Eighteen

One of the directives for the California house was that it be easy and casual to live in most of the year, but ready to spring into action on those occasions when large formal entertaining was planned. There are now three multipurpose rooms that can serve as dining rooms. All of them can hold a table for ten with ease, and the original dining room

can take a much larger table. (Although that seems to exagger-
ate the number of guests for a seated dinner, even for Hollywood.) The living room is not included among the rooms to
be used for seating dinner guests, though it could also accommodate quite a few. It can remain empty for the guests to
gather in before dinner and escape into afterward.

The main dining room (photographs 19 and 20) is a thor-
oughfare to the kitchen, the supper room and outside. When
I first saw the house, the ceiling of the main dining room was
painted the same chocolate brown as the ceiling of the living
room. It has seven doorways. That shouldn't happen to any
room, least of all a room only 15' × 18'. Two of the doors were
also painted chocolate. There is an open arch leading into the
room from the hall, and another open arch into the supper
room. A third arch with a glassed-in door leads to the garden,
and two French doors (with a window on each side of them)
lead onto the terrace.

It seemed sad to totally ignore the intricate beamed effect
of the ceiling. Although I didn't find it particularly beautiful,
to paint it white and forget it was too feeble. Brown it couldn't
stay—not that brown. Wanting, as I did, a nineteenth-century
flavor to the room, I painted the ceiling to look like *bois clair*
—in this case walnut. (See pages 100–2 for how this is done.)

As the room is a passage to the outside and the only light
room in the house, I wanted it to be "gardeny." I found and
bought four modern wicker armchairs for it (see photographs
19 and 20). The ceiling, in combination with the chairs, made
the room look like what I had originally promised—a set for
A Month in the Country, by Turgenev. I could envisage the
characters sitting around a table in the wicker chairs playing
piquet. When I saw the brass chandelier in New York (page
59) it fitted the scene perfectly. It could be pulled down to light
the game of piquet and pushed back up to leave the table free
for dining.

More and more, the room developed a Biedermeier look,
which combines a lot of lightwood with black inlay. Biedermeier rooms often had material-covered walls, usually a patterned stripe. The material I stapled on the walls had a very
nineteenth-century, middle-European flavor, and as I had
turned it the wrong way around to avoid its too-bright color,
it also looks as if it had been fading in middle Europe for a

hundred years. (See Chapter 2 for how to put up material on walls.) In the corners I hid the staples with strips of wood painted black. I further accentuated the "walnut" ceiling by adding more strips of black wood to it. To hide the staples around the French windows and to give the windows a frame, I glued picture framing around them. I painted that, as well as the doors, "walnut." (See Chapter 16.)

For the windows we made shades out of lace. For years I have looked away from the bolts of thick cotton lace in department stores. They made me think of rows and rows of identical lives hidden behind identical lace curtains. Not having them would be a sign of originality. Lately, however, I eye the bolts with a certain curiosity. Machine-made cotton lace is not expensive and can be used for any number of things. In Los Angeles I found one that had scallops of flowers in the pattern. We cut panels the same width as the windows and cut around the scallops to form the borders. (Cutting around the edge of a design in lace saves hemming it; it also accentuates the design and gives an attractive finish to the bottom of the shade.) The shades are on rollers, the rollers fitted into the window frames. (See page 188.) A small loop in the lace just above the bottom scallops has a brass rod threaded through it with brass acorns protruding at each end. This again is typically Biedermeier, and the weight of it holds the blind straight. (A)

I used cotton lace, again cut into scallops, to decorate food barrows for a wedding party. (B) The cost of the lace was well

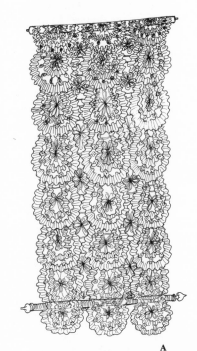

A

B

worth the effect it created. For each barrow I needed only
1 1/2 yards of lace. (The barrows were borrowed—for a consideration, naturally—from a street fruit vendor.)

I have cut strips out of leftover inexpensive lace and used
them as very grand ribbons for Christmas presents. (c) Leftover lace flowers I cut out, spray-starched and used for Christmas tree decorations. (d)

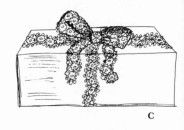

C

The sideboard in the dining room (photograph 19) came
from an auction. It was mahogany and heavy. (e) Under the
drawers was a cupboard, and between the top of the sideboard
and the shelf was a mirror. We gutted everything but what is
left in photograph 19. Then I painted it. (See page 64.) The
pieces I had removed later served as a mahogany cupboard for
a washbasin and as the mirror above it in a bathroom of the
California house.

I found the dolphins that support the central table (photograph 20) deep in downtown New York. They were waiting,
hidden in a corner, for their climb uptown. In London, which
is smaller, I have often been able to watch the rise, and sometimes the fall, of a "cooked-up" piece of furniture. It starts out
at a London market—not something as smart as the Portobello
market has become, but a market further out of London, fre-
quented by dealers. From there it travels to a shop in the
outskirts of town, where it gets mended, painted and transformed into what it is to become. After that it can travel
through as many different shops (mostly catering only to the
trade) as it can stand price rises. Finally it ends up, if worthy
enough, on Bond Street. (Close to the top of its rise, it can pass
through a chic auction house as well, but there it won't be
bought by a dealer, who knows it by this time, but by an
individual looking for that sort of furniture.) What can happen
is that the piece of furniture, which is usually more decorative
than valuable, has such an inflated price due to its travels that
it gets stuck. It then goes to a less "good" auction house, and
so the piece and its price can travel downward again. Somewhere along the way it might go to an antique shop in the
country, where it could, of course, be "discovered." There is
always the foolhardy traveler who believes what he finds in the
country to be a bargain.

D

A genuine antique often travels the same road, but its path
is more secure. It starts out, usually, in a mess, but as its price

E

rises, so does the quality of repair work on it, and the quality of the wax (should it need wax) that gets rubbed into it.

Had the dolphins remained for a while with their original owner (and not traveled to Los Angeles wrapped in Indian cottons), they would have been repaired (regessoed) and re-gilded and eventually a marble tabletop would have been found for them. By then they would have become astronomically expensive.

Gesso

Gesso is a combination of plaster of Paris, glue and linseed oil that makes a form of paste used for intricate decoration on furniture. Gessoed pieces are often gilded. I didn't regesso, but repaired the dolphins as best I could with wood putty. Wood putty, or plastic wood, comes in various colors, but I make my own coloring by buying the lightest variety and adding to it from my oil paints, as I would for wood graining. I use wood putty to repair any damaged wood or plaster carving. I build it up in layers, allowing each layer to harden before adding to it. When I have finished and it is quite set, I sand it smooth. For the dolphins I didn't color the putty but used my usual mixture of Liquid Leaf (see page 65) to gild the repair.

Liquid Leaf

(Wood putty sometimes shrinks. This is a nuisance, because gaps can mysteriously appear in the repair work. There is now a new form of epoxy putty—E-Pox-E Ribbon—on the market. Two different-colored strips of rubbery substance get mixed together, which begins their hardening process. Working

epoxy putty
E-Pox-E Ribbon

against the clock—to beat the hardening—you can mold the most wonderful shapes with it, either for repair or for ornamentation. The designs can then be sanded and painted, and they won't shrink.)

To make the tabletop (photographs 19 and 20), we cut a round piece of plywood and I stippled it to look like brown marble. (See pages 103–6.)

Nineteen

The little room (photograph 18) leading off the California dining room had an indeterminate use. Small, with two rather squat windows and connected to the dining room by an open arch (photographs 19 and 20), it might have been meant for a breakfast room or to hold an extra dinner table.

I was delighted by its vaulted ceiling, although it is a little on the low side. I thought it called for a bit of Victorian exoticism—not really suitable for a breakfast room, so perhaps I could call it the supper room. I painted it to look like tortoise shell. (See page 105 for how.) Then we built the banquette. The only variation on the banquettes already described (page 55) is that the corners are "cut off." (A) This makes the seat more comfortable for eating (less deep) and creates shelf space for the dark-blue pots (photograph 18).

The blue pots were yet another auction find—ordinary brown clay pots, but with a nice shape. I've always admired Chinese vases where the glaze only partially covers the pots and the original unglazed clay can still be seen. So I painted most, but not all, of each pot with yacht's varnish (from a specialized paint shop). This sealed the porous clay. When the varnish was dry, I painted the varnished parts with cobalt-blue artist's oil paint (thinned only slightly with turpentine. As I had thinned the paint down so little, the pots took a week to dry. When they were dry I gave the blue color three coats of yacht's

A

varnish to make it shiny. Had I given the pots ten coats, they might have looked as if they had been glazed in a kiln during the Sung dynasty nine hundred years ago.

For the window of the supper room, we adapted three panels of a carved Indian latticed screen, sprayed white, into sliding shutters. This furthered the Oriental feel of the room, while the white cotton lace shades of the dining room echoed the white lattice in a more European fashion.

The low chairs (photograph 18) are Indian as well. The paisley that covers the chair cushions and the banquettes I had admired years ago when I saw it used by the decorators Denning and Fourcade. They had had it quilted and had a whole room covered with it. I couldn't have been more surprised when I found the same pattern on a very thin and inexpensive cotton in a downtown Los Angeles dress-fabric shop. It cost $1.98 a yard. Because the material was so thin, I stole another idea from Denning and Fourcade and quilted it. I quilted only the pieces for the banquette seat cushions and the chair cushions, which would get the most wear. To do this, I bought ready-made quilting by the yard (see pages 172–3 on covering quilts) and sewed the material to it on the machine, following the squares on the quilting.

Around the edges of the chair cushions I sewed some brown woolen cord and used red woolen cord to hide the staples on the base of the banquette. I bought the first in the trimming section of a Los Angeles department store, and I made the other. (See pages 219–20.)

So as not to hide any more of the already too square and squat window by cushions, I put a low bolster in front of it. One bolster went on each side of the banquette. Bolsters, like stripes, borders and cushions, appeared in all nineteenth-century decoration that had an Oriental influence. They also appeared on Empire beds and sofas. It's easy to cover them. The only decision to be made is how to cover the ends: whether to have two flat circular ends or to sew a strip of material to the edge and gather it into the center. (B) If gathered into the center, it must be finished off (and the edge of the gathers hidden) by a button or a knot and tassels. (See the bolster ends in the chaise longue, photograph 5; on the bed in photograph 33 and banquette in photograph 18; and on the sofa beds in photographs 47 and 54.)

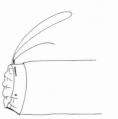

B

How you make a bolster depends on what quality you want. The easiest but nastiest (and not all that cheap) is a ready-made foam one. Nothing, but nothing, makes it lose its all-too-regular shape until it totally disintegrates (which it does, in time). The next, slightly better but not ideal bolster is made of chopped foam. This is the cheapest, but a canvas cover has to be made for it. The cover is the shape of a tube, with a circle at each end. One circle is sewn on completely and the other partially. (The circles have to be notched at the edges to lie flat. [c].) The tube gets turned inside out, stuffed full of chopped foam, and then the half-open circle is sewn closed.

c

Bolsters can also be stuffed with kapok or, best of all, feathers. Feathers mold to the body when leaned against, instead of aggressively leaping back up as foam does. I stuff feather bolsters by cutting a hole in one corner of an inexpensive feather pillow, pushing the corner with the hole into the canvas tube and squeezing the pillow. The principle is rather like the one for using a piping bag to decorate a cake. If it works, one avoids the flying feathers; if not, it's a disaster.

The low central table in the supper room is a leather trunk on a stand (photograph 18). I bought it for the room. If necessary, a square board covered with a cloth can be placed on the trunk to enlarge it, but this means eating at knee level. For a more formal dinner the trunk can be removed and a table for ten people slotted in; five people would have to sit on the banquette, five on chairs. If it is a served dinner, the person in the middle of the banquette is definitely in "starvation corner."

Trunks are extremely adaptable things. They have many uses apart from the obvious one of storage. They make excellent coffee tables or side tables. A trunk between two single beds in a small room looks good and works well. (D) It also looks smart standing at the foot of a bed. And if there are a lot of trunks furnishing a house, moving is a lot easier.

Trunks, especially the very badly made tin-and-plastic-cum-paper ones, are not expensive. Concocting disguises for them, however, can be time-consuming. The easiest is to throw a piece of material over the trunk that matches the room the trunk is in. A carpet hanging over and completely covering a trunk looks wonderful, especially if it is an old kilim, which makes the trunk look like the tables appearing in many nineteenth-century Orientalist pictures. Another way to disguise a

D

trunk is to glue material over it and paint the tin bits in some matching color or in black. Or, of course, to paint the whole trunk using my method for painting tinware. (See Chapter 9.)

If I had been really ambitious and had had an extra month to spare, I would have tried to make a trunk like the one in the supper room. I would have bought the cheapest trunk I could find and cut a stand for it out of plywood. Then, over the trunk and stand, I would have glued one of the good imitation leathers now on the market and painted the leather with the old faithful Liquid Leaf (page 65).

One of the things I watch out for at flea markets and junk shops are old tin trunks. The small ones, either trunk-shaped or round (hatboxes), make wonderful bread bins. I first clean them properly, then spray them with car spray—inside and out—and paint them. I either pick out the bands that usually run around them in a different color, or paint a design overall (see pages 61–62). Once I stippled a bottle-height tin to look like tortoise shell (see page 105) and placed it on a tray and trestle. (E) It made a really good-looking bottle holder for a drinks table.

E

nother of the rooms in the California house that could be used for dining was called the "den" in the realtor's prospectus—perhaps because it had two bookshelves. Now, in addition to being an occasional dining room for grand galas (the table on the right of photograph 53 can be drawn up to the sofa bed and surrounded by chairs), it is a music room (a piano faces the sofa bed) and a guest room.

A batik from the East Indies (via Holland) covers the walls. This particular one comes in panels: Two thirds of each panel has a blue background, a third has a green background. Each panel is surrounded by a border. (A) We stapled the material to the walls as described in Chapter 2. We made a chair rail around the room using the border.

Our original plan had been to put the green material below the rail, the blue above it. Alas, the green material had an angled stripe in its pattern that looked very strange on the wall —uneven and crooked. So we covered the sofa bed and lined the bookshelves with it instead and used only blue on the walls. As each panel had lost its green section and its border, we now had to construct the wall covering out of many little pieces. Where a seam would dissect a flower too obviously, I cut another half flower out of remnants and glued that on over the seam. (B)

We stapled material over the door leading into the bathroom. The fact that the music room is separate from the rest, has its own entrance and an adjoining bathroom, makes it a convenient guest room—or even a self-contained studio. Unfortunately, the bathroom is also the only downstairs cloakroom. As the door to it is now practically invisible (on the right wall of photograph 53), it leads to occasional consternation for some of the dinner guests.

How a door is covered in material depends on whether both sides of a door are being covered or only one side. If both, the material can be stretched over the one side, pulled around all the edges of the door to the other side and stapled. (c) (The padding, which of course is thicker, must not overlap the edges

A

B

of the door, or it won't close.) When stretching the material around the spine, the hinges obstruct. Little flaps the same size as the hinges have to be cut. The flaps are tucked under, and the material above and below the hinges is wrapped around the edge of the door and stapled. (D) An opening must also be cut out for the door handle and the door catch. The material for the back of the door, cut slightly smaller than the size of the door, can be stapled on so that it covers the first lot of staples. The second lot of staples must be hidden by something—a border or a molding or simply by a strip of the same material, glued on. (See page 21 for how to make the strip.)

A door handle, whatever its shape, is usually held to the door with small screws. The spindle on which the opening and closing mechanism of the door depends is a little iron stick that pierces the door and goes from handle to handle. When I'm covering a door, I make sure that the padding under the material has a large hole for the handle and comes nowhere near the small screws that hold the handle. Nothing is quite so maddening as getting a screw caught in the padding. It seems as if the whole wall will become entangled on the one screw. Whenever attaching anything to an already padded and material-covered wall, it is important to cut a larger hole in the padding than in the material. This sounds impossible to do on an already covered wall, but it isn't. I make a small slit in the top material, push in the tips of a pair of nail scissors and snip out as much of a little circle from the padding underneath as I can reach. (E)

C

D

E

When I am padding a door, I give the door handle a wide berth. When I'm putting the material on, however, the hole I cut for the handle is smaller than the base of the handle. I thread the handle through the material. Then I loosen the small screws holding the handle with a screwdriver, and with the help of the same screwdriver, I push the material under the base of the handle. (F) Then I tighten the screws again.

Although the door handle and spindle can be completely removed and the door covered more easily that way, my way is faster and it avoids the risk of not being able to put the whole thing back together again.

If I'm covering only one side of a door in material (and this applies to cupboard doors as well), I end the material on the spine of the door, where the hinges are. I turn the material under, to avoid a frayed edge, and staple to the spine. But if the material is stapled in the same place on the other edge (where the door catch is), it complicates opening and closing the door. The material must, therefore, end on the face of the door or on the other side of it. To cover the material's edge and the staples, a molding all round looks best. If this is too difficult, a thin band of material (page 21) also works. (G) The door must, of course, have padding under the material of the same thickness as the padding on the walls.

The bookshelves of the music room were originally painted the chocolate brown the previous owner loved. The parts I hadn't covered in material (shelves and molding) I painted an imitation lightwood. (See Chapter 16.) For the small window within the bookshelf (and for the large window, not visible in the photograph), we bought two split-bamboo blinds from one of the many Oriental import shops. They only needed a wash of yellow ocher oil paint greatly thinned with turpentine and then a coat of French polish to make them the identical color of the bookshelves.

The sofa bed in photograph 53 is an example of my favorite way of arranging a bed that is also used to sit on. I borrowed the idea from the late eighteenth- and nineteenth-century beds called *lits à l'anglaise,* which have a headboard and footboard of equal height. (See page 167.)

To make the sofa bed in the music room, we first bought an ordinary twin-bed box spring and mattress. In the same shop where we bought the bamboo blinds for the windows, we found

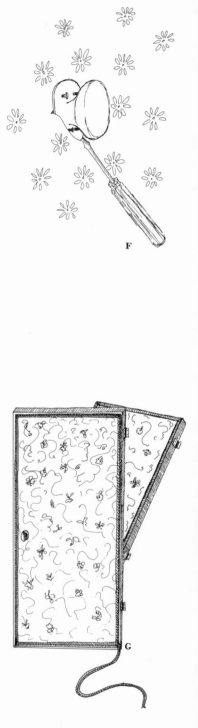

F

G

H

wicker headboards in natural straw. We bought two of them
and made them the same tone of wicker as the blinds. (For this,
I needed more yellow ocher, less turpentine and a slight addition of raw umber.)

The headboards were too high to use in the way I wanted,
so I sawed 6″ off each leg. The headboard was the sort that
seemed to have no visible means of support, but depended on
the box spring and mattress to hold it in place against a wall.
The bed could hardly do that now, freestanding as it was. Nor
did the headboards have any solid wood left (I had sawed it off)
that I could screw to the box spring. So I screwed two rows of
picture eyes along the top and bottom edge of the box spring,
then wove some picture wire into the wicker, in and out of the
eyes and back in and out of the wicker. (H) After wiring the
headboards to the box spring in this way, I painted the wire
with more yellow ocher to cover up its golden shimmer.

A head and foot board prevent the cushions and bolsters—
if there are any—from slipping off. Similarly, the bedclothes
and pillows don't slide off when the sofa is used as a bed.
Because the two headboards are of an equal height, the bed
looks like a sofa. The back cushions are the bed pillows, hidden
by pillow shams.

To make a pillow sham, I sew two pieces of material together
on three sides by machine. I make the pieces the same size as
the bed pillows they are to cover, plus 1″ all around. On the
fourth side I sew some Velcro or snaps to close the sham.
Sometimes I make pillow shams that close at the back, sewing
on the back panel of material in two sections, one half overlapping the other. (I) This way they don't need snaps or Velcro,
but they are slightly more bother to sew.

If the bedcover is quilted, as this one is (see Chapter 30 for
how to quilt), it can serve three purposes. Tucked in and
around the mattress, it looks as if the mattress is upholstered,

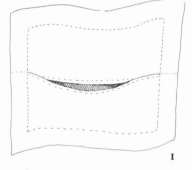

I

especially if a border outlines it, giving it shape. When the bed is made up, the cover can still be used—either for warmth or just as a good-looking blanket cover. If the bed is to stay made up while the room is used to sit in, the bedcover, tucked around the bedclothes, hides them. The pillow shams can hide the bed pillows even in their pillowcases.

If the bed is to be sat on a lot during the day (like the one in the tropical studio, photograph 47, and New York studio, Chapter 41, figure A) and if the bedcover is not very thick, it is helpful to sew it like a fitted bottom sheet. The material must be as large as the mattress plus the sides plus a couple of inches (after hemming). An elastic a few inches shorter than the circumference of the mattress can then be threaded through the hem and the whole thing pulled over the made-up bed like a bonnet.

For the armchairs in the music room, I made new slip cushions. (See pages 85–86 for how to do this.) I covered them with pieces cut out from an old quilt, avoiding the holes. The quilt was a tattered patchwork one I had found at the Pasadena market. The colors matched the walls, and the diamond shapes matched the carpet.

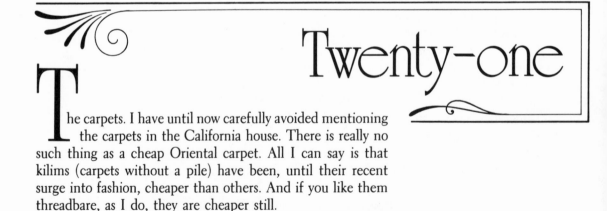

Twenty-one

The carpets. I have until now carefully avoided mentioning the carpets in the California house. There is really no such thing as a cheap Oriental carpet. All I can say is that kilims (carpets without a pile) have been, until their recent surge into fashion, cheaper than others. And if you like them threadbare, as I do, they are cheaper still.

The one in the music room (photograph 53) is a Caucasian kilim, the one in the supper room (photograph 18) a Turkish one. Where to find reasonably priced kilims now, however, has become a problem. Sometimes they will crop up at an ill-attended auction or at a market. The runner in front of the barn sofa (photograph 52), for instance, I bought in a flea market in Brussels. But, sadly, I have given up going to carpet shops. Years ago I bought two geometrically patterned Persian kilims (known as dazzles) quite cheaply in a shop. One is in my blue-and-white-striped dining room (photograph 14) and the other in the blue denim room (photograph 16)—where it gives a splash of tidy color to the white-painted floor.

The carpet in the batik living room (photograph 15) comes from Scandinavia. It is modern, with a thick pile, and I bought it in a sale in a department store. I placed it in the living room for the usual "hot" injection of red in the otherwise cool blue and white. I must admit I would never have bought the red carpet if my budget had stretched further—I would have preferred something older, more worn, more "lived in." But with the blue-and-white batik, it looks good enough.

The carpet in the California living room (photograph 6) is probably Turkish, on account of the pastel coloring. It exactly matches the paisley shawl with which I covered the S-shaped settee. In the same room, in front of the two striped banquettes, are two raffia runners, also in stripes and matching in colors. (The tip of one can just be seen on the left-hand side of the photograph.) I picked them up by chance in an Oriental shop for $7 each. The carpet in the California library (photograph 55) and the one in the New York studio (photograph 50) are, respectively, a good and a less good version of Spanish carpets. (The earliest European carpets came from Spain. Eastern knotted carpets were first brought to Spain by the Arabs and Moors around the tenth century, and the Spaniards copied them.) The California library carpet is rather subtler than the one in the New York studio. Neither is very old.

The studio carpet was a loan to the tenant from a kind friend. When it arrived, rolled up, I was delighted. I unrolled it, full of excitement—and fell into despair. The colors were so strong, they leaped out of the carpet with furious force. I quickly rolled it up again. That looked better. So I laid it on the floor the wrong side out.

If there is even the remotest possibility of getting at the floorboards, I try to do so. Sometimes even parquet turns up. The tropical studio (Chapter 40; photographs 47 and 48) had a wall-to-wall carpet that was literally nailed to the parquet underneath. Had we sanded the parquet to get rid of all the nail holes, we would have had no parquet left. So we sanded only superficially to get rid of splinters. By the time I rubbed in a few layers of wax, the holes, which were small, were filled. It may be a waste of wax—and it certainly was quite hard work —but the result is a good-looking floor.

Plain floorboards can look lovely, but it helps if they are wide and if they don't have huge crevices between them. If they are narrow, with gaps, they are better off covered with wall-to-wall carpet, plywood or any other flooring wood that can be painted. Painted floors can be marbled (pages 103–6), stenciled (pages 62–63) or painted with a freehand design (pages 61–62).

I prefer the least-expensive kind of wall-to-wall carpeting. I can quite often make something out of cheap materials and like it better than a finished, expensive version. But it is rare to prefer a cheaper version of something without changing it. Yet I feel that way about wall-to-wall carpeting.

I like cord and coconut matting far better than the expensive woolen kinds of wall-to-wall carpeting. (See photographs 28, 31, 37 and 54 for cord and photograph 58 for coconut matting.) The only wool wall-to-wall carpeting I like is a dark chocolate brown (in the brown living room, photographs 1–5, and barn bathroom, photograph 44). It comes the closest to looking like a floor and shows dirt the least.

Small carpets can look well thrown on top of a wall-to-wall carpet, especially if the background color of the small carpet is the same as the color of the wall-to-wall (as is the case with the Chinese carpet, photographs 37 and 38).

If there is a wall-to-wall carpet that is still in good shape but a terrible color or full of spots, it seems a shame to throw it out. It can be completely covered with a thick material. (The kilim material on the armchairs of the California living room— photographs 8 and 9—would do nicely if it were cheaper.) Or small rugs can be made out of a heavy material. But then the material that is used must be backed with thin foam rubber or lined. It should, of course, be a material with a border that can be mitered (see page 107) to create a frame. A really thick material doesn't even need backing.

To cover a worn and ugly wall-to-wall carpet in a small room, I once glue-seamed together three lengths of thick canvas with carpet glue and, using carpet tacks, nailed it around the room

A

on top of the old carpet. Then I glued a border (page 21) around the edge of the canvas, thereby hiding the tacks. (A)

It's possible to make a number of smaller carpets out of an old wall-to-wall, cutting it at home with a utility knife, but the edges should be immediately painted with some carpet glue so that they don't unravel.

Stair carpets, I am always told, should be the most expensive woolen variety because they get the most wear; the cheaper kinds (the ones I like) become slippery with use and dangerous. I had stairs covered in a cheap cord carpet anyway, and when it becomes dangerous, I intend to stretch a piece of red canvas over it and hold it down with brass stair rods. (B)

When a stair carpet starts wearing out, it does so on the edge (or nosing) of the step. It can then be moved so that the worn bit is on the rise of the step. (A well-laid carpet usually has some extra inches tacked to the bottom riser.) Unless the carpet is moved long before it becomes threadbare, I find that the worn bit is more noticeable on the riser than it was on the nosing —but, of course, it *is* less dangerous.

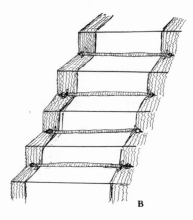

B

When the red stair carpet (see photograph 17) starts going, I have a plan for it. I will have it moved and will cover the worn risers with some of the same paisley material as on the walls, of which I kept extra for just this purpose (see Chapter 22, figure E).

Twenty-two

Apart from hiding faults, such as uneven walls or worn-out carpets, material can be used for architectural effects. When I first saw a blue-and-white batik with a design of large ovals on it, I was enchanted. At the time I was working on a living room of a rather formal eighteenth-century house, and I bought the batik for it. The material rather resembles a trellis: trellised ovals. I tried holding up the ovals against a wall. They looked awful. A door or a window kept interrupting, cutting off a slice of an oval. (A) I decided to piece the material in order to make arches out of it. Trellised arches would suit the lightness of the eighteenth century admirably and give depth to the walls.

I made the arches by slicing off the bottom bit of some ovals, the top and bottom bit off others. I formed long arches and sewed the pieces together on the machine. (B) (The only unspliced oval can be seen nearest the window on the left wall in photograph 15.) Above the fireplace I shortened the original oval into a near circle. Whenever I needed extra width (left and right of the circle above the fireplace, or to fill in between the arches on the wall opposite), I used long white strips made out of remnants.

Batiks are wax prints, hand-printed, and often have irregularities. The stripes can be crooked, the colors varied, the printing uneven or even smudged where the color has "bled." I am delighted by these defects. They give new material instant age. The subdued tone that is otherwise acquired only through years of fading, washing and wear is immediate. It also provides me with an excuse when stripes go askew and patterns don't quite match: It's the fault of the fabric, not mine.

The cover on the couch in the otherwise rather delicate and light room is made out of blue jean material—indigo denim. All indigo blues fade. I don't know the reasons, but since I like faded things, I don't care. The couch and the batik are in the same tone of indigo, and they are fading together. The couch and the batik-covered armchair—this time a flowered batik, but in the same color as the wall batik—are slipcovered (see

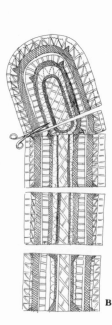

A

B

Chapter 5). Although they are both in materials that hide dirt successfully, they are leaped on by muddy dogs and children and need to be put into the washing machine quite often. The color of the sofa cover improves after each wash, but as with my jeans, it takes force to put the slipcovers back on.

The dining room in photograph 16 has blue denim walls, the same quality as the blue jean material, but in a royal blue. Around the windows and on the ceiling of the alcove I stapled Indian crewelwork bedspreads. The alcove wasn't there when I began the room. It is an extension, a glassed-in and roofed wooden box, sitting on what used to be a narrow balcony. It has a lower ceiling and is not as wide as the rest of the room. By covering it in a different material, I stressed its separateness.

I copied the shape of the windows from an old mirror I had seen, and then I copied the mirror. The mirror is painted black and hangs on the wall opposite the window. Under the mirror a shelf, also painted black, serves as a sideboard. (c)

The mirror was made on the same principle as the one in the tented dining room (pages 107–9). I used three inexpensive store-bought mirrors and then had the half-round ones for the top cut to size professionally. The mirror I was copying had moldings out of bentwood, but the one we made has moldings out of two layers of plywood, one narrower than the other and cut with a portable saw. The narrower arch is glued on top of the other.

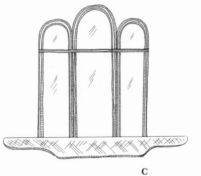

c

Under the arched windows there is a large curved sofa. It is made out of what was left of a curved seat that had stood in a courtroom. I took off the back (high, broken and uncomfortable), gave the horsehair seat additional padding with a thin layer of foam rubber, painted the wood that was showing white and stapled on the crewelwork bedspreads. The staples—on the sides of the sofa, around the windows and around the alcove itself—I covered by gluing on woolen cord and braid (pages 218–20).

I didn't know how to curtain the alcove. The only way I thought would look all right would be to curtain it off completely with a blue denim curtain (same as the walls), which I couldn't do: For larger dinners a collapsible oval table is placed in front of the curved sofa; by curtaining it off, I would have curtained off the guests from their food. I would also have lost the best stage effect of the room: the arched windows reflected in the same arched mirror, in which trees appear to grow (at least in daylight). To have curtains or blinds inside the alcove would also have hidden the shape of the windows. But something was necessary for protection from the draughts and for privacy from the houses across the garden, especially in winter, when the trees are not in leaf.

Finally I had ordinary white Holland shades made (see page 188) for each of the eight windows. (Two of the windows are left and right of the alcove and can't be seen in photograph 16.) Instead of attaching them to the top of the window, I attached them at the base. I screwed in small brass hooks on the wooden separations between the curved glass and the straight glass. To the bottom of the shades I attached rings. The shades pull up instead of down and are held up by the hooks.

When they are not being used, the shades are hidden behind the cushions on the sofa. To make the shades into more than just plain white Holland shades, I painted them in the same flower pattern as the crewelwork walls. (D)

I found in my stores what was left of a Samoan screen carved out of pale sandalwood. The blue room had a chimney-breast where a fireplace must have been. We blocked in each side of the protruding chimney-breast with plywood and cut curved openings into it. Into the openings we fitted two of the least-broken leaves of the screen. (One is visible on the left of photograph 16.) The screens are hinged and work as doors. They are lit from behind, which creates a lacy and dramatic effect. Since the color of the sandalwood clashed with the dark brown of the four carved Indian chairs (see photograph), I sprayed the screens white.

I used the outside edge of a more broken-down leaf of the Samoan screen to frame the mirror that the blue-and-red batik bedroom is reflected in (photograph 38). There the original color of the screen has also been toned down, but less drastically.

The two dining room armchairs in the Renaissance style (partly seen in the foreground of photograph 16) I found years ago at an auction; no one was bidding for them. I think they may well have been made for an opera set: They were dripping with gold fringe and velvet. Covered in a bright paisley cotton —a cut-up inexpensive Indian bedspread—they are unpreten-

D

tious. With the rest of the bedspread I made slipcovers for the cushions on the window seat.

The Victorian wrought-iron staircase in photograph 16 still had most of its curving handrail when I bought it—except for the circular top section. This left more than half of the round stairwell unprotected. An impossible trap. First, out of a large sheet of plywood we cut a section of handrail in the same way we had cut the curved mirror frame—with a portable saw. I bought ten extra, but unfortunately different, upright stair rods (balusters), screwed them in to support the curving handrail downstairs (where their lack of uniformity is less noticeable) and used the ones that had been downstairs to support the new top section of the handrail, which had been sanded down and screwed on as if it were the original iron one. Then I painted the stairs and handrail white.

In the California house there was a black wrought-iron staircase, part of which can be seen in the photographs 8 and 9. It looked hard and coarse. I longed for the shimmer of polished iron (see page 201). I took a bottle of pewter Liquid Leaf (page 65) and painted it. Not completely, but lightly, letting some of the wrought iron show through. It looks softer that way.

The red-carpeted staircase (photograph 17) is outside the blue denim room (photograph 16). It is narrow and the handrail had deep dents in it. To make the stairs appear wider, we added wooden curves to the three last steps. To the dented handrail we added an extra wooden "swoop." The stair rods, like untended teeth, were rotten or missing. The rods that I was able to salvage I moved to fill in gaps further upstairs, and for the most visible flight I had some simulated bamboo ones made out of aluminum. These I painted (page 102). Onto the dented handrail I stapled a thin layer of foam rubber, then some red velvet, and to hide the staples I glued on fringe. The fringe was rather white-looking compared to the yellow in the paisley on the wall, as well as to the yellow ocher of the bamboo and baseboard, so I dipped it in some strong tea to yellow it (page 196). A wooden pineapple or knob or even some brass ornament should have been screwed to the top of the "swoop" above the newel post, but I never got around to it. (E)

The staircase outside of—but part of—the blue-and-white-striped dining tent had a wonderful mahogany handrail. (The stairs can be seen reflected in the mirror in photograph 14.) The balusters were less prepossessing. I stippled those and the cupboards under them imitation maple and made the knobs on the rods "mahogany." (See Chapter 16 for how this is done.) It looked a little dull, so I rubbed a bit of red (alizarin crimson) over the brown knobs to echo the red of the dining room sideboard.

E

III

The Kitchen

Twenty-three

Whether, for utmost convenience, a kitchen should be large or small is a moot point. A large kitchen, if well planned, is versatile. You can sit, eat, cook and talk in it—all at the same time. There are, however, more steps to take in it and, if you tend to be a fast and messy cook—as I am— more spaces in which to spill and misplace. A small kitchen, on the other hand, has everything within easy reach. Sink, burners, dishwasher and so on can be reached from one position, and strangely enough, there can be more storage space in a tiny kitchen than in a large kitchen. I have cooked for forty in this (A) tiny cubicle of a kitchen and found it less daunting than cooking in a larger kitchen—but I had to do so without help. Had there been a willing pair of hands, I'd have fallen over them. The small kitchen is indeed far less practical if there is a family to cook for or with. To lug three meals a day

A

into another room in order to eat them is a nuisance. If, on the other hand, the kitchen is too small to eat in, it forces one out of the squalid atmosphere of dirty pots and pans and cooking smells. It turns a meal into more of a production, thereby helping to justify the time that went into cooking the food.

It is just as well to be satisfied with the size of the kitchen one has and adapt to it. The lack of space—or too much space —can always be used as an excuse when a dish has failed. If you are in the enviable position of planning a new kitchen, however, there are certain things to remember. Refrigerators and ovens can be bought with the door opening to the left or right. It is important to know which one you need in order not to block your access by the open door. There are priorities among labor-saving devices. For a small family (as mine is), I have found a small refrigerator sufficient, but need an equal-size deep freeze in which to store food in case of unexpected guests. Although I love eating and buying food, a daily trip to the supermarket is too much even for my appetite (and certainly for my pocket). If I don't have a dishwasher, I'm grateful for a double sink. Suds in one, clear water for rinsing in the other. If I have a dishwasher, a double sink seems a waste of space. I think a garbage disposal is a wonderful thing. Given the choice between it and a dishwasher, I'd wash dishes. To have the garbage disposal next to the chopping board means one gesture can send peels and leftovers into oblivion. Two ovens have always seemed a totally unnecessary luxury to me, whereas a separate broiler does not. To be able to brown a previously made first course while the oven makes the roast, or to let the soufflé rise undisturbed while the chicken broils, is a great help.

If I were starting from scratch and investing in new appliances (and gas existed in my kitchen), I would have two electric rings and two gas rings. For high and fast heat, gas is unbeatable, whereas the electric burner is better for the slow-simmering stew. Also, should costs, strikes or malfunction hit the one, the other could be used. If possible, I find an eye-level oven preferable. I'm bad at bobbing up and down if the oven is under the burners. In both the green kitchen (photographs 21–23) and in the tiny kitchen (A), it is possible to look at the fish poaching in the oven while stirring the hollandaise on the burner.

The arrangement of the kitchen appliances should be obvious to anyone who has ever boiled an egg. The water, the egg, the icebox from which to fetch the egg, the burner on which to boil the water for it and the sink for pouring the boiling water away should be within easy reach of one another. In other words, there shouldn't be a large table blocking the sink from the stove. If they are next to each other, however, there must be enough space between them to be able to put down the boiling pot when removing it from the heat. Also, it is dangerous to have the water immediately next to the electric fixtures.

Cooking is easier with the kitchen equipment in view, and kitchen equipment can be decorative. For this, the pots, pans, ladles and strainers can't be bent, rusty or dirty. Those are better off hidden in a cupboard, although I'm not quite certain that those hanging up, attractive though they look, don't eventually become rusty and dirty. Grease and grime cling to a kitchen with remarkable tenacity. The glass bottles in my green kitchen (photograph 23) become opaque after a few heavy meals. So one has to make a choice: A lot of pots suspended from the ceiling or around the stove look wonderful and save rummaging around a cupboard—thereby saving time. But the saved time will soon be spent again, with interest, when the pots get dirty from just hanging there and must be washed.

If I am going to paint kitchen appliances (and I have painted refrigerator, oven, dishwasher, freezer and washing machine quite successfully), I buy them in secondhand shops or slightly dented or chipped from factory outlets. These exterior imperfections reduce their price drastically, although they are actually in perfect working order. Once I have stippled them with my different shadings of smudged-looking color (for how, see pages 66–68), even the deepest craters in the appliances don't show up. If pristine white is preferred in a kitchen, there is no need to disdain the cheap chipped icebox—there are excellent white-enamel products on the market. One dab with the paintbrush at the offending spot and the fridge is as good as new.

I am fanatical about cooking smells. As most of the houses or apartments I've done are material-covered, I suspect, rightly or wrongly, that the onion smells creep out from the kitchen and lodge themselves permanently within the padding of the next-door or upstairs rooms. I have not had great success with the charcoal-filled smell extractor, which is to be found easily (but for a lot of money) and which can be hung up above the stove, plugged in and is ready to go. I have never quite understood where the fumes *do* go or how much of them the charcoal can assimilate before becoming overtaxed.

I have had far more success with an ordinary extractor fan, camouflaged by some form of hood or simply set into the wall above the burners, where I can hide it when it's not being used by hanging a frying pan over it, as in photograph 27. For a fan of this sort, the burners have to be on an outside wall.

A fan can also be set into a window, but there it becomes increasingly difficult to disguise its unsightliness. In the green kitchen it is hidden by paneling (photograph 22), and the air is ducted, through a false cupboard, to an opening on the outside wall. In the cubicle kitchen (A) the air is drawn upward through a chrome hood onto the flat roof above the kitchen.

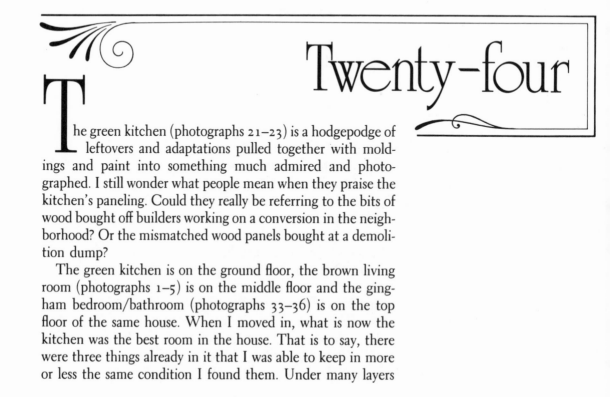

Twenty-four

The green kitchen (photographs 21–23) is a hodgepodge of leftovers and adaptations pulled together with moldings and paint into something much admired and photographed. I still wonder what people mean when they praise the kitchen's paneling. Could they really be referring to the bits of wood bought off builders working on a conversion in the neighborhood? Or the mismatched wood panels bought at a demolition dump?

The green kitchen is on the ground floor, the brown living room (photographs 1–5) is on the middle floor and the gingham bedroom/bathroom (photographs 33–36) is on the top floor of the same house. When I moved in, what is now the kitchen was the best room in the house. That is to say, there were three things already in it that I was able to keep in more or less the same condition I found them. Under many layers of paint I discovered the window shutters. Under a coat of dirty white paint was a marble mantelpiece. (It is not a very beautiful mantel—more reminiscent of a hunk of salami than any marble I know—but it was there: a discovery. And I'd used up so many days freeing it from paint that I felt obliged to be pleased with the results.) The third find was the ornamental plaster molding on the ceiling. This, too, was obscured by paint.

I wanted to turn the kitchen into a Pennsylvania Dutch or Austrian-type country kitchen. I had some Welsh quarry tiles put on the floor professionally. This was an investment. Not as great a one as if I had had French, Spanish or Italian unglazed tiles put down, but expensive nonetheless. The large octagonal tiles are on the floor, and smaller octagonal ones are on the counters, behind the sink and around the burners. I attached the tiles to the counters and to the walls with glue—a tile cement.

I dislike most tiles: They look hard, cold, shiny and uniform. But I like unglazed tiles: Each tile is slightly different and the terra-cotta color is warm. But they are porous, mark easily and are hard to seal. I have tried various sealers and have come to the conclusion that boiled linseed oil rubbed into the tiles works best. I despaired when I first tried it. It took three days to dry, was extremely sticky and looked spotted. But once the oil had settled in, it became more regular. Now I simply shine up the tiles from time to time by rubbing them over with a colorless wax furniture polish.

The pieces of wooden paneling that I had virtually picked up off the streets were all different. There were square pieces, recessed inward; rectangular ones, with the molding protruding; and four flat carved columns with a sort of ribbon-work design (photographs 22 and 23). And there was yet another remnant of a mantelpiece.

I didn't know Mr. Lewis in the days when I was trying to build the kitchen. I had a helper who could follow only that which I was able to explain exactly. So as not to appear too incompetent and to justify my insistence that "of course it can be done," I spent my nights measuring. Would a piece of paneling fit here? Could I cut off a piece of it there? And so on. Realization came slowly. If I painted the whole thing—and I had to paint it, since each bit of paneling was different—it wouldn't be noticeable if I faked some panels. I used 5/8" moldings. I glued them on all the drawers, on the edges of the plywood shelves (page 21) and wherever I ran out of real paneling, including the huge water-storage tank to the right of the fireplace (photograph 23). To camouflage this, we first put up a framework of 2″ × 1″ pieces shaped to the tank, covered the framework in plywood, which we nailed on, and then glued on the molding in squares and long rectangles.

I can manage to miter a narrow and not too ornate molding without a mitering block. I can also manage a wider flat piece of wood or a half-round. The method is simple. I take two pieces of molding, lay one on top of the other at a 90° angle and draw a line across the width of the bottom molding. (A) Then I draw a diagonal from the line to the opposite corner of the molding. This diagonal is my miter, and I cut it with a small backsaw or, if thin moldings, with a utility knife. (B) It is only when the molding is wide and ornate or has to go around a corner that this method doesn't seem to work and a mitering block becomes necessary.

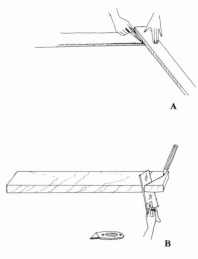

A

B

To make a mitering block, I take two pieces, each about a foot and a half long, of 3″ × 2″. I behave almost exactly the same way with the two pieces as I did with the two moldings just mentioned. I lay one piece on top of the other at a 90° angle, this time not on the end, but somewhere around the middle of the other piece. I draw two lines and dissect them with a diagonal line. I saw the diagonal line with a backsaw, not all the way through but about halfway, to create a channel.

About 6″ away from this first cut, I repeat the whole procedure and make a second cut, but in the opposite direction. Then I hammer the two pieces of 3″ × 2″ together lengthwise to form an L shape. When I want to miter an ornate molding, I lay it into the corner of the L and saw the molding through either the right or left channel, depending on which way the molding is to face. (c)

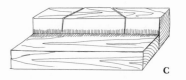

C

To miter a molding that will go into a corner or surround a valance, as in the California bedrooms (photographs 40 and 41), it has to be held upward in the L of the mitering block and cut that way. (D)

The paneling above the marble mantelpiece in the green kitchen (photograph 23) is a composite of three different bits of wood, all of them old. The top is part of a scrapped wooden mantelpiece bought off some builders working on an old house

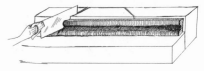

D

down the road. It is not dissimilar to the marble mantelpiece under it. Obviously they were put in at about the same time, the time the house was built (around 1880). (I think the people down the street may have had the nicer mantelpiece, whereas the people in my house must have been a little richer and had marble.) The piece of Victorian paneling under the scrapped wooden mantel I found in a different place, and the two ornate columns left and right of the paneling are from a third. (Even the columns are composite, as they had no capitals. The ones they have now are part of the wooden mantelpiece above them.) When I painted the kitchen, color joined all these bits together.

The colors I wanted for the paneled kitchen are the ones used for those wonderful old Austrian chests and cupboards: shaded greens with yellow, brown and rust decoration. They are, surprisingly, the same as the colors in a William Morris material I had and with which I eventually covered the kitchen sofa (photograph 23). Perhaps not so surprising—after all, the same pigments have been used for centuries. It's curious, however, how easily a modern color—a modern chemical dye—can jar with the old colors that were obtained from earth, rocks, semiprecious stones, vegetables and insects. The colors that were used—and the ones I try to use—are chrome yellow and yellow ocher, burnt sienna, raw sienna, burnt umber, raw umber, Vandyke brown, Venetian red, cadmium red, vermilion, alizarin crimson, terre verte, viridian or chrome green, cobalt, ultramarine and Prussian blue—and, of course, black and white. (Again, I buy the cheapest variety of artist's oil paints in tubes.)

This collection of colors should suffice to achieve, when mixed, almost any tone. I seldom have them all on hand and can manage with fewer, but getting fully equipped for a project is a great pleasure—before the real work begins. I had a complete supply of these colors when I started painting the green kitchen.

Working on the principle that as in really good gilding, a color has a special luminosity—especially a cool color—if there is a warm undercoat, I first painted the whole kitchen terra cotta. (In furniture gilding, red was often used under gold leaf.) For the kitchen undercoat I started with a flat white household paint, oil-based, and colored it with burnt-sienna and burnt-umber stainers (from a specialized paint shop) until I got the color I wanted, as close to the terra-cotta tiles as possible. I could have had the color mixed in a paint shop, but by now I am used to—and enjoy—mixing my own. If I can't achieve exactly the shade I want with stainers, I add a little of my stand-by artist's oil paint. It will mix with any oil-based paint; the only trouble is the mixing. Left to its own devices, the oil paint will just lie there at the bottom of the pot of paint, to reappear as a nasty surprise when the pot is nearly empty. It has to be mixed into the paint bit by bit, a good squeeze from the tube into a cupful of household paint, the mixed cupful stirred into the larger pot of paint.

I gave the green kitchen two coats of terra cotta: ceiling, walls, all the woodwork, refrigerator and oven doors. When it dried, I smeared—and I mean literally smeared—the walls, woodwork and appliances with terre verte and viridian green. I wore a pair of rubber gloves. I had a large plate with equal amounts of the two green oil paints plus a small quantity of white. I also had a bowl of gum turpentine, a second bowl of glazing coat (page 69) and quite a few rags. I dipped a rag into the turpentine, then into the glazing coat, and dabbed at the paint. Then I smeared the wall. The only bit I tried to paint neatly, and with a paintbrush, was the cornice (see photograph 23). First I painted it green and then I picked out the flowers —which were hard to recognize as flowers, due to a century of paint—in yellow and red (chrome yellow and Venetian red). Where the layers of paint had transformed the shape of a flower to a mere blob, I painted a flower.

I used the same colors I had used on the flowers to pick out the carving on the four columns (one on each side of the fireplace and one on each side of the stove, photographs 22 and 23). I sealed all the paintwork with one coat of flat polyurethane (page 68). Then we drilled holes for wiring into the columns and attached four Victorian brass lights with green glass shades, one to each column.

If you are fortunate enough to have a fireplace in a kitchen or dining room, or if there is an existing flue, it is ideal to use it for a barbecue. I built the barbecue in the green kitchen fireplace quite easily in an afternoon, but I made a tiresome mistake. I have an extremely heavy iron grill on top of the firebricks. If I haven't put enough wood or charcoal under the grill, I have to lift the food I am cooking off the grill, then lift the heavy grill to add more fuel, and then replace it all. I should have made an opening between the firebricks, with perhaps a small door, through which to push additional fuel. (E) The hibachi barbecue in the blue-and-white tented dining room (photograph 14) is more convenient, although the one in the green kitchen is larger and I can cook a greater amount on it. I can also use it (the kitchen fireplace) as a wood-burning fireplace when I'm not cooking.

I built the barbecue by stacking firebricks, one on top of the other, into the fireplace opening and securing them with sand and cement. I played around with them for a long time, placing them crossways and lengthways so as to have an even front to the barbecue without having to cut any bricks. I left a small square space in the center. A small iron grill, found in a junkyard and cemented in between the bricks, holds the fuel. The heavy ornamental grill lies on top of more bricks and across a larger opening. If I am cooking a leg of lamb, for instance, I place it directly onto that grill. (The heavy grill cannot be properly seen in photograph 23—it is hidden by the various other grills I use.)

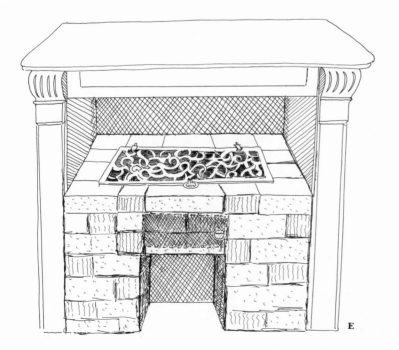

E

A sofa in the kitchen was something I had always longed for (photograph 23). Why not be comfortable while shelling peas? I think the idea had been with me since the time when, as a young girl, I was taken to see a very grand old French lady living in a beautiful castle. I sat nervously on the edge of a gilded, carved, tapestried and certainly signed Louis XV settee. I was nervous, that is, until the grand old lady pulled out from under a network of old chintz—which I had presumed to be her embroidery—two large bowls and started shelling peas. "So uncomfortable doing these things in the kitchen, you know."

The sofa is covered in a slipcover (one of the few I've made; see Chapter 5) so that it can be removed for washing. The cover is in a darkish color, so that it doesn't need washing too often.

On the paneling above the barbecue I hung a small ornamental shelf. I painted it in the same colors as the columns: chrome yellow, Venetian red and terre verte. The shelf holds old tea tins, in which I keep fresh tea.

The cooking utensils that I want to use often I keep visible in a tin ("tole" is the smarter word) flower vase (photograph 22). The vase is tiered, and it had sprung a leak in one of its tiers. The flowers on one layer would die, and the next layer would flood the table. This happened quite a few times before I discovered the cause. When I did, relegating the vase to the kitchen gave me the best spoon, sieve and whisk holder I could possibly have.

Baskets—the kind meant for plants—also make attractive kitchen utensil holders. Utensils grouped together and pushed into a basket, with perhaps a bunch of parsley in a water glass in another basket, make a cheerful and useful arrangement in any kitchen. In fact, I keep quite a few baskets round my cooking area. I have stock cubes and bouquets garnis in one, a plastic bowl with sea salt in another. Various herbs—some in water in lined baskets and others growing in their basket-covered pots—stand near the window. (F)

Sometimes I think that if I see another basket or some chic lady tells me where to buy a new kind of basket, I'll be sick. Twenty years ago they were original, wonderful and, in combination with white walls, modern furniture, light-flowered materials, houseplants and sunshine, a delight. Twenty years later there is nothing original about baskets. From the Philip-

F

pines, from the People's Republic of China, from Poland or France—in they come, an ever-changing variety in every price bracket. The trouble is, I can't find anything around that I like as much for the price.

So although I may be bored to distraction by baskets—above all, by treating them as some new discovery—I end up using them a lot. I change them, however. Having abandoned white walls and light wicker some ten years ago, I am now deeply steeped in the dark colors of the nineteenth century and the aged look of wicker. Dark wicker (that is, antique—or what they say is antique) costs a lot. So I buy the shapes I like in modern wicker, give them a coat of Vandyke brown or burnt umber, and seal it with French polish—not as durable as polyurethane, but it has the greasy shimmer time gives. (See pages 102–3).

Baskets, in lieu of anything better, can be used on a desk for papers. Newspapers and magazines can be stacked in baskets, as can sewing, embroidery or anything else to be stored publicly and attractively. I carry my paints and tools around in baskets (see book jacket), as well as unanswered letters and bills. (It's remarkable how often I misplace the latter.) I also like to use baskets in bathrooms for toilet paper, Kleenex and hand towels. (G)

To the right of the windows in the green kitchen is a pot stand (photograph 21). I think it is something that was formerly used in restaurants to store cooking pots. I painted it terra cotta along with everything else that was turning terra cotta (walls, ceiling, tiles). Then I found breadbaskets, graduated in size, and slotted them into the pot stand. Practically all fruits and vegetables look wonderful, and if they are going to be eaten soon, why hide them in the icebox? They are just as nice as having a bunch of flowers around. I pile the fruit and vegetables into the baskets, reserving the lowest two for onions and potatoes. They make the most mess, so I line their baskets with plastic.

I don't like to have ingredients that I use often hidden in a cupboard where I can't immediately see, without looking inside the package, how much of it is left. Also, I have a bad memory, hate waste and resent the open box of biscuits gone soggy through my forgetfulness. So I keep provisions in glass jars. The best glass storage jars are the least expensive kind, with screw tops (the kind used for preserving). In one case I painted the tops of such jars with Liquid Leaf (page 65). Then I labeled the jars in an ornamental script (also with Liquid Leaf) "Coffee," "Sugar," "Flour," and so on. The kitchen I did this for had copper pots, so I chose copper Liquid Leaf, but jar tops would look fine painted in any color to match the kitchen. Old coffee tins—the kind with the plastic tops—can be made into extremely ornamental storage jars, painted to look like tole. (See Chapter 9, figure D.)

I keep oil and vinegar in two large bottles on the mantel (photograph 23). I bought them at an Italian market and they didn't have stoppers. Glass stoppers from broken decanters or old medicine and perfume bottles can be picked up at a local flea market for a few pennies. The large yellow earthenware pot on the mantel holds flour, the smaller one on the counter, coffee. When I'm making pastry I take advantage of the marble and make it on the mantel shelf (when I am not using the fire below it, naturally).

G

Twenty-five

Photograph 24 shows a kitchen breakfast setting. It is laid out on an oak table which, when I bought it some time ago, was dark. I first painted it with a wood stripper, and after scraping whatever scraped off, I painted it with wood bleach.

It was a pleasure to see it fading before my eyes. Then I scrubbed it to prepare it for its multiple roles of chopping board, worktable and dining table (photograph 21). The first time I chopped, huge stains appeared on the pale surface. So I had to darken it again, with a coat of boiled linseed oil. Now, every three months or so, when all the linseed oil has either been completely absorbed by the wood or been scrubbed away, the grease stains reappear and another coat of boiled linseed oil suppresses them.

The breakfast setting illustrates my point that things don't need to match. They can be held together by color (as they are here) or by shape (as, for instance, the chairs around the kitchen table in photograph 21). The place mat, the napkin, as well as the potholders hanging next to the stove, are made out of Provençal cotton. Their patterns are all different, but the colors are all the same: yellow, green and rust red.

Each of the objects in the table setting echoes one of those colors. The two plates are modern Italian, the cup and orange-handled silverware are modern French. The rest are finds from antique markets. The butter dish was never meant to be a butter dish, nor the little gold-colored bowl a bowl for jam. Visual improvisation is for me the fun in doing the ordinary —in laying a table, in cooking, in furnishing.

I am a big fan of TV dinners. I like to prove that to eat dinner in front of the television doesn't necessarily mean eating plastic off plastic. Nor does it mean being some sort of lesser mortal, mentally and visually impaired, for enjoying television and food at the same time. Also, I like to prepare the setting: light up the fire, lift up the Persian shawl which—surprise, surprise—hides the television (the shawl can just be seen in the corner of photograph 25), produce—also from under the shawl—two small trestles (pages 149–50) and bring in two prettily laid and deliciously spread trays from the kitchen. And I defy anyone to say that gaping at the television while eating is uncouth.

But even without TV it is nice to have a meal on a tray. I have organized myself to feed up to four people in this way. I own four large plastic trays that look like tortoise shell (photograph 25). I have made tray cloths and napkins for them. The tray cloths I usually quilt. For the napkins I use the same material, but unquilted. I edge them with a bit of cotton seam binding. The binding can be bought at Woolworth's and comes in a large selection of colors. It comes double and on the bias, or single, like a ribbon. Sometimes I scallop the edges and bind them with the bias binding, sometimes I just bind them straight, with the single binding. (A) I find it as quick to edge a napkin in either one of these two ways as to sew a neat hem. (See page 84 for more on napkins.)

The trays are large. I set each one as if I were setting a table. I include a glass, a little jug of wine (in photograph 25, a bottle in the shape of grapes), a tiny bread basket, and an individual saltcellar and pepper mill. If I possibly can, I put the first course and the dessert into little individual pots or ramekins. I have a collection of various china lids in assorted sizes with which I cover the first course (eggs cocotte, a mini-soufflé, a pâté) and the dessert (crème caramel, mousse). The dishes I own tend to dictate the food I serve.

I like using lids on food not only because they keep it warm but because the hidden always seems more tempting to me, just as the wrapped present is for a child. I get a definite thrill lifting the lid off a pot on a friend's stove, expecting some delicious bubbling nectar underneath. I don't feel much of a thrill looking into an open pot of stew or seeing the food sit exposed for a while before it's eaten.

For a breakfast or coffee tray, I like to use a small tray and make a nest of material in it, using some remnant or even just an old-fashioned linen tea towel. Into the nest I arrange the china and a piece of hot coffee cake or a croissant, closely packed—nestling. (B)

There are many reasons for my obsessive preparations. I think I'm quite a good cook, more because I hate to waste food by cooking it badly than from any special pride of achievement.

I want to get the best out of the food. This means also giving it a good setting. I want to feel like the artist feels when the cloth is pulled off the picture at the unveiling—even if the lid is only being taken off a well-cooked chop.

I prepare the trays ahead of time in the kitchen. Unless it is something that must literally go from pan to mouth, I put the hot food into the heating cupboard (above the oven in the green kitchen, photograph 21) or onto the hot plate (in the blue-and-white tent, photograph 14) while guests have drinks. Then I carry in the trays and put them in front of a chair or sofa on the trestle stands I made myself.

The stands are made out of pieces of 1″ × 1″ for the legs and 2″ × 1″ for the top supports. I first cut four equal-sized legs out of the 1″ × 1″ pieces. I make mine 2′ long. Then I take a piece of 2″ × 1″—15″ long—and attach two legs to it, using glue and screws. I form a sort of croquet hoop or pi sign. Then I take a second fifteen-inch 2″ × 1″ and attach the other two legs to that, but I don't attach the legs at the same points as on the first hoop. The second hoop must be 2″ narrower so as to fit inside the first one and enable the trestles to open and close flat. (c)

For the open trestle to remain firm, I use L-shaped pieces of wood. To make the L's I cut four pieces of 1″ × 1″ three inches long and four pieces two inches long. I glue them together to form the L's. (For extra strength they can also have a nail hammered through them or be screwed.) Then I attach all four L's to the wider hoop with glue and nails (D): one L facing downward on one side of a leg, and one facing upward on the other side. (E) Then I place the smaller hoop inside the larger hoop and drill a hole through the two legs on each side. To secure the legs to each other, I use a nut and bolt, with a washer between them.

At this stage the finished trestle will not stand, nor can anything be put on it. The tops of the trestle will now have angles facing upward. For the tray to rest on the trestle firmly, the ridges must be pared off with a small carpenter's plane, which can be bought at a hardware shop. To enable the trestle to stand firm, the legs must be angled (mitered—see page 140). This can be done with a hand or back saw. (F)

I use these trestles not only to support trays for fireside meals (photograph 25) but for countless other purposes as well. I

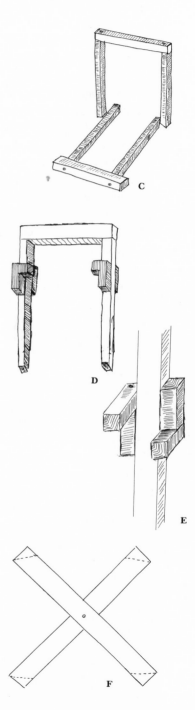

C

D

E

F

whip out a trestle and put a suitcase on it to ease my own packing and unpacking—or to give a good first impression to an overnight guest. (Bottled water, biscuits and carefully chosen books by the bedside are my other first-impression ploys— after which the needs of the poor guest are usually forgotten.)

I make bedside or coffee tables out of the trestles by adding a tin tray and painting trestle and tray the same color. (See Chapter 9 for how to paint tin.) For coffee-table height, the trestle legs have to be cut down.

A backgammon board can sit on a trestle, as can a chess board or any other game that I never have enough space to set up when children or adults want to play. To make a backgammon board I take a flat piece of wood, surround it with a little fence, put in a divider and paint the points to look like two different-colored woods inlaid into a third—maple and ebony on mahogany, for example. (G)

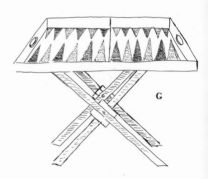

The same sort of trestle, only taller, can be set up to hold a drinks tray, either permanently or just for a party (Chapter 19, figure E).

Here is the easiest and quickest way I have devised to make a large covered table that will remain in place permanently: First, I make two X-shaped legs, the X forming right angles. I use four equal-length pieces of 2″ × 3″ and miter each end. (See page 140.) Then I screw the X together. To strengthen the X, I screw a piece of wood onto it on the top or bottom or both. The two X's must be joined by a strut to keep them from buckling. I make the strut out of another long piece of 2″ × 3″. I cut notches in it that slip into the top angles of the X's. (H) As I usually use an old door that is already full of holes (from the knob, locks and so on) for the top of the table, I hammer a nail or two through the tabletop into the two top X supports for additional strength.

⇉1

London living room:
czar's carriage (*Chapters 1, 2*)

2 ⇇

London living room:
homemade sofa and bookcases
(*Chapters 1, 2, 4*)

⇉3

London living room:
picture montage and detail of door
(*Chapters 1, 4, 6*)

4 ⟨≪

London living room: shutters
and three-seater "conversation"
(*Chapters 2, 4*)

≫⟩ **5**

London living room
(*Chapters 1, 2, 3, 4*)

7 ‖‹

8 ‖‹

9 ‖‹

Blue-and-white-striped
dining room: two
table arrangements
(*Chapter 14*)

15 |←
Batik living room
(*Chapter 22*)

⇒| 16
Blue denim dining room
(*Chapter 22*)

17 |←
View of red stairs
from blue denim dining room
(*Chapter 22*)

California
dining room
(*Chapter 18*)

21 |❦

Green kitchen and details of stove and barbecue, *right* (*Chapter 24*)

24 |⟨
Breakfast table setting
(*Chapter 25*)

25 |⟨
Dinner on a tray
(*Chapter 25*)

Two sides of barn kitchen
(Chapter 26)

28 |❦
Dining alcove
with kitchen hatch
(*Chapter 31*)

29 |❦
Hallway of tropical studio
with doorway to kitchen
(*Chapters 27, 40*)

❦|❖ 30
Flower paintings (*Chapter 26*)

≫| **31**
Yellow gingham bedroom
(*Chapter 28*)

32 |≪
Green-curtained bed (*Chapter 33*)

33 |⊱
Pink gingham bedroom
(*Chapter 29*)

⇥| 34
Pink gingham
bathroom/dressing room
(*Chapter 36*)

35, 36 |⊰
Pink gingham
bedroom:
quilt-covered table
and window
(*Chapters 30, 32*)

37 |◄
Red-and-blue batik
bedroom, and detail of
built-in chest of drawers
(*Chapter 35*)

►| **38**

►| **39**
Blue-and-white
guest room (*Chapter 35*)

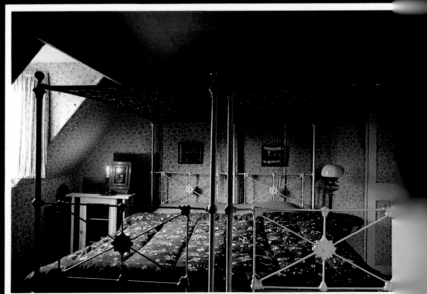

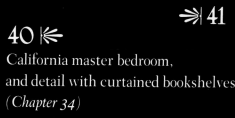

40 |←

California master bedroom,
and detail with curtained bookshelves
(*Chapter 34*)

≫| 41

42 |←

Green batik bedroom
(*Chapter 34*)

43 〰

Barn: double-decker sleeping alcove
(*Chapter 42*)

 44

Barn bathroom (*Chapter 38*)

≫| 45
Bathroom in tropical studio
(*Chapter 39*)

46 |≪
Country bathroom
(*Chapter 38*)

47 |≪

≫| 48
Two views of
tropical studio
(*Chapter 40*)

49 |⟨

⟩| 50

New York studio and detail, *above*
(Chapter 41)

View of barn; *below*, painted
shutters and barn dining table (*Chapter 42*)

53 ❦

California guest room/music room
(Chapter 20)

❧ 54

The all-purpose orange room
(Chapter 43)

55
California library
(*Chapter 44*)

56
Green library and detail
(*Chapter 44*)

57

Twenty-six

I have no great love of laminated kitchen cabinets. First, they are abominably expensive. Second, they look plastic. Third, I think I can utilize space more efficiently by building new inexpensive wooden cabinets or chopping up and reconstructing cheap wooden unpainted ones. If I am planning a new kitchen and am confronted by graph paper with the dimensions of the kitchen and a huge catalog of laminated cabinets that I'm supposed to fit into the plan, all I come up with is hours of puzzlement and a large total cost.

If there were existing Formica cupboards in a kitchen I was asked to do something to, I would, of course, keep them. No matter how much I dislike a thing, "A bird in the hand" and so forth. But I would hope that they had fallen into disrepair so I could have an excuse for repainting them.

For all my ways of painting, which in the end is only one way of painting—a sort of texturing with oil paint and turpentine—the best surface to work on is enamel. Its smoothness swirls the paint into fantastic patterns with only minor help from the paintbrush. The next best surface to work on is Formica. A kitchen I did had brown Formica cupboards. Imitation wood. The wood imitation on the Formica was probably better than my wood imitation, but the evenness of it betrayed it for what it was—identical sheets of plastic imitating wood. By dragging a paintbrush dipped in turpentine and burnt umber over it I lost some of the too obviously repeating grain. By giving it two coats of polyurethane—sanded between coats —I made the paint watertight. Now it is not immediately apparent what the cupboards are made of. It could even be mahogany.

The kitchen cabinets in the converted barn (photographs 26 and 27) are made of unpainted plywood. They are the cheapest ready-made kitchen cabinets available. They are also rickety, the doors come off their hinges and the handles fall off. But once they were screwed to a wooden base and weighted down with stone slabs on the counters, they stopped wobbling. I gave the doors stronger hinges and replaced the knobs with brass ones that have a nut on the screw. (A) (The original ones pulled out easily because they were screwed into the plywood, which was too thin to grip sufficiently.)

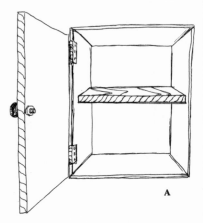

A

Then I sprayed the units with car spray. Car sprays both seal the wood and create a hard, enamel-like base to paint on. Instead of using expensive spray cans, I borrowed a large spray gun from a garage. I filled it with beige car spray. The beige is the same as the lightest color in the stone of the barn walls. When I had sprayed all the cabinets, the dishwasher, the refrigerator and the freezer, I squirted patches of a darker beige on them—this time using spray cans. It gave me the variety of tone that the stone has.

The barn kitchen is an extension, a sort of tongue protruding out from the rest of the barn (Chapter 42, figures A and B). The entire barn has no walls or doors dividing it, but I felt it should look, as much as possible, like one entity, one room. Wherever I could keep the stone—which is the main beauty of the place —I did. And whenever I could extend the impression of stone by improvisation, I did that—hence my reason for spraying the kitchen cabinets and appliances in colors to match the stone walls (photographs 26 and 27).

When spraying a large surface with car sprays, it is wise to wear a mask. (A handkerchief tied around the nose and mouth works fine.) Otherwise, there is a most unpleasant sensation in the throat, not to speak of the unfelt harm the fumes may be causing. To avoid this, I tried to spray the kitchen cabinets out in the open air, but the day was windy and the spray flew sideways, missing the cabinets and hitting the trees.

Once I had sprayed the cabinets, I tried to make them look even more like stone by painting outlines of stones on them in wobbly lines with a thin paintbrush. I used raw-umber oil paint with white added to it. Then my mother and I painted the trompe l'oeil pictures. My mother is a far more talented and patient painter than I am, but has other eccentricities. She refused to go where the cabinets were, although she was willing to help me. What I was able to bring to my mother (drawers and doors) she painted—beautifully. What was impossible to move (icebox, dishwasher and cupboard bases) I painted. For models we used whatever was at hand: vegetables and fruit, flowers and some of the copper utensils that would eventually be used in the kitchen. We used artist's oil paints thinned with turpentine.

My mother had previously painted flowers for the front hall of a country house where the paneling had become cracked and warped from newly installed central heating (photograph 30). The flowers, illustrating those that grew in the garden behind the house, were painted with oils onto cardboard. What remained of the paneling I painted to look like oak (see Chapter 16 for how this is done), and my mother did the same for the background color of the flowers. Then we stapled the cardboard trompe l'oeil inside the panels.

I can never see why, in house decoration, a kitchen should look like a kitchen, a bathroom like a bathroom and so on. That may be the reason why I like trompe l'oeil—fooling the eye. With even a minimal drawing ability, one can achieve charming still lifes. Charming because of, not despite, a slightly abstract and misproportioned quality to the drawing. But anyone completely determined not to draw or paint can achieve a similar effect by cutting out magazine illustrations or pieces of wallpaper, composing a still life and gluing that on. Quite a few coats of polyurethane are then necessary to ensure a durable coating over the cutouts and to smooth out and obscure their edges.

There is a catch to polyurethane. Although it dries quite rapidly to the touch (within twenty-four hours), it doesn't achieve real hardness for about three weeks. If lacquering surfaces that will take a lot of punishment (kitchen counters or floors), it is best, if at all possible, to paint yourself out of the house on the day you leave for a vacation.

I gave the painted barn kitchen only two coats of polyurethane (page 68). I didn't worry about drying time, since the cabinets are used neither for cutting nor for walking on. I was just careful for a couple of weeks. The painted surfaces can now be washed quite safely and even quite roughly.

The counters are made from stone from a local quarry. They were cut by the man who owns the quarry. To prepare the stone counters for the uneven spills of grease they would be getting, I pregreased them evenly. I did this the same way I did the tiles in the green kitchen (page 139)—with two coats of boiled linseed oil. I would have liked to have put stone all over the kitchen floor, but the cost would have been exorbitant. Even if it hadn't (the stonecutter has a very unmaterialistic nature), it would have taken him, single-handedly, too long to cut so many stones.

As the kitchen is an extension of the rest of the barn, I wanted all the flooring in the barn to be the same. I thought I could use old flagstones—if I could find them. From time to time sidewalks made of timeworn paving stones are pulled up and replaced by cement. I toured the roadworks in my district and found some, but not enough. Then I found more, but they were too expensive. The search went on. In the midst of it, I was at a builder's yard. Someone was delivering a load of cement paving stones, the kind that are put into gardens. Gray, even-colored, even-shaped, with ridges on top. They came in two sizes. I bought both sizes and enough to floor the whole barn. But instead of using them as they are meant to be used, with the ridged side up, we turned them the wrong way around. On the wrong side they are smooth. The difficulty was in the way they were cut: They were cut so that they butted together on the ridged side and left enough space on the underside for the cement to hold them together; turned the other way around, they needed a very wide line of grouting. (B) For the grouting not to look too much like cement, which it was, I had to mix a larger-than-usual quantity of sand into the cement. The sand makes the cement a better color, but it also makes it less solid. I painted the grouting with three coats of polyurethane in the hope that this would prevent it from crumbling.

The finished floor looked just like a cement floor. Horrible. The first thing I did was to take a screwdriver and hammer and chip away at the cement here and there. (The slabs are made out of some form of composition cement and are rather soft.) I dug little holes into some and scratched up others, anything to make them look worn. Then I covered the floor with beeswax and turpentine, which changed the floor from the dead gray of the cement to more of a honey color. Natural beeswax can be bought in any good hardware shop and comes in cake form. First it has to be melted and then turpentine has to be added to it—half and half. (I was about to melt it on top of the stove and add the turpentine when I realized that I might have caused a disaster: The turpentine would have ignited.)

I applied the beeswax and turpentine onto the floor with a

B

large paintbrush. When the wax dried I tried to polish it, using an electric polisher. Not a glimmer came from the floor—the wax had been completely sucked into the cement. I had to give it another coat. This time, mainly because it was so boring to do the same job over again, I mixed a little oil color in with the wax and turpentine solution. I squeezed a bit of raw umber into one pot of the solution, a bit of burnt sienna into the next pot. I didn't paint tile after tile, but picked out one here and one there, trying to make them all slightly different shades of honey-colored stone, and as close as possible to the color of the stone walls. (See photographs 26, 27, 51 and 52.)

After this procedure the floor was so thoroughly saturated with wax that it could now be waxed with ordinary floor polish and shined quite easily with an electric polisher. When the color becomes too even (and as there is no painting equipment left in the barn), I tone a few squares here and there with a dark shoe polish. It works perfectly.

Twenty-seven

A friend had a very large old-fashioned kitchen she wanted redone. It had to serve a double purpose: be convenient enough for caterers to prepare large-scale entertainments in, and work as a family kitchen in which to cook and eat comfortably. There was very little, I felt, that needed to be done to the kitchen. It already had—my great wish—one of those marvelous black iron restaurant stoves. There is nothing better to cook on or in, unless perhaps my English wish, the Aga. It is a miracle of good fortune if either one of these stoves is already in a newly acquired kitchen—but they are a nightmare of expense and complexity to buy and install.

As for the rest, the large, rambling and impersonal kitchen had off-white Formica counters, a lot of wooden (also painted off white) cupboards and a linoleum floor the owner hated.

Once more, my motto: Never get rid of anything that is already there; it will only be more expensive to replace. Adapt. All that was necessary here was to give a certain balance to the existing cupboards by adding two more. What additional balance was needed I tried to achieve with paint. The kitchen already had a central table made out of butcher block. I painted the cupboards and walls to match it. (See Chapter 16 for how to imitate wood.)

My friend complained that the occasional invasion of caterers left her in a total quandary about her own kitchen. Where had they put what? In the hope of saving her such future difficulties, I painted on the outside of each cupboard what it had inside: china on one, mixers and bowls on the next, packaged goods and cans on another. I also painted on the outside of the refrigerator what was likely to be on the various shelves inside. I did the same to the freezer. (A)

A

The black iron stove had a stainless-steel hood. To make the hood seem less obvious, and to camouflage the unevenly spaced, silvery downlighters on the ceiling, I painted the ceiling of the kitchen in a "pewter" metallic paint.

The disliked linoleum floor had large white squares interspersed with small black diamonds. The white had become discolored and permanently stained. Ripping it up would have entailed the expense of putting down something new. And put down what? I experimented. I stippled yellow ocher and burnt sienna onto the white squares, making them the same color as the walls and using my usual method—oil paint and turpentine. (See Chapter 16.) Then I sealed them with polyurethane. I chose a time when the owners were away and painted myself out of the door three separate times. I gave the polyurethane four days to dry between coats. Had I allowed more time, it would have been better. Or so I am told. Although I left insufficient time between the coats (the owners were returning), the floor still looks all right despite two years of heavy traffic over it.

B

A pair of plain white roller shades already on the kitchen windows were revitalized with paint and a bit of trompe l'oeil. (B)

On another occasion I was asked to decorate a tiny kitchen squeezed out of the space left over from an obsolete stairway. It was terribly ugly and I was baffled by its shape, but the owner felt—and he was right—that something ought to be done. The appliances looked a little worn, but they functioned and they were in the right order. (Not that there was much choice possible in the placement.) The refrigerator, oven, a foot of counter space and a sink were all that fitted in anyway. Where there was space—and a vast amount of it—was high up. Dozens of very ugly cupboards. Apart from lowering the ceiling drastically and digging a hole into the studio next door in order to turn the space into a sleeping alcove (c), I couldn't think of anything to do. And the alcove, though interesting, would have been far beyond the budget I was given. To change the existing appliances for more streamlined ones would have simply been a waste of money. They would still have looked cramped and misproportioned.

C

The best solution seemed to be to disguise the entire kitchen —unending cupboards, walls and appliances—by covering it with a mural. And as the studio was tropical in tone (photographs 47 and 48), a jungle seemed the right thing.

I didn't have the talent—nor the head—to paint a 14' high mural. Also, I would have been unable to get the right perspective in a room only 6' × 4'.

My helper, Fran, however, has a brother, Chris, who is full of talent. We pried him away from his book illustrations and persuaded him to think big. The result was the most enchanting forest, mountains, sky and waterfall full of animals, birds and fish, which covers walls, ceiling, cupboards and appliances. (D) In photograph 29 a tiger on the wall seems to be eating the real fruit that stands on the kitchen's collapsible table, itself painted with foliage so well that it virtually disappears.

D

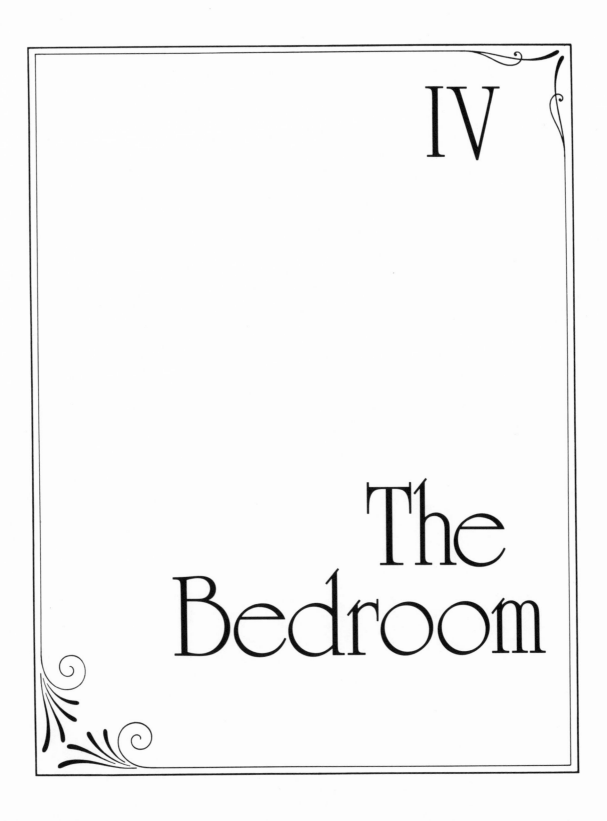

IV

The
Bedroom

Twenty-eight

The easiest way to turn a box spring and a mattress into something splendid is to shroud and drape it in material. There is no limit to possible styles. Sixteenth- and seventeenth-century state beds were the grandest. They had ornamental and carved canopies sometimes topped by ostrich feathers—real or carved—the whole thing sitting on four posts and covered in swags, festoons, rosettes, *choux* (cabbagelike puffs), and curtained with embroidered hangings. (A)

A

Extremely understated versions of these flamboyant beds are not difficult to make and, if cotton materials are used, not expensive. I use a lot of gingham. It comes in most colors, and as it has been around for hundreds of years, it combines with furniture of every period. The yellow gingham bed (photograph 31) is my modern-day version of a *lit à la duchesse*. A *lit à la duchesse*, or angel bed, is a seventeenth-century bed whose canopy is not supported by the more usual four posts, but is attached to the wall or to the ceiling. (B) The pink gingham bed (photograph 33) is my homemade eighteenth-century bed—a *lit à la polonaise*.

The valance for the yellow bed (photograph 31) is made out of three pieces of 2″ × 2″ wood nailed together. It is supported on a fourth piece of wood, which is screwed to the wall. (C) Later, the pieces were all covered in the gingham fabric, which was stapled on.

On top of the material-covered wood is an additional valance. I made it out of a strip of a doubled material twice the length of the valance and gathered. To gather it, I drew two pieces of cord through channels formed by three rows of stitches sewn across the doubled material on the machine. I attached the cords at one end of the strip and pulled. (D)

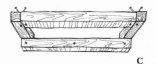

On top of the valance I placed two mock Prince of Wales ostrich feathers. To make them, I first constructed a wire armature out of gardening wire, then wound a long row of ruffles around the top of the armature and wrapped some straight strips of material around the neck. (E) I fastened the material to the armature with the help of a needle, thread and some glue, and then nailed the finished feathers to the top of the valance.

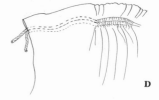

To make the ruffles for the armature, I cut long strips of material. I doubled the strips, turning the edges in, and sewed them on the machine. I gathered them by hand, taking long stitches and pulling them together as I went along. Every 6″ or so, I took a few stitches, one over the other, to tighten the gathers. (F)

Each bed curtain (there are two; see photograph 31) is made of two lengths of cotton gingham seamed together and edged in ruffles. (The ruffles are made the same way as the ones for the feathers and then sewn to the curtains on the machine.) The curtains are stapled to the inside of the valance. It would most probably have been wiser to put curtain rods within the valance and thread the bed curtains onto them, but I stapled: It's quicker and easier. When the curtains need washing, I pull out the staples with a pair of pliers and restaple them when they are clean. (I use the term "pliers" loosely. I don't really own a pair, but the old pair of nail clippers that I do use works excellently.) The yellow curtains have been washed twice in five years and look perfectly respectable, but of course the room is in the country. For town and constant use, I'd either use a darker material or hang the gingham on rods, as it would need washing more frequently.

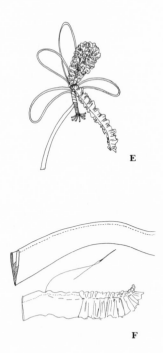

E

F

The headboard was a rather horrible ornate one I already had (page 212), but its shape was all right. First, I covered it in interlining, to soften it, then in the gingham with which I covered the whole room. As always, I did the covering of both the room and the headboard by using the trusted staple gun. (See Chapter 2.)

I placed two iron bars (curtain rods painted black) on either side of the bed to look as if they support the pelmet. The black gives a bit of a kick to the otherwise scrambled-egg effect of the all-yellow room. Covering everything in a room in the same material—bed, bed curtains, shutters and walls—makes the room appear larger. The huge curtained bed blends into the wall and shrinks, the shuttered windows disappear. But a room in which everything is the same can also become very bland, especially if the color covering everything is a pale one. So whatever else I put into the scrambled-egg room I painted black or chose because it had some black in it. Two terra-cotta flowerpots (an edge of one can be seen to the left of the valance in the photograph) I painted black and gold. (See page 62 for method.) A mahogany pillar I had once bought to support a bust I never found I also painted black and gold; it supports the bedside lamp. The small bamboo desk already had a chinoiserie design on its black top when I bought it; otherwise it, too, would not have been spared the overgilding brush.

The panels on the doors, which are the same as the panels on the window shutters, I picked out with yellow lines. I used yellow ocher lightened with enough white to match the yellow in the gingham.

The bedspread for the yellow room was made in the same way as the valance. The gingham material for it is twice the length of the bed and of a width to just cover the sides of the bed; it is lined. (In this case with the same gingham, but any cotton material would do.) It has six double rows of machine stitching running the length of it. Through the channels I threaded strings, sewing them in at one end and pulling them to form gathers. I edged the bedspread in ruffles. When it was first done it looked rather nice, but repeated washing made it lose a lot of its crispness, and I changed it shortly after the photograph was taken. Now I have a new bedcover. I covered an old quilt in the yellow gingham and sewed some white eyelet trim around its edges. I threaded a black velvet ribbon through the eyelet for the same reason as I put up the black rods—for accent and to somber up things. (G)

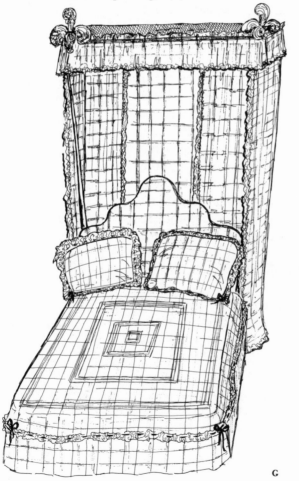

G

During the twentieth century, the eighteenth century has been the period most in fashion with chic decorators. This has made the houses of those using decorators as similar to one another as the houses furnished with matching suites from the local department store. Both are equally over-priced, considering the lack of self-expression they produce (though overpriced at opposite ends of the scale). It isn't that I don't find eighteenth-century furniture and its houses beautiful. It was, after all, the time that gave us the most wonderful ideas in art, architecture and decoration, ideas that I want to steal and adapt again and again. It is simply that I have admired the eighteenth century and its furniture too long. I've sighed over too many thin, spindly and afflicted-looking legs. I've praised delicate carvings, fine gilding, silks and brocades too often. Given the choice now, I would take a set of stiff, solid nineteenth-century Biedermeier chairs (A) over a Louis XV or Louis XVI set any day, even though if I resold them they would, for the moment, fetch less. I think I would even prefer the matching suite—at least I could recover and mismatch that.

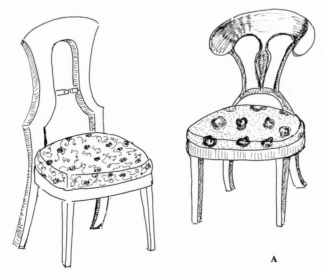

A

There is one piece of typically French eighteenth-century furniture, however, that I will never tire of. And if I ever owned one, I'd feel no compunction about its grandeur. I would in no way wish to redo or underplay it. This miraculous bit of furniture is the *lit à la polonaise*. (B) A *polonaise* bed is a fourposter that usually has curved iron supports, a dome or wreath on top

B

C

and drapery that swoops and swirls, with a *chou* or two (see page 193) along the way. The headboard and footboard are more often than not the same height.

If it has a headboard and footboard of equal height (as in photograph 53), it could be called a *lit à l'anglaise*. A *lit à l'anglaise* is meant for an alcove, but if it's in an alcove, it might possibly be called a *lit d'alcove*. (c)

The pink gingham bed (photograph 33) is my homemade version of an eighteenth-century *lit à la polonaise*. It is in my own bedroom, a floor above the brown living room (photographs 1–5), and the floor plan is the same (see Chapter 1, figure A). For the living room I used the entire floor space, but on the bedroom floor I have a bedroom (the bed stands where the czar's carriage is on the floor below), a bathroom/dressing room (photograph 34) and a small laundry room (description on page 217).

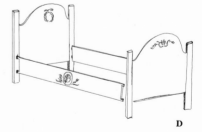

D

The bed is, by now, a very altered version of what I first bought. What I bought were some pieces of wood that screwed together to make a 3′ 6″ wide bed. They were old and rather wonderful. The headboard had a little garland on it, the footboard some other decoration. There were also two very pretty medallions on the pieces of wood that made up the sides. That was all there was to the bed: no box spring, no mattress. (D) As I owned a 4′ 6″ box spring and mattress and anyway wanted a slightly wider bed, I decided to enlarge the original wooden frame.

I made the bed a foot wider. I did this by adding four 3″ × 3″ wooden bedposts, 10″ taller than the existing ends of the headboard. I filled in the space between the old and the new posts with 3″ of plywood. The medallions on the sides of the bed were too attractive not to be properly seen, so I decided to put a side of the bed facing the front. So that both the footboard and headboard decorations would be seen when the bed was placed sideways, I turned the footboard to face inward. I also raised it to make it equal in height with the headboard. To do this, I cut all four new legs to an equal height. (E)

When the bed was in place I hammered a rectangle of molding to the ceiling above it. The molding has the same proportions as the mattress, but is much smaller. To the first molding, which I mitered, I added another, unmitered strip of wood to give the canopy slightly more depth and me more space into which to hammer and staple. (F) I covered the unmitered piece of wood by gluing on an embossed strip of paper. Once painted, it looked like an ornate wooden molding.

To make the curves between the canopy and the bedposts I used copper water pipes. They can be bent to shape even by a weakling. To prevent the pipes from bending too sharply, one should have a plumber's bending spring, an articulated tube that gets put into the pipe before the pipe is bent. I bent the first pipe into a curve that I thought looked best, the next ones to follow the curve of the first. When I had four similar curves, I hammered their tops and their ends flat and made holes through them by hammering in a large nail.

I screwed the tops of the curved pipes into the four corners of the canopy. I used a long screw, pushed it through the hole and screwed it into a small wooden block that I had attached into each inside corner of the canopy. The bottom ends of the pipes are held in place by wooden pineapples that screw through the pipes into the bedposts. (G) (If I hadn't had the wooden pineapples, any brass knob or wooden knob on a screw would have done.)

If the bed has to be moved (to clean under it, for instance, or in my case, to find the many things stored under it), the four knobs can be unscrewed to release the bed. The pipes stay dangling from the ceiling.

The border left and right of the front medallion (photograph 33) is the same sort of embossed paper as the border around

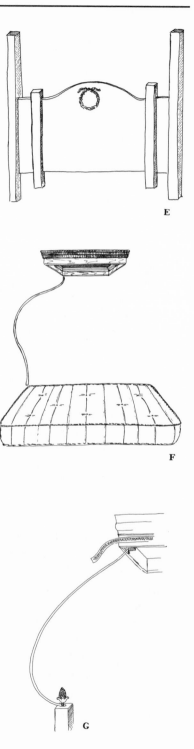

E

F

G

the canopy molding. Borders of that sort are extremely useful —if they can be found. If not, the most surprising things can be made to look like carved wood or plaster, once they are given a coat of paint to match whatever they are glued to: a row of plastic discs or counters, any embossed paper, a plastic mousse mold slightly cut down, a child's sand mold, chocolate boxes that sometimes come in relief. (H) If the decoration is not going to be hit or kicked too often, it can also be sculpted out of an epoxy called E-Pox-E Ribbon (see pages 115–16). I painted the bed gray and picked out the original wood or-namentation as well as the paper additions in white.

H

The bedroom walls and ceiling are covered in pink-and-white gingham. (For how to cover walls, see Chapter 2; for ceilings, page 23.) I had bought lots of it at a sale and covered everything I could with it. What I couldn't get the staples into, I draped. I even wound material around the copper pipes that "support" the bed curtains. To do this I cut strips of material and, starting at the top, twisted the strips, like a bandage, around the pipes. So that the uncovered edge of the strips wouldn't look frayed, I ironed a fold into the strips, and when I wound them, I left the folded edge visible. To make the curtains puff out even more I covered four pieces of gardening wire in the same way, made circles out of them and wired them onto the pipes. (I)

I

The bed curtains are a length of material each. I scrunched up a length at one end and stapled it into an inside corner of the canopy, below the wooden block that holds the copper pipe. I did the same with the other three pieces. They balloon out over the wire armature and are tied back to the wooden pineapples on top of the bedposts with a bow. The bow is made from a strip of the same material, cut, hemmed and slightly starched. The border on the curtains is a pink-and-white woolen one I already had. I gave it an extra kick by crocheting some extra red wool into it (pages 218–19). The sunburst in the center of the canopy is made in the same way as the ceiling of the czar's carriage (pages 26–27).

A bed like the pink gingham one is totally ruined by bedside tables. There would have to be two of them, matching—some form of delicate little table which holds nothing and which I dislike. The bed stands free from the wall. This enables it to have the puffed curtains and also makes it possible for there to be a huge low table hidden behind it. The table consists of two boards on top of a dozen bricks, and is covered in a patchwork quilt. It holds the phone, books, papers and all the clutter I like to have near my bed but which is not necessarily very nice to look at. The bed pillows are hidden under the quilt.

Thirty

One of the more boring of life's occupations is making beds. Using only a duvet (down comforter) to sleep under is obviously a solution for some. You shake the bloated sack from time to time and that's that. Though they originated in the part of the world I come from, I hate them and thank God for the Anglo-Saxon sheet and blanket, tightly tucked in. The duvet is fiendishly hot in the middle, frozen feet stick out at the bottom, and the mound slips off at the slightest movement. During the day the bed looks like a not-very-tempting heap of cottage cheese.

For my taste, a bed should go as follows: The sheets should harmonize with the bedroom. (There are almost too many pretty flowered sheets on the market, and lately I find my eyes resting with relief on plain colors or, even better, white.) Everything should match—top sheet, bottom sheet, pillows. I know a fitted bottom sheet is both neater and easier to put on, but I never seem to buy the right size. Also, they are so difficult to fold properly that I find them a nuisance in the linen cupboard. I have no special preference for blankets, as I like to cover them with a blanket cover anyway, for which I use a matching third sheet.

I like a lot of pillows. They make a bed comfortable and look luxurious, and if there is no headboard on the bed (photograph 42), they prevent you from banging your head against the wall. In the United States, pillows come in many varying sizes. For a double bed I would ideally have two king-sized and two queen-sized pillows of the least expensive quality (Dacron) and, for the heads to actually lie on, two standard feather pillows. All would have pillowcases to match the sheets. There is no need to launder all the bedclothes at the same time. Using the blanket cover sheet (if using a sheet) as a top sheet, the top sheet as a bottom sheet, slotting pillows from front to back and so on may challenge the memory, but will save on laundry time and bills.

Making beds is easier if the bedspread and comforter are one. An unmade bed can be quickly hidden by pulling the bedspread/comforter over it. Its bulkiness hides the bulges underneath. If the bed consists of only a box spring and mattress, the bedcover should be large enough to cover the bed all the way down to the floor (photographs 38 and 42). If the cover is made out of a duvet or a ready-made comforter and the bed to be covered is a double one, it won't work. They don't exist quite so large. But it must be at least large enough to cover the sides of the mattress. (A)

Even if the cover goes all the way to the ground, the box spring will also have to be covered. When the bedcover is removed or even if it is only turned back, part of the box spring is going to show. Ruffles to cover the box spring—and to match the sheets—can be bought. Quite expensive, they tend to match only one set of sheets and clash with the rest.

A

I prefer to slipcover a box spring in the same material as the bedcover. This is a fast job that takes comparatively little material but requires some determined strength to lift the mattress off the box spring, turn the box spring upside down, staple the material on the bottom side, turn the box spring back up and stitch the material around the top with a curved upholstery needle. (B) This way the feet of the bed still show. They can be either covered (page 43 and photograph 40) or hidden by a straight skirt (page 35 and photographs 2, 43 and 53).

I make bedcovers in various ways. Sometimes I buy plain quilting by the yard and cover it with material. If I can't get plain white quilting—which is often the case—I buy a cheap quilted material in a color that harmonizes with the one I am about to use. I cover the plain side of it with my material, and the quilted material acts as a lining. This method makes rather thin covers, but it is fast and the least expensive. I used it for the mattresses in the czar's carriage, the layered ones in the converted barn, the large mattress in the tropical studio and the one in the California music room (photographs 1, 43, 47 and 53). Another way to make a bedcover is to buy an inexpensive ready-made comforter or a duvet (more expensive) and cover that. I did this for the green-curtained bed, the pink gingham bed, the two batik beds and the double bed in the barn (photographs 32, 33, 39 and 52).

Quilting comes sewn in small squares. The new material can be sewn to the quilting on the machine. When sewing it, the new material must be on top, the quilting underneath. If it is the other way around, the material, which is covered by the quilting, can get scrunched up without being noticed. With the quilting underneath, however, the squares in the quilting are hidden and can only be followed if the material is plain and basted to the quilting or if it has a geometric pattern that helps to work out exactly where the squares are. If the material is flowered irregularly I usually forget the squares in the quilting and sew around the shapes of the flowers. (C)

To quilt a whole bedspread is too cumbersome for the sewing machine. It is better to cover the lengths of quilting separately and then sew them together. Because of the even larger bulk of a comforter or duvet, only the outer edges can be covered in a new material using a normal sewing machine. The rest of the material must be attached by hand.

The bedcover on the pink gingham bed started out as a duvet. It had parallel lines of stitching running the length of it. To cover it in the pink gingham, I stitched along those lines and sewed new lines across. It looks neater with squares (photograph 33). If I had a large washing machine, it could go into that, but as I don't, when it needs a wash it goes to the laundromat. During the day I keep two bolsters on the bed (as can be seen in photograph 33) and hide the bed pillows.

Combing antique shops and markets, one can sometimes unearth old patchwork quilts at reasonable prices. But those few that are still reasonable are often permanently stained and irreparably torn. A quilt like that looks awful on a bed—dirty and worn. But as a cover for a table (see photograph 35) the same worn quilt can look like a valuable antique. The especially bad bits can be turned in the direction that is seen the least. If the table must take the occasional wet drinking glass, the quilt can be protected, its tears held down and the whole thing ennobled with a glass lid the same size as the top of the table. If the quilt is small, it need not cover the whole table, but can hang—square-shaped or round—over the top. In that case, some other plain cloth draped under the quilt must cover the rest of the table down to the floor. (D)

C

D

From time to time small pieces can be salvaged from totally ruined quilts. These pieces can be appliquéd onto a new base. I have bought nonfitted white cotton quilted mattress covers in whatever size I wanted my quilt to be, and appliquéd bits from an old quilt onto them, either following the existing pattern or making up a new pattern while still using the old bits. A border in a corresponding color (and out of new material if there is not enough of the old available) gives a neat finish. (E)

E

Although it is useful, I am becoming slightly bored with the round, covered table that goes well with eighteenth-century furnishings. I have a complete horror of the very small, round, covered table. It usually has a lamp on it that is too large for it, and together they look like two lampshades sitting one on top of the other. (F) If a round table is to be acceptable at all, it must be large and stacked with things: lamp, books, pictures on stands, objects. The cloth covering the table should be too long for it, so that it balloons on the floor. The table should be covered in thickish material if possible (a quilt is perfect), and if it isn't, there should be an old blanket or length of interlining under the thin material to give it body. (See photographs 35 and 49).

I would never cut a too-large rectangular blanket or quilt into a circular shape, no matter how old or worn it is. It is unnecessary. The corners, tucked under the table, do a lot to help the puffy look of the covered table, while saving time and not limiting the covers to only one life.

I prefer the tailored look of the earlier rectangular Renaissance-type covered table. It is easier to make (trestle and boards —pages 149–50), takes less material to cover and blends in— or, better still, is unobtrusive in—most surroundings. It can be used as a desk, side table or games table (see hall table, photograph 7, and side table, photograph 49). If it is a desk (see Chapter 41, figure A), a large blotter, which proclaims it to be a desk, is difficult to find. I've made one out of a piece of cardboard (the back of a large sketchpad), to which I glued leather corners to hold the blotting paper. The corners I painted with Liquid Leaf (see page 65).

A rectangular table covered in a velvet or a false suede looks elegant and formal, as if it came out of a seventeenth-century Italian town house. In a blue-and-white gingham, with some

F

tailored bows on the side, it looks very seventeenth- or eighteenth-century French, straight out of a château. (G) The same table with a standing mirror on it makes a very nice dressing table, especially if covered in some lighter material with perhaps a swag or two. Done up in organdy and lace (or nylon covered in some cheap cotton lace curtaining), it is a dressing table out of the nineteenth century and could have belonged to the Empress Elizabeth of Austria. (H) It was usual at the time to give the mirror a veil, as if it were a bride. This can be done with one staple or a dab of glue, depending on whether the mirror has a wooden frame or not.

Thirty-one

There are many useful everyday things around the house that I prefer hidden. The television set is one of them. The best thing is to put it into an off-the-ground cupboard directly in line with some comfortable place from which to watch, as in the New York studio (photograph 50), where there is a large sofa directly opposite the cupboard. The television set stands in the central section. Of course, a hole had to be drilled in the back of the cupboard, through which the electrical wires and aerial could be threaded.

The next best way to hide the television is to push it under a table and throw some form of cover over the table. To be watched from various angles, the television can be placed on a small platform on wheels. None of the commercial TV stands are low enough, but a board approximately the same size as the television does nicely. Four castors (small wheels or ball-like rollers bought in a dime store) are easily screwed into the four corners of the board. The set can be pulled out from under the table and turned in any direction. Such a device is hidden under the quilt-covered round table in the pink gingham bedroom (photograph 35) and under the paisley shawl–covered table, the corner of which is just visible in photograph 25. The cupboard under the bookcase in the California living room (photograph 9), the corner cupboard under the bamboo bookshelf of the tropical studio (photograph 48) and the lower cupboard to the right of the fireplace in the blue-and-white batik living room (photograph 15) all hide roll-out platforms with television sets. In the converted barn, the television set has to travel further (on its platform on wheels) for comfortable viewing: from under the table within the right arch (photograph 52) to the front of the large sofa.

I have always wanted to be asked by someone to hide a television more resourcefully—but it would, unfortunately, also cost more. To begin with, the television would have remote control—no longer such a luxury in the United States, but still so in Europe. I would build a false wall opposite a bed and hide the television behind it. (The wall would also hide a walk-in closet.) I'd cover the television with a large mirror or picture. According to how much I was allowed to spend, the picture would either slide aside electronically or be lifted up and down like a sash window. If electronically, the bedside table would have the control button. The picture would move up or down or sideways—depending on space—to expose the screen. If funds didn't allow for the electrical machinery, I'd uncover the television by moving the mirror/picture by hand.

I used this last method to cover the hatch between the dining alcove and the kitchen in photograph 28. An ordinary sash window, instead of having glass in it, has a picture of a ship. To surround the picture, Mr. Lewis made a heavy frame, which I painted "mahogany." (See Chapter 16 for method.) The alcove is used to work in, have meetings, sit and talk. When it is used for a dinner, the picture is pushed up and the food handed out from the kitchen. If the food is prepared beforehand, it can be kept warm on a sunken hot plate on the kitchen counter and left hidden by the picture. When everyone is seated around the table, the host can lift the picture and hand the food from off the kitchen counter and around the table without leaving his seat. He can put the used plates back on the counter and pull down the ship.

I could have used an ordinary set of small plywood double doors, as I did in the country kitchen (photograph 10) and saved on the expense of the window mechanics, but they take up more space and would have hit guests or dishes, depending on which way they opened. And to cover the doors with a picture would have meant cutting a picture. (A, *see next page*) It is almost criminal to cut a picture in half, at least one painted by someone else. (One's own is another matter.) But a poster can be cut guiltlessly, as can a magazine illustration or a piece of wallpaper. An attractive flower or series of flowers from a wallpaper or magazine can be cut out, collaged into a still life and glued to the wooden doors.

The paper can be livened up with oil paints so that it looks less flat. The paint can be applied thickly, straight out of the tube, following the existing colors. This gives dimension to the flat paper. If paint is applied to parts of the paper only, oil stains may appear around the paint. It might be necessary to seal the paper with a coat of lacquer before beginning painting. The oil paint will take a long time to dry thoroughly. (Some

colors, especially reds, thickly applied, take up to a month to dry.) Then the entire creation will need another coat of lacquer. A frame around it will further the illusion that the picture is an oil painting.

Bottles and glasses, like TV sets, I would also rather keep hidden. If I were living in a large country house, surrounded by people who helped, and could afford to have a collection of every conceivable kind of liquor, I would keep all the bottles exposed on a vast marble-topped sideboard in the huge hall that the house would be certain to have. Perhaps I would even have a small icebox, marbled to match the marble tabletop (see pages 103–6 and photograph 57), in which to keep the champagne chilled. As things are, however, I prefer to keep the two or three half-full bottles of liquor and the row of additive bottles and cans hidden.

Various things make good liquor cabinets. The better ones are waist high so that you don't have to grovel on all fours looking for bottles and can mix the drinks at counter level. In the batik living room (photograph 15), the bar is in the upper cupboard to the right of the fireplace, with the television, on wheels, below it. (B) The bar also holds a small refrigerator; the kitchen is on another floor, and running up and down stairs for ice would be a nuisance. For those who can afford it, I'm sure an ice machine is a help, but the only one I've come across made the most off-putting noise while regurgitating.

In the New York studio (photograph 50), I built three shelves into the right-hand portion of the maple cupboard. I stapled a curtain to hang down from the counter-high shelf to hide the supplies stored behind it. On top of the counter there is space for a tray of drinks and space on which to mix them. Glasses and tools are on the two smaller shelves. (C)

In the tropical studio (photograph 47), a few bottles of drink and the ice bucket stand on the lowest of the bamboo bookshelves, but glasses and the many little bottles and cans are hidden in the cupboard below it.

I like to build narrow shelves onto the doors of liquor cabinets—in fact, onto any cupboard doors. If the shelves are narrow enough, they use space that would otherwise be wasted. (They must, of course, if closing in on other shelves, be spaced between those shelves.) In a liquor cabinet, they can hold the glasses, the bottle openers, the tonic-water bottles, and so on.

B

C

When mixing drinks it's faster to pull all these out from cupboard doors than from hidden interiors.

In the pink gingham bathroom (photograph 34), I built narrow shelves into every cupboard door. They hold bags, belts, gloves, scarves, socks and stockings—anything narrow. The shelves in the cupboard doors of the dressing table hold makeup jars, reserve soaps and toiletries. By being able to see the things in the cupboard doors at a glance, I reduce the time I spend on dressing or packing for a trip.

In the shelves on the door of the linen closet, I store sewing equipment. Kitchen cupboard doors can hold spices and sauces. The broom closet can have shelves for all sorts of cleaning necessities.

I make the shelves out of 1/4″ plywood. They are like small troughs. I cut the plywood with a portable electric jig saw into narrow pieces, the shelf part usually only 4″ wide, the back part 4″ high, the front 2″ high, the sides slanting between the two. (The length depends on the width of the door.) I glue them together with wood glue. (D) After they're assembled, I screw the shelves to the door.

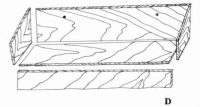

D

In most cases I paint the shelves to simulate mahogany or the usual *bois clair,* or lightwood (Chapter 16). In bedrooms and bathroom/dressing rooms, if the shelves are to hold accessories, I line them. I choose a material from my stack of remnants, paint the shelf with fabric glue and stick on the material. For the inside of the trough I sew a removable little cloth which can be shaken or washed out when it gets dusty.

I like clothes. It comes, I imagine, from my mother's and my having to, at one time, sew our dresses from an ever-shrinking pair of curtains we had brought from Czechoslovakia. Apart from encouraging me to think myself Scarlett O'Hara, this remnant sewing didn't thrill me, especially as my sewing was hurried and insecure and fell apart at inopportune moments. I spent a great deal of time dreaming of boxes filled with tissue paper and dresses out of the pages of *Seventeen* magazine. I am sure it is from these times that I have preserved my interest in the containers for clothes as well as the clothes. When I don't paint the inside of my closets to look like wood, I line those as well, using some inexpensive cotton dress material or a large remnant.

I have two ways of embellishing cheap hangers. I used to buy single wooden ones and cover them in material. I would attach brass hooks to them for skirts or wooden laundry clips for trousers. Now even wooden hangers are becoming expensive, but I've had some quite good results buying quilted material —again in some pretty cotton print, which can be bought in any department store—and making a sleeve out of it for an ordinary wire hanger. Around the hook part I wind bias binding, which can be bought in a multitude of colors. (E)

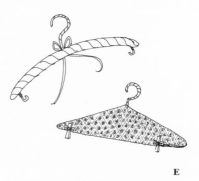

E

Thirty-two

The window curtains in the pink gingham bedroom (photograph 36) are gray denim. The room was becoming a little light on its feet: pink and white (even though a strong pink), a "floating" bed, patchwork quilting . . . I decided to put up gray curtains to quiet the pink, and to make them out of denim—a cheap and strict-looking material.

The room has curved windows. I made curved valances out of thin plywood. To do this, I nailed three pieces of 3″ × 2″ around the upper third of the window frame. To this framing I nailed the plywood. With a portable jig saw, I cut a curve into the plywood that corresponds to the curve of the window. (A) (I could have used thick cardboard instead of plywood, which is easier to cut, but it would also need the wooden framing.) I padded the valance and covered it with the gray denim. The curtains are pinch-pleated and on rings, the rings threaded onto a rod. The rod is attached beneath the valance.

Another easy way is to make a framework out of three pieces of wood (page 162), keeping wide and well away from the curtain rod or track, and staple some form of swag onto the framework, like, for instance, the swags on the bed canopy in photograph 32 (pages 191–92). The same sort of framework can

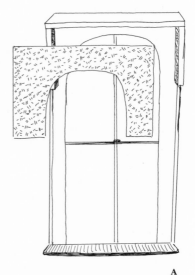

A

be draped with a piece of material in the Empire style, with cascades on the side (B) or just swagged like the valance of the czar's carriage (page 22). (I must admit that I don't much care for draped valances on window curtains. To look right, the windows must be excessively tall and swathed in a mile of material. Not economical. But I like draped and ornate valances on beds a lot, where they make a bigger splash for less outlay.)

To pad a valance—which immediately improves the look of it—I place the cut plywood or cardboard on top of a strip of padding and cut the padding to the shape of the valance, but add 1″ overlap. (C) I cut a lot of notches in the overlap and then staple it onto the back of the valance. I repeat this procedure when I cover the valance with material.

For curtains that need to draw back—as opposed to the ones I prefer, that only loop back—I use rings. This is mainly on account of the tedium of putting up a curtain track with cords. I never quite get that one right: Something is constantly getting knotted or stuck or slipping off. Also, I have a block about reading and understanding instructions. On the other hand, I've never lacked curiosity about how someone else does things —which I hope may apply to whoever is reading this book.

For those who have mastered how to put up a curtain track, just pulling a string to open and shut the curtains is a grand and easy gesture. When the curtains are open, however, a nasty bare piece of plastic or tin shows, and it should be covered by a valance. With rings on a rod, a swish of the hand opens and closes the curtain. (Light-colored curtains, however, may soon develop a handprint if "swished" twice a day.) If the top of the curtain is hidden by a valance, it is possible to improvise in secret under it. For instance, with loops of material instead of rings, or by threading the curtains straight onto the rod. If the rod is too weak for the weight of the curtains, tying the rod with string to the top of the valance or to the ceiling will help to support it. (D)

If the curtain rod and rings are to be visible (no valance), I prefer them to be wooden and as thick as possible. (Keeping in mind that the thicker the rings, the less far back the curtains will draw.) I buy them in any finish—the least expensive—and then paint them, rod and rings alike, using my usual method of simulating wood (Chapter 16). I paint them to suit the room they are going into.

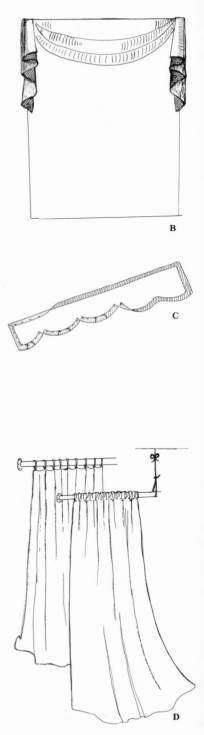

B

C

D

Curtains aren't difficult to sew, although getting them to look just right does take time and a lot of measuring and can be expensive. A curtain should look full, heavy and voluptuous. To hang properly, it should be lined and interlined. Whenever I make curtains for myself, I prefer to make them out of a material thick enough to hang in rich folds without needing to be lined or interlined. If I can staple them straight into the top of the window frame and loop them back, all the better (photograph 2, pages 21–22). This is the simplest way and looks the best, but it does keep out a certain amount of light. To have curtains *and* maximum light, the curtains must be the kind that can be drawn back.

The windows of the pink gingham bedroom are narrow (only 3′ wide). I didn't want to block the light, so I couldn't make the gray curtains very full. To make up for their lack of fullness, I gave them thickness. There is one length of 36″ wide denim per curtain. I cut the interlining 2″ narrower and 2″ shorter than the material. The lining I cut the same as the material.

If I have the space to do so, I like to cut and pin my curtain on the floor, as I did with the denim curtains. I laid the length of denim down, wrong side up. On top of the denim I placed the interlining, and on top of the interlining the lining. I pinned the denim over the interlining, creating a 1″ frame of denim all around the interlining. Then I pinned the lining, folding 1 1/2″ of it under, just over the gray framing. I sewed the lining to the gray edge, occasionally catching the interlining with a few stitches. (E)

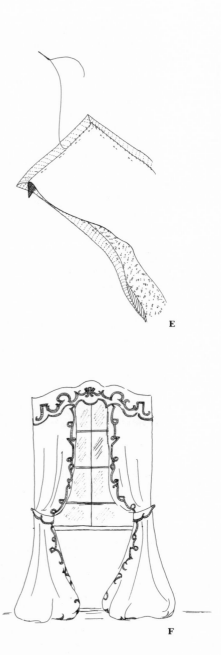

E

F

Among the things I find visually very depressing are curtains that are too short. As depressing as a man who wears trousers that are too short and who has short socks. The space that appears between the floor and curtain is as offensive as that space between trouser and sock. It is easy to avoid. A curtain dragging on the floor is better than one that is too short. Many curtain designs dating from the eighteenth and nineteenth centuries had the curtains dragging on the floor by what must have been at least a foot. (F) I added 5″ to the length measurement for the gray curtains: 2″ for the top and bottom turn-ins, 1″ extra in case of incorrect measuring, the rest to drag.

The correct curtain has a 4″ to 6″ bottom hem. Mine usually has only a 2″ one—to ease calculations. To make up for that casualness, I weight down my curtains to make them hang properly. The weights I use are usually a couple of obsolete English pennies sewn into each corner of the curtain hem, but proper curtain weights can be bought at Woolworth's.

After the gray curtains were sewn, I put in pinch pleats. As the tops of the curtains were going to be hidden by a valance, I didn't necessarily need to make the pleats; I could have just sewn the rings to the top of the curtains. But I feel that curtains hang better with pinch pleats.

There are all sorts of theories on how much material is needed for pinch-pleated curtains. It ranges anywhere from one and a half to three times the width of the window. I am usually influenced by the amount of material I have and how much light I can afford to steal from a window. (Obviously a full curtain drawn back blocks more light than a meager one.) To find out how many pleats I need, I cut a ribbon or a piece of string the width of the window. I lay the string on the floor above the curtain I am about to pinch-pleat. Then I pin in the pleats, one at each end, another in the center, and fill in the pleats between them until the width of the curtain or curtains is reduced to the length of the string.

Pinch pleats are triple pleats. They should have some form of tape to give them more body, but if the curtains are lined and interlined, I find the pleats quite thick enough. I concertina three equal folds and pin them. Next, I sew 4″ down the back of the pleats to hold them together. Then I sew across the pleats. I sew the ring, if I'm using rings, into the center of each middle pleat. (G)

When I am asked to make curtains for someone, I hope that they already own a pair of old, well-made ones. If so, I buy some cheap cotton material and cut it (and seam it if necessary) to the same width and length as the curtains plus 1″ all around to turn in. I pin the new material to the old curtains. Then I cut open the pinch pleats, one at a time, push the new cotton material around and into the old pleats and sew the pleats up again. I don't sew the two hems together—it might pull the curtain out of shape—but leave the new material flapping, with a hem of its own. Should the new, lighter material look as if it might creep up the old curtain, a weight can be sewn into the hem. I sew the new material to the old along the sides, using large, loose stitches.

G

If there are no old curtains around, I go to an auction and buy, cheap, some really ugly tattered pairs which no one wants but which are well made. I use the pair most suitable in size, cover them in new material and hoard the rest. In addition to hoarding old curtains, trimmings and every variety of rag, I also hoard pieces of new material. If I see a reduced bolt or remnant of some pretty fabric, I tend to buy it. A cushion, chair, bed or room, depending on the quantity of material I have, is bound, sooner or later, to call for attention.

Just as I believe each piece of furniture needs pushing about and trying out before it finds its true position, so I believe a piece of material can be extraordinarily helpful in trying out furniture coverings and colors. Color is very dependent on light. Light is different in every room, according to how much of it there is, which way the room is facing, what does or will cover the walls. If the walls are to be painted, holding up a piece of material gives a better and easier idea of color than painting a lot of samples. Draping chairs in large bits of different materials enables you to see which type of material and color look best. Holding up 2″ samples (which is all shops seem to give away free) gives no idea at all.

The gray curtains and valance in the pink gingham bedroom are trimmed with a pink border (see photograph 36). I bought it by the yard, in white, and dyed it at home with Rit dye. I first dyed a small piece, timing it to find out just how long it took to get the right intensity of color to match the pink in the gingham. I wetted a swatch of gingham as well to help compare the wet colors. When they matched, I dipped the rest of the border.

The most extraordinary curtains can be made by using ribbon work or appliqué. Curtains reminiscent of those found in state apartments as early as the seventeenth century can be re-created by using plain, inexpensive materials (denim and lining material) and the sort of tape binding that can be bought in a dime store. Strap work, ribbon work or galloon (tape braid) —whichever you want to call it—appears also in architecture and in wood carving. (See photographs 22 and 23 of carved columns.)

The pattern I used for trimming the nicest curtains I ever made I copied from a design on the outside of a late seventeenth-century Austrian house. (H) I made the curtains out of blue denim (ordinary blue jean material). I made them like the gray curtains, only longer and wider. The valance was more intricate, but also made in the same way as the gray one: cut out of plywood with a portable jig saw. (See figure F.) For the ribbon work I used an off-white ribbed binding. I pinned it in intricate loops and curls to the material until I was satisfied with the design and then sewed it onto the curtain. I had to make a lot of little pleats in the tape to form the corners and curves. (I) The tape braid on the valance was glued on, but I had to sew it first into the shape I wanted. Because the tape was white, I didn't dare use glue to secure the many pleats. Most material glues tend to yellow with time. This is hardly noticeable when it's on color, but on the white pleating it would have been. Sewing this kind of ribbon work takes a long time. But it is the sort of handwork I enjoy, and friends have stopped considering it an eccentricity when I appear laden with a curtain instead of, genteelly, with a piece of needlework.

I once painted the same sort of design on muslin curtains. It was for a beach house that some friends of mine rented summer after summer. With the excuse that the place didn't belong to them—so what was the point of spending money on it?—they returned every year to the same gloomy interior. I talked them into buying some cheap muslin, and with water-proof magic markers we painted ribbon work onto the muslin in two tones of green (two tones so that the ribbon would appear shadowed. (J) We did the same on more muslin and made it into bedspreads. In one room a 12″ shelf bracket made a quick and cheap support for an Empire-style bed hanging, the hanging also out of painted muslin. (K) Eventually, spurred on by the ease of using the magic markers, we whitewashed the interior of the whole house, and ribbon work appeared over doors and windows, making the house look rather like a cross between an Austrian chalet and an embroidered Slavonic petti-coat.

Sometimes if I find a pretty remnant of a chintz in a sale or, even better, an old, faded and tattered piece at an auction, I cut out such flowers or garlands as it might have and sew or glue them onto a plain background material—that is, a mate-rial the same color as one of the colors in the chintz. This can

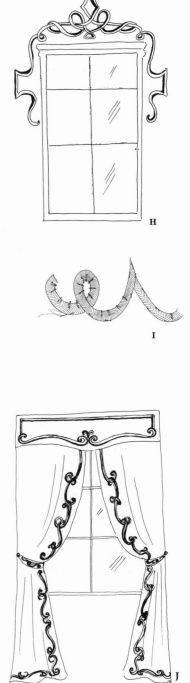

be done on curtains, bed hangings, cushions and even upholstered furniture. It can also look effective and very nineteenth
century glued around window frames or doorframes. (L)

Good-looking borders, which can be bought for this purpose,
are expensive. A border can be made much more reasonably by
cutting strips out of material in some floral stripe or paisley
bought by the yard. (See photographs 42, 43, 45, 49, 50 and
53.)

When appliquéing flowers or joining stripes, there are certain things to watch out for. Half of a flower looks odd. A
second half cut out from a remnant of the same chintz should
be added to the first half to make it look right. (See Chapter
20, figure B.) If attaching a design above a door or window or
to a valance, the design should be centered. By using cut-out
flowers, one can build up or shrink a flower arrangement to the
size needed. If a striped border is used, the stripes must meet,
and if framing something (a door or window), the corners must
be properly mitered (page 107). (M)

After all this talk of curtains, I must confess that of late I have come to prefer shades. In fact, I avoid using curtains for windows whenever I can and try to use shutters or shades instead. Shades need less material (not *much* less—but a bit). They eat up less light. But mainly, once pulled up, they are out of the way, not flapping uselessly left and right of the window like two wobbly fangs in an otherwise toothless mouth. Shades fit flush inside of the window frame; therefore they take up less space. If there is a seat or a boxed-in radiator under the window, a short shade looks fine. (N)

N

Short window curtains I won't even mention, I find them so horrible—like something that has been accidentally cut off or forgotten.

There are many types of shades, and all have different names —often different names for the same type of shade, which can lead to confusion. There is the ordinary roller shade, a stiff flat thing on a roller. It can be made at home with supplies available in department stores. The material used, which can be bought by the yard, is called Holland; hence the name "Holland shade." The Holland can be bought in a variety of plain colors, in monumentally ugly designs and sometimes, when in luck, in some pretty stripe (as the yellow striped shades in photograph 31). It is cut to the size of the window and stapled to the roller. (O) The roller, equipped with spring, comes ready-made in standard sizes. If an irregular size is needed, it can usually be cut down in the department store. If this fails, the roller can be cut down at home, using a backsaw. The mechanism must then be reattached to the shorter roller. Instead of Holland cloth, a spray can be bought to stiffen ordinary material, which can then be stapled to a roller. I have found this to work quite well when the shade is first sprayed, but in time it turns back into a pumpkin—in this case a piece of floppy material. I have also glued and sewn material to existing Holland shades (photographs 36 and 41). Gluing is better, but it's not easy. Once the material is covered in glue, it tends to stretch and squirm in a really mean way. Sewing, on the other hand, tends to leave a thickish edge where the material is turned under, which can impair the rolling of the shade.

Then there is the Roman shade. When it's down, it looks like an ordinary roller shade; up, it's a series of folds. It works by pulling up cords through rows of rings, the rings attached

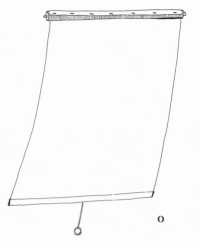

O

to vertical tapes on the sides of the shade. A tape with plastic rings already attached can be bought by the yard in a department store. Should that tape be unobtainable, there exists another tape into which separate spiral brass rings can be inserted. Or a tape can be made at home by sewing rings to a ribbon or to a binding. (P) If I'm in a hurry, I tend to use no tape at all, but sew little plastic rings at equal intervals straight to the material. The shade in the czar's carriage (photograph 1) is made this way. Once the rings are attached, cords are tied to the bottom rings and drawn through the row of rings upward.

Some really well made shades of this sort have a series of pockets sewn into the back of the shade, into which wooden slats are placed. These shades, weighted down by the wood, seem to look neater when drawn up and straighter when down. (Q) But this difference doesn't seem to me worth the extra material that is needed for the pockets, nor the extra trouble of finding, buying and cutting the wooden slats.

A version of the Roman shade, but one that is gathered on top, is sometimes called a festoon curtain or shade or sometimes a balloon shade. If a shade has many festoons and (because it is gathered along the sides as well as on top) remains in festoons when down, it is sometimes called a Vienna shade or—perhaps naturally, considering where Vienna is—an Austrian shade. (See photograph 34.) Although, like the English muffin, which doesn't exist in England, they have certainly never heard of the Vienna shade in Vienna.

To make a Vienna shade I take material double the length and a quarter more than the width of the window. For six festoons, as in the pink gingham bathroom, seven tapes with rings are needed. The tapes are the same length as the window. The material is gathered lengthwise first and then sewn to the tapes. The Vienna shade looks best when it is finished off with a ruffled edge on the sides and at the bottom. (For ruffles, see pages 162 and 194–95.)

In the California supper room (photograph 18) and the living room (photograph 6), the shades are slightly different again. They both have an added fullness, achieved in this case not with gathers but with pleats. Pleats make them flat on top, ballooning out further down. They look their best not completely drawn up (when they are, they become a squashed

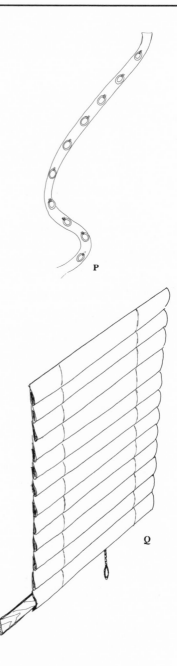

mess) but somewhere almost up, so that they still swoop and bulge (as in photograph 6). They must be longer than the windows—an additional quarter of their length—so that when they are down and covering the windows fully, a bulge still remains at the bottom.

In the supper room (photograph 18), the material for the shade is one and a quarter times the length of the window and one and a quarter times the width. There are three festoons. There is a small pleat in the material left and right of the central festoon to use up the extra quarter of the width. This makes the shade puffier. At the back of the material there are four vertical equidistant tapes with rings sewn to them. The best way to get the vertical tapes straight and equidistant is to first iron lines into the material: Fold the material into as many sections as tapes, and iron the edges. (R)

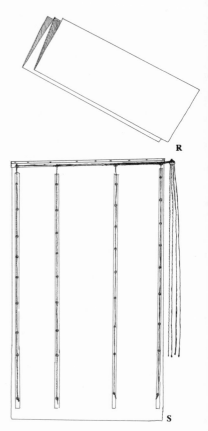

The professionally made shade starts with a slat of wood 2″ × 1″. The wood must be the exact width of the inside window frame and eventually gets screwed into it. The shade is stapled to the top of the wood. The underside of the slat of wood has picture eyes screwed into it. The cords run up through the rings, through the picture eyes, and are all drawn to the right, where they converge into one larger ring (s) and hang down. All the cords (four in the case of the supper room shade) are tied to some fastening on the wall or window frame to the side of the shade—a cleat, a knob or a hook. I usually make a knot in the cords at the three places I am most likely to want my blinds—for the most light, for the best looks and down—and loop the knot onto the knob when the blind is at the level I want. (T)

I have to shamefully admit that when working for myself or for someone who also appreciates shortcuts over perfection, I skip the wooden slat and screw the picture eyes straight into the window frame. I then staple the shade to the window frame on the underside so that the staples won't show. (U)

The shades in the California living room (see photograph 6) had to have a curved top to further the illusion that they were hanging within a tall curved arch (which didn't exist; see Chapter 7). They are out of unbleached muslin. (It is the cheapest and, to my mind, one of the nicest materials for making shades, since it billows.) To make the shades, pieces of wood were cut 2″ wide and the same shape as the arches above the windows.

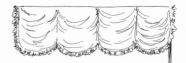

The muslin was stapled around and to the back of these pieces of wood, and the wood was nailed to the wall just under the black arches. Each shade has three large pleats and is drawn up by three tapes with rings, one tape in the center, the other two on each side. When the shades are up, they form two large balloons. They are not lined. If they were, they would lose much of their airiness. When festoon shades are made for a bedroom, they should be lined so that they shut out light more effectively.

U

Thirty-three

A different form of festoon, or swag, hangs from the canopy above the green bed (photograph 32). This is purely a decorative swag, but one that can do a lot for a plain curtain, dressing table, or box spring and mattress. (A) It is a straight bit of material, double the length the swag is to be, the sides cut slightly on the bias, the bottom already cut in a curved shape. I hem the curved part and gather or pleat the sides. Two or more separate swags can be attached (and the join and gathers hidden) by a straight strip of material between the swags. A swag can also end with a cascade (see page 182, figure B.).

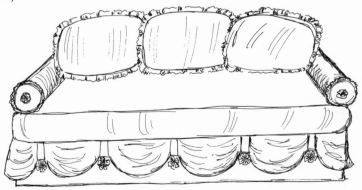

A

To make a cascade, I cut a straight piece of material the length of the longest part of the cascade. I cut off a triangle at the bottom to give the material a slant, hem it and pin in the pleats. (B)

The green material I used for both the swags and the curtains is lining material—a very thick, good, chintzlike material called satinet, but lining nonetheless.

Both the swag and curtains on the green bed have a wool fringe. It is in the colors of the flowered Liberty cotton—coral, white and green—that I used to line the swags and curtains. The same cotton covers an old quilted bedcover. (See pages 172–74 for how to cover quilts.) The quilt was the first one I covered and I didn't do it very well. In photograph 32, you can see the large fold that shouldn't be there and that I eventually got rid of by cutting out the extra material and sewing it to the nearest seam. Rather like a face lift.

The top of the green curtained bed is one of four old wooden curtain valances I bought at an auction. I had used three of them on some other job, and the leftover one joined the rest of my varied remainders in the cellar. When I saw the plaster cornice of the bedroom, I remembered the valance. Both cornice and valance have the same aptly named "dental" molding.

To make the valance smaller without having to remiter the corners, I sawed a piece out of the middle of it. I attached the two pieces back together again by screwing a piece of wood behind and across the join. I smoothed some plastic wood, or wood putty (see pages 115–16), over the cracks my uneven sawing had made, until they virtually disappeared. I made the join even less noticeable by giving the valance a coat of flat white paint. To the top of the shrunken valance I screwed a piece of plywood. I attached two 12" metal L-shaped brackets to the wall with a toggle bolt and screws. (A toggle bolt, which can be bought in any hardware store, is used to hang heavy objects on hollow walls.) Then the whole toothy coronet got placed on top of and screwed to the L-shaped brackets. (c)

I stapled the green swags, lined in the Liberty flowered cotton, to the inside of the canopy. On top of the swags, also from the inside, I stapled the lined curtains. "Lined" is once again an exaggerated term: All I did was place a length of flowered material on top of the green material and staple an

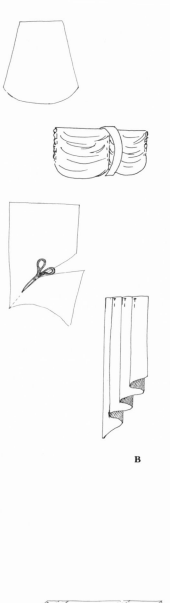

B

C

occasional pleat into both of them. I caught the two materials together with a few long stitches.

To hide the mess of staples inside the canopy, I made a sunburst. I started by stapling bunched-up pieces of the flowered cotton in the center, and drawing them to the outside edge of the canopy, where I stapled them over and below the staples that held the curtains. (D) This gives the effect of a small tent within the canopy, as well as hides one row of staples. To hide the sunburst row of staples, I used some more woolen fringe. Over the bunched-up material in the center, I made a little round shower cap of material, otherwise known as a *chou*. To do this I cut a circle and sew it irregularly, using a curved needle, over and around the bunched-up center bits. I put a few extra stitches into the middle of the *chou* so that it looks as much like a cabbage as its name suggests. (E) If I am making a *chou* on bed hangings, I knot a piece of string around a bunch of material in the curtain. If the bubble that this forms is high up and won't be touched, I stuff it full of tissue paper, but if it's within reach I stuff it with some wadding or leftover bits of material. (The tissue paper crackles.) To hide the string, I sew the *chou* back to the curtains with a stitch or two. (F)

When I can, I like to put my feet up, so I flop on the bed whenever I have the chance. The telephone is near. I write my letters and do my paperwork half-sitting, half-lying on the bed. I know a lot of women who do the same. Fewer men I know seem to want to spend their day with their feet up. I think they have better circulation. By making a bed look part bed and part sofa, I don't feel as if I've gone to bed during the day. The simplest way to make a comfortable and easily convertible sofa bed is to bank the thing with cushions. (See photographs 1, 43, 47, 53, 54.) Even the beds that are more bedlike (photographs 32, 33, 39, 40 and 52) don't become too "unmade" if used during the day on account of the padded quilts that cover them and the pillows that are left exposed. You can pull and shake the one and punch at the others to tidy them up quickly.

The bed pillow covers, whether pillowcases or pillow shams, must fit in with the color scheme. In the green bedroom (photograph 32), the bed pillow, in its white, flower-bordered pillowcase, is in the center. The two large square pillows on either side are also bed pillows, the kind used in France. They have white pillow covers, which I bought at a market for old

clothes and which I use as pillow shams. They needed a bit of repair and a lot of careful bleaching, and then I threaded some ordinary white cotton seam binding through the eyelet holes. When I tried to find more the following week for someone who had admired mine, I couldn't, but I found a plain old-fashioned linen pillow cover and a very ruffled baby's dress. A few bad-tempered hours later, the two were united into a pretty good copy of my original *broderie anglaise* pillowcase.

Photograph 32 also shows cushions out of the remnants of a Provençal material and a matching border, and a cushion in the same Liberty material as lines the curtains and swags and covers the bed quilt. Color and a certain laciness bind all these cushions together.

I made a ruffle to surround the Liberty cotton cushion. It's a ruffle I find good-looking, fun to do and hell to iron. So I just don't. I hope I'm making it out of a material that can get by without being ironed. To make the ruffle, I use a doubled strip of material. (See page 162 for how to make this.) Then I make box pleats, the width of the pleat depending on the width of the strip (the "box" should be square). I take three or four stitches per box pleat, through all three layers, to hold the pleat. (G) I make a row of box pleats, the "boxes" almost touching one another, until I have enough to surround the cushion.

Then I sew the row of boxes to the cushion. I do this by hand and am once again sparing with the stitches—both for speed and so that there won't be too many stitches showing. Once the ruffle is attached, I take each "box" and catch the top and bottom of it together with another two or three stitches. (H) As the thread must be torn off and restarted after each pleat, the ruffle takes a bit of time. But when it's finished I think it's worth it. It is, in fact, a ruff. Not the kind that encircled an Elizabethan lady's neck but the later, more frivolous kind that might have encircled Mme. de Pompadour's neck above a deep décolletage.

To make the cushion covers for the blue-and-white-striped dining tent (photographs 12–14), I adapted an idea I had seen at Colefax and Fowler, the grandest and best English decorating establishment. Colefax and Fowler make, among other things, the most wonderful ruffles with which they sometimes encircle their cushions or curtains. The material forming the ruffles is pinked with a special machine into little half-moons of scallops. Not having such a machine, I cut strips of material with ordinary pinking shears and gather them. For these cushion covers I cut 4″ strips of plain blue cotton and 4″ strips of striped cotton. I gathered them on the machine. Then I placed the striped strip on top of the plain strip, gathered them and sewed both of them onto a square of striped material, the square the size of the cushion. I sewed them to the square 3″ away from the edge. (I) When the ruffles were on, I sewed the ruffled square (ruffles on the inside) to another, plain square of the same size and the cushion cover was finished.

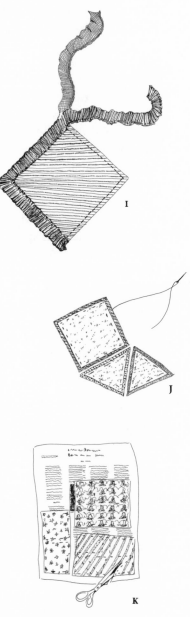

I

The cushions in the czar's carriage (photograph 1) are made out of an Edwardian velvet-and-satin patchwork. I bought bits of patchwork that were falling apart (in fact, I have never seen any satin-and-velvet patchwork in the markets that wasn't falling apart) and I made cushion covers out of the pieces I salvaged.

Even for as uncomplicated a patchwork as the one of the cushion covers in the czar's carriage, the squares, triangles and rectangles have to be paper-lined before being sewn; otherwise, they pull and stretch out of shape.

The normal method for patchwork of this sort is to make a cardboard templet, baste the pieces of material to it, leave an overlap of material around the edges of the templet for seaming (J), sew the overlapping material together and remove the templet. I stitch my bits of material to a newspaper, cut the newspaper and the material the same size (K), and sew the pieces together on the machine, with and through the newspaper. Then I tear the paper away. The newspaper is sufficient to give the material body and to prevent it from stretching, but not so thick that it can't be sewn through on the machine.

If I am making something out of a collection of faded and worn pieces of material, which I prefer to new material, and I am suddenly short of a particular color or quantity, there are various ways of aging new material. Lemon juice, sunshine and patience is one way. Bleach is the other; it may be more dangerous, but it's faster. For material in solid colors, I start with very diluted bleach, immerse my material in it and, if nothing happens, pour in more bleach. (Into the water on top of the material—not onto the material!) This way, since I haven't mixed the bleach in properly, if the material does fade (instead of falling apart), it fades slightly irregularly, the way time would have faded it.

For a patterned or flowered material that I want to bleach into an aged look, I use a small quantity of bleach slightly diluted. (Trial and error tells how much to dilute; it depends on the dyes, the material and the strength of the bleach.) Then I dip a paintbrush (large watercolor brush) into the solution and paint it onto the flowers or the design in the material.

Velvets, contrary to belief, are not ruined by water. It's what to do with them after they've been wet to make the pile stand up again that's the problem. A tumble drier works the best, but if it's unavailable, holding the velvet over a kettle and brushing it (or holding a steam iron over it and brushing) also works.

Tea is excellent for aging (yellowing) a too-new-looking piece of material. My heroine of decorating, Nancy Lancaster, reputedly jostles her guest as he sits holding a teacup in any newly upholstered chair she owns. That way the spilled tea is an accident, she gets the effect she wants, and she feels less guilty about staining the recently paid-for upholstery work.

Thirty-four

Draped beds tend to be considered feminine. Why this should be so I can't quite understand, since men as well as women slept in them for hundreds of years without, as far as I know, having such worries. As it's the cheapest way of making a really grand-looking bed and the most fun to do, I hang on to curtaining beds like a dog hangs on to a bone. For a more "masculine" bed, however, I try to keep the colors toned down, or mix a rough-looking material with the softer material used for the drapery. I did this for both bedrooms in the California house (photographs 40 and 42), with canvas on one bed and a wool plaid on the other.

In the California master bedroom (photograph 40), I

cheated. It has a ready-made bed. The owner wanted a king-sized bed, which is extremely difficult to make look like anything but an oversized modern bed. With its curved and padded headboard and footboard, this one looked rather like a huge ship. It came "ready" in natural-color canvas only. I might have preferred a brown one—in a darker color the bed would have appeared smaller—but we were in a hurry. Except in a high-ceilinged room, a very wide bed lends itself badly to canopies and drapery. Here, there was anything but a high ceiling—I could practically touch it—and there was no cornice. Since a cornice can do a lot to give the illusion of a heightened ceiling, we made one.

A wooden cornice can be put up by a patient amateur. It really only takes a hammer, some thin nails and a bit of wood glue. More difficult are the corners that jut out (as on the bed cornice) and the ones that go in (inside corners of a room). They must be mitered (page 140).

I made the cornice out of 2" half-round moldings, bought by the yard and attached to the wall one below the other, with a gap between them. I painted the moldings "mahogany" (see Chapter 16 for how to do this) before attaching them, so as not to spot the ceiling or the walls. I nailed up one row of half-rounds just under the ceiling. A 2" space of wall below this molding I stippled to look like walnut. When it dried, I stapled up the yellow-and-brown batik wall covering. (See Chapter 2 for how.) I used the second molding to hide the edge of the material and the staples. This left an inch of "walnut" between the moldings.

The jutting-out cornices above the bed and above the windows (photographs 40 and 41) are marginally wider to make them more noticeable. Instead of using two half-rounds, I used a half-round and a flatter, "nosed" molding. The valances, as I shall call them to distinguish them from the cornice, have the moldings mounted onto 6" wide boards. Three boards are nailed together, the moldings mitered and glued to the boards. The valances above the windows and bookshelf jut out about 5" from the wall. They are painted the same as the cornice: mahogany, walnut, mahogany. The three-sided rectangle above the bed is the same width as the bed and juts out as far as a third of the bed. It is screwed onto three shelf brackets, the brackets positioned so as to enable the whole structure to be screwed into the ceiling joists, or beams, where they hold firm. (A)

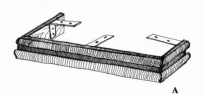

A

To find out where the ceiling joists are is quite a business. Usually they run in the opposite direction of the floorboards and are about a foot apart. Some people can tell by tapping, others just have to make a few false starts with a thin nail until they hit lucky.

The voile bed curtains are stapled to the canopy in the same way as the other bed curtains I've described (pages 162–63 and 192–93). This voile, which I found on sale in a downtown Los Angeles shop, was a dollar a yard. Although made out of some synthetic fiber, which I usually avoid, it looks exactly like the wonderful cotton voiles I have always admired floating on the welcome current of air in the hot climates of Italy or Greece.

I've described how to make a sunburst for a ceiling on page 27 and for the inside of a canopy on page 193. But here, as voile is transparent, I couldn't staple it directly onto the ceiling: The shelf brackets would have shown through the sunburst. I had to cut a piece of plywood the same size as the bed canopy, make the voile sunburst on that, and then screw the completed thing inside the canopy.

The upstairs windows of the California house rivaled the downstairs ones (see Chapter 7) in peculiarity of shape. They were small squares. I tried to fool the eye into believing they were taller by curtaining them from ceiling to floor. I hid the gap between ceiling and window with a shade (photograph 41). I covered plain white roller blinds with brown lining material (page 188) and hung the blinds above the window frames instead of inside them. (B) For this the shade has to be longer than the window measurement, and space must be allowed for it between wall and curtain.

B

On one wall of the master bedroom there is a wide and rather low French window leading onto a balcony. I curtained it in the same way as the other windows. The wall opposite was blank and seemed endless. I decided to build a bookcase there the same size as the French window and to curtain that as well (page 25, and photograph 41.) The shelves I stippled "mahogany" (Chapter 16), the plywood doors under them I covered in material (pages 120–22) and the plain wooden handles, also stippled "mahogany," I screwed into the doors once they were covered.

The doors and the doorframes (one to be seen left of the bed in photograph 40) I painted to look like walnut. In the other California bedroom (photograph 42), there is a blatantly white door. Eventually it became the same color as the one in the master bedroom. When the photographs were taken I hadn't yet painted it. I was waiting to see if I would keep the walnut tallboy desk next to it, in which case the door would be painted "walnut"; if not, it was going to be "mahogany," a better match for the brown curtains and mahogany chair.

The gilded canopy over the bed in the green batik bedroom (photograph 42) was made to continue the style of the Chinese carved curtain valances. It is a square box—a wooden delivery box—with mitered pieces of molding stuck onto the lower three edges. The molding is a piece left over from the one that forms the baseboard in the library (photograph 55). The gilding on the canopy is Treasure Gold (page 65) rubbed on with a finger over a coat of red paint.

The batik on the walls is a more colorful one than the ochers and browns of the neighboring master bedroom, but harmonizes with it. The window curtains are green lining material, the bed curtains brown. Both colors are picked from the batik. An advantage of lining material, apart from its low cost, is that it can be found in virtually any color.

The plaid woolen bedcover has the same colors as the batik on the wall. I bought the plaid material by the yard (7 1/2 yards, 36" wide, at $4.95 a yard) in a downtown Los Angeles dress fabric store. I seamed together three 2 1/2-yard lengths (making sure I matched the squares), hemmed the edges and threw it over the bed. The blanket is both a bedcover and an extra blanket. I had planned to quilt it onto a duvet (following the squares would have made it easy—see pages 172–73), but I ran out of time.

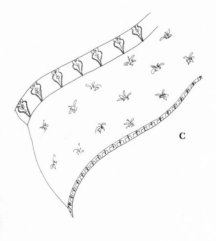

c

The batik on the walls had two borders, one wide, one narrow. With the help of the wider one, I gave the room a "cornice." Originally, the border's points turned inward, toward the material. (c) Used as a cornice, it looked a great deal better—almost architectural and Gothic—to have the points pointing upward. I cut the border away from the material and hemmed both edges on the machine. After I covered the walls with the rest of the material (see Chapter 2 for method), I glued it on to hide the staples and the edge of the wall material.

As the border is wide, it would be a terrible waste to have the material that covers the wall go all the way up to the ceiling. It ends lower down and the border covers the gap as well as the staples. (D) I used the second, narrow border on the batik to trim the bed and window curtains, to frame the doorways and to form a nonexistent baseboard between floor and wall.

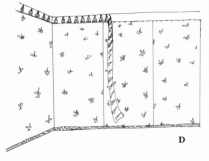

D

For rooms without a cornice, another way of neatening up the transition from wall to ceiling without too much expense is to glue on some jute webbing—those canvas-colored bands that hold in the springs on chairs. Department stores or upholsterers often carry smart-looking striped webbing. I once bought a brown-and-black one for 35 cents a yard and used it to frame a room I had covered in beige denim. It supplants a cornice, forms window and door frames, trims shutters and hides the staples, as well as gives the room a rather masculine air. (E)

A really cheap and quick (by "quick" I mean it will still probably eat up a whole day) means of acquiring a cornice (and moldings) is to cut long strips of paper and glue them onto a painted wall. The paper can be painted by dragging it (pages 69–70), stenciling it (pages 62–63) or painting it freehand. It can also be cut out using the paper-doll principle.

Nancy Lancaster, one of the founders of Colefax and Fowler, the British interior design establishment, has the best taste I know. Her sense of scale in house and gardens is perfect: well-planned, voluptuous disorder. Her country living room,

E

which is one of the nicest rooms I have ever been in, has white painted walls, a cornice, baseboard and borders made out of strips of paper dragged in blue paint, sofas and armchairs covered in blue-and-white striped slipcovers, the whole thing splendified with some black Regency furniture.

Also, I have often thought how attractive a room painted bright blue would be with a cut-out white paper motif around the ceiling and running down the corners of the walls. (F)

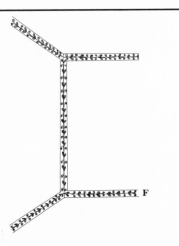

F

Thirty-five

More tented and draped beds appear in photographs 38 and 39. The top one is a Victorian iron fourposter I was delighted to have found for a client. It was rusty and had to be sandblasted to make it the silver color it is now. A sandblasted piece of iron is the most wonderful shade of silver. Not as bright as polished silver or as sharp as stainless steel, it has the mellow look of pewter, only more alive. To prevent it from reverting to spotty rust, it can do with the occasional scrape from some steel wool, followed by a bit of oiling. It can, of course, be lacquered, though personally I think that it loses its silky look that way.

I had also been longing to sandblast the two narrow Victorian beds (photograph 39), which are mine and which started out even more rusty, but I was too miserly to do so. I settled for covering them with a liquid rust remover (which can be bought at hardware stores) and making a frightful mess peeling and scraping. When they were more or less free of rust, I painted them white and put them in my attic guest room.

The bedroom with the sandblasted fourposter bed (photographs 37 and 38) was based on a red-and-blue batik, which now covers the bed. The walls and the tented ceiling of the room are also batik. For quite a while batiks were the most attractive, least expensive wall covering I could find. Not only do their colors tend to match (same dyes), but so do the designs, even though the batiks may come from places as far apart as Malaysia and Kenya. To match the red-and-blue swirls of the bed batik, which comes from Bali, I found a Dutch indigo one. It looks like a lot of swirling eyes. As the room is high and since I was to give it a very gathered ceiling, I needed a lot of material. It took 60 yards of 48″ material to cover the walls and the ceiling. (See Chapter 2 for how this is done.)

Although I have moved on to Indian cottons in preference to batiks because they are cheaper, I am still often asked to make a batik room, as I was here. I snuck in, however, two Indian striped cottons. (Again, they are dyed with the same vegetable dyes as the batiks, so they match.) The existing curtains—heavy, ugly damask ones—I covered with a thin red-and-blue-striped cotton (page 184). The bed curtains are out of an even thinner, voilelike cotton in dark blue with the thinnest of white lines. They are tied to the polished iron crossbars of the bed with ribbons made out of the same material.

The fourposter in photograph 38 is iron, but it is easy to make one like it out of wood. The upright posts can be square, out of 2″ × 2″ or even 3″ × 3″. They can be material-covered (glued or stapled on) or painted. Covering them in silver foil might be rather nice, or there are very thin sheets of brass and chrome on the market that could be wrapped around the posts. (I haven't used the latter, since the edges would be terribly sharp and would need soldering. Lately, however, I have heard of a small amateur soldering kit and I have been meaning to try it out.)

A

To prevent the posts from wobbling, it is best to build them into a wooden frame. The posts should go all the way down to the ground, where they serve as legs for the structure. The box spring and mattress simply drop inside.

To make the top of the bed more solid, the uprights must be joined. There are various ways: I've used the same 2″ × 2″, just hammered on (A) and covered in the same way as the posts. Boards can be used to encircle the posts, rather like those enclosing the box spring.

An ornate valance can be cut out of plywood, screwed to the top horizontal pieces of wood, padded and covered. (See pages

181–82 for how.) It can face either upward or downward, or
both. (B) A curtain rod can be screwed to the inside of the
canopy and the curtains suspended from it.

A piece of material stapled over the top of the whole structure makes a flat "roof." A few pleats stapled into it make a
gathered "roof." Or a widish board can be nailed across the
middle of the canopy and a sunburst stapled to it underneath.
(For how, see pages 26–27.) A tidier way is to make a separate
frame out of 3″ × 1″ with a board nailed across the center,
staple the sunburst onto that and place the completed "roof"
on top of the bed. This way it can be lifted down from time
to time to have the dust shaken off.

A fully curtained fourposter bed has four curtains and some
form of hanging—usually from the same material as the roof
of the canopy—behind or instead of a headboard. This is best
suspended from a curtain rod in the back of the ornamental
valance, if there is one, or simply stapled to the back of the
canopy (as in figure B).

I treated the twin iron beds I bought for my attic guest room
(photograph 39) as if they were a double bed. They would have
been prettier each with its own little canopy (C), but I didn't
have sufficient space because of the mansard roof (left of pho-

B

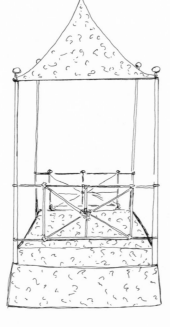

C

tograph). Each bed has four horizontal iron bars joining the four posts, the bars secured to the top of the posts with brass knobs. To make one canopy over both beds, I had to remove a horizontal bar off each bed so that they wouldn't obstruct the center (see figure E).

I made the pagodalike canopy as follows: I measured from the central point of the ceiling above the beds to one of the corner posts (as usual, with a piece of string—see page 26). Then I added 3″—2″ extra for tubes through which to thread horizontal bars and 1″ to staple to the ceiling. I cut four lengths of batik, 48″ wide, to this measurement.

I shaped the roof right over the bed. I stapled the point of one corner of material to the ceiling. The other corner I left dangling. I pulled the material to a horizontal bar and pinned the full width of it around the bar. I cut off the excess triangle (now hanging) (D) and used that (the wrong way around) to form the next triangle. When I had the whole space above the two beds covered, I stood on the bed and pinned the triangles to one another. (E) I shaped the canopy while I pinned it. By pinning in a few extra darts, I accentuated the conelike top of the canopy.

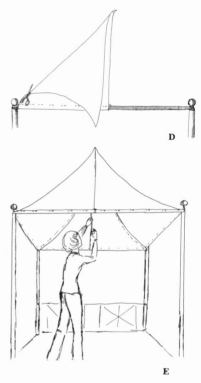

D

E

With the whole structure pinned, I pried out the staples from the central points, pulled out the iron bars from where I had pinned material around them and took it all down. Then I sewed what I had pinned on the machine.

This left all of my seams, pleats and darts visible on the inside of the pagoda, where people, lying in bed, would have little else to contemplate. To minimize the visible seams, I made French seams. This means first sewing a narrow seam on the machine (or by hand) in the normal way, then turning the cloth right back over the seam and sewing another seam that encloses the frayed ends of the original one. (F) (This meant the French seam was now on the outside.) In order that even the minute extra thickness of the French seam didn't widen the tip of my pagoda, I dabbed a bit of glue along the seam and pressed it flat. (Incidentally, I could have done none of this had I not been working with a material that had the same print on both sides.)

Two eiderdowns cover what now appears to be a double bed. They are ones I had, which I re-covered by sewing the same batik as the one I used for the canopy straight to the old

F

covering. (See page 172 for method.) The walls I covered in
a blue-and-white cotton dress material—another summer sale
find. (See Chapter 2 for how to cover walls.)

The blue-and-white guest room had no closet. Nor did it
have much space for one now that I had crammed two beds
into it. The only space I had was in the two corners opposite
the beds, but there the mansard roof cut the wall space in half.
So I made two little tents: one a closet, one a dressing table.

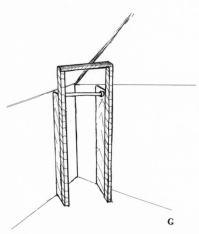

For the closet tent I put up a 5' tall squared-off arch—a sort
of pi sign made out of 2" × 4". I wedged it in across the corner
under the slanting beam. About a foot down from the top of
the pi, I attached a piece of plywood on the back side of each
upright, from the uprights to the wall (where the wall was still
flat). (G) Between those two pieces of wood I attached a clothes
rail. It won't hold many clothes, but the guest room is planned
so as to keep the guests only for short stays.

To create the tentlike effect, I stretched and stapled a piece
of material—the same blue-and-white cotton I used for the
walls—around the horizontal 2" × 4" and the two pieces of
plywood. The other end of the material I gathered and
stretched upward to the top of the slanting beam, where I
stapled it. (H) From the horizontal piece of wood I hung a

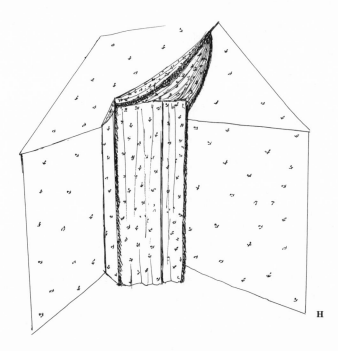

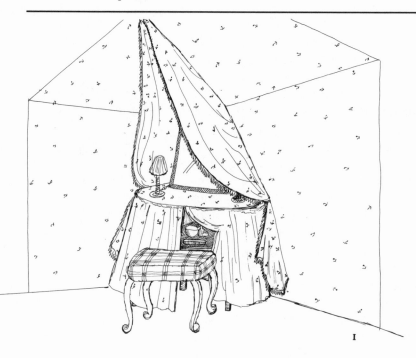

I

curtain. To make it, I gathered and stapled on two lengths of material, which I had previously hemmed. I accentuated the triangular shape of the tent by trimming it with some dark-blue cotton fringe (pages 218–19).

In the other corner of the room I put up a nondescript broken-down table bought in a junkyard for the equivalent of a dollar. I made a plywood top for it with a curved front and a triangular back to fit into the corner. I covered it in the same material as the walls and closet. The cover has a skirt that hangs to the floor. The skirt is divided in the middle so that a storage shelf under the table can be used. (1) The cover is lined and only draped over the dressing table—not stapled on—so that it can be easily removed for laundering.

Over the dressing table and above the dressing table mirror, I made a second little tent. I stapled a length of gathered material to the top of the slanting beam and let the material hang down. Then I tucked it behind the table lid. I edged the material with more blue fringe.

An innovation I am quite pleased with is the way I made and covered the shutters for the dormer windows (on the left of photograph 39). The windows are so small that I could use thin plywood without too great a worry that the shutters would warp. (Larger shutters have to be made out of a thicker wood; otherwise they tend to twist and turn in time, and not shut properly.) Each window has two shutters, split in half, so that when open they can fit flush into the slant of the dormer. (In the photograph, however, the double half is fully open.) The covering is the same material as the walls, gathered. It is not stapled on at all, but works like a pillowcase: You slip it on the two plywood doors and then pull strings, sewn into the top and bottom of the "pillowcase," to form the gathers. Tape for this purpose, with the string already in it, can also be bought by the yard in a dime store or department store. (J)

J

When I was asked to decorate the blue batik bedroom (photographs 37 and 38), it already had a great deal of closet space. But what closets! I was confronted by an appalling set of plywood doors—three rows of them—from floor to ceiling, each door with a delicate little flower knob handle—a dozen of them. (K)

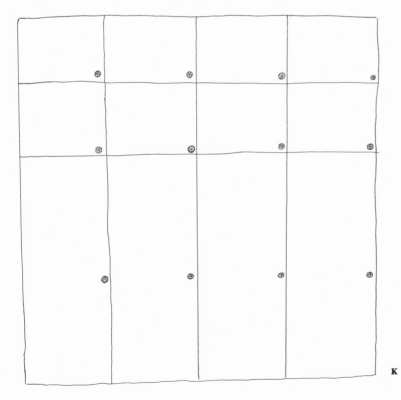

K

I would never have the heart to demolish existing closet space, but these were truly too ugly to remain the way they were. My client owned an extremely good-looking mahogany tallboy. Mr. Lewis, the carpenter, cut a hole into the closet doors for me, and we slotted in the tallboy (photograph 37). I removed the offensive knobs from the many remaining closet doors, changed them to touch catches, padded the doors (this made them less flimsy) and covered them in the same material with which I covered the walls. (For covering doors, see pages 120–22). Then I hung pictures on the covered doors. Now it looks surreal. Like a wall with a very flat chest of drawers.

A wall of built-in closets in a bedroom ruins the wall, no matter how much you do to disguise it. I have tried mirrors, material, paint. It remains a row of doors against which no furniture can conveniently be placed.

If building new closets for a bedroom, it is better, if at all possible, to build a false wall and so somehow manage a walk-in closet behind it, with one door, then to have all those wretched doors. If there is no space for a false wall, it is better to cut off corners to form closets (Chapter 32, figure к), build tents or create, using either wood or material, two closets on either side of a *lit d'alcove* (Chapter 29, figure c).

Whereas a row of closets in a bedroom seems wrong to me, a row of mirrored, painted or material-covered closets in a bathroom/dressing room looks right.

V

The Bathroom

Thirty-six

I spend more conscious time out of my twenty-four-hour day in the bathroom than in any other room in the house. For most people it must be the same—except, of course, for those who spend their whole day at home. If I were one of those, I'd probably spend all of my day in the kitchen. How efficiently bathrooms and kitchens work, as well as how they look, is therefore very important to me.

The bathroom is the room in which I want to relax. I want to read in the bath, make lists, plan and think. This is where I want to see and decide what to wear, do the exercises I never do and have the well-lit table at which to do my face. Given two rooms to make into a bedroom and bathroom, one larger than the other, I'd take the small one to sleep in, the larger for a bathroom. But this is personal and probably eccentric.

Ideally, I like to have bathroom and dressing room combined. This, of course, is only possible if starting from scratch, or if converting a room into a bathroom, or if the existing bathroom already has closets or is large enough to squeeze closets into. With bathrooms, as with kitchens, one might as well be dictated by what is already there, and try and suit that to one's needs. If there is an existing bathroom and it is tiny, make that as livable as possible.

I had the luck of being able to convert a bedroom already full of closets into a bathroom for myself. Less lucky was that I had to sacrifice the bedroom to make the bathroom, but as the existing bathroom needed replumbing anyway, I had the excuse to change it.

Above the apartment that turned into my brown living room (photograph 5) there was another, identical two-room apartment. I made that into my pink gingham bedroom (photograph 33), bathroom/dressing room (photograph 34) and a laundry room. A greater effort toward decoration had been made by the previous owners of the top apartment than by the owners of the one below. In fact, it was decorated with a vengeance. I couldn't believe my eyes when I first saw it. The bedroom had very nice floor-to-ceiling cupboards, but they were trimmed to distraction with plastic moldings, all painted gold. The room was a fitted bedroom—a corridor of closets except for one dent, where there was space for a bed. Although the bed was gone, even there something ornate remained: a curvaceous headboard awash with more plastic moldings picked out in gold. Left and right of it were two curved bedside tables with half-round shelves, the plastic shell motif within the shelf picked out in yet more gold. What wasn't gold in the room was painted antique white.

I am constantly going on about making things look old and gilding with Liquid Leaf. Criticizing the antique white and the gilding of the bedroom is not necessarily a contradiction. For a piece of furniture or a wall to look old, it has to be worked on until it does look old. Giving it a coat of some form of plastic paint called "antique white" and one coat of harsh gold paint doesn't do the trick. Paint needs to be rubbed in, wiped off, shaded, smeared and generally tortured into aging. Not just applied.

If there is anything I really dislike, it is the fitted bedroom. It is extremely expensive. One pays not only for the closets and cupboards, but for the design—and in this room, for all those hideous plastic moldings. If bought ready-made, it still has to be adapted to whatever room it is going into, at still more horrendous cost. As all the wall space is taken up by doors, it is virtually impossible to add a bit of furniture to make the room individual. Here, the result was a room screaming for pink satin lampshades on top of lamps held by badly gilded cherubs. (A) In effect, an ideal set for a not-very-high-class brothel.

A

This well-frosted addition to the house, of course, increased its price. In vain I begged the owners to remove it and charge less. As it also wasn't very well made, dismantling and rearranging it would have been dificult, if not impossible. I had to keep it and make the best of it.

I tried to dislodge the plastic moldings. Hopeless. The glue was stronger than the wood the moldings were attached to. I ripped out the headboard. Eventually it came in useful. Its curlicues covered, it now looks comparatively austere in the yellow gingham bedroom (photograph 31). I bought a bathtub and placed it where the bed had been (photograph 34). The bathtub is modern and made out of fiberglass. Ten years ago they were not as horrifically expensive as they are now. If I were doing the room now, I would settle for an old cast-iron one and paint the outside of it (see Chapter 39, figure E).

The outside of the fiberglass tub is laminated in pink gingham. There is a pink stripe laminated around the edges of the white inside the tub—the stripe the same color pink as the border I used to hide the staples and trim the gray denim curtains in the pink gingham bedroom (photograph 36).

I found some old brass taps and a very nice water spout. But how to attach them? The bathtub was shown in the shop with an unaffordable network of gold taps, shower fittings and pipes, soap dishes and towel racks. At the time I was working with a good plumber. Together we built a wooden box around plain copper pipes. The box looks like a table. The taps are on the top, the spout on the side (photograph 34). I had a piece of glass cut for the top of the table with holes for the taps to fit through. A few bottles and jars with gold-colored tops confuse the eye, and the taps are hard to find among them. I have been accused of wanting to secrete away all of the more basic bits of plumbing. Perhaps this is true, but I don't think it's a result of some deep complex. I find most bathroom fittings ugly and better hidden. This bath ended up looking more like a sleigh or some strange chaise longue. That it should mysteriously fill with water seems appropriate.

Behind the bathtub I put up two shelves, and above the shelves a large mirror cut to the shape of the arch where the bed formerly was. The shelves connect with the rounded shelves of the bedside tables (right-hand side of photograph 34), and I use them for books. (B, *see next page*) This way I can reach a book while sitting in the bath.

I find nothing nicer than reading in the bath, though it doesn't do the books much good. David Hicks is a great master at designing bathrooms. He puts bookcases, desks and commodious bath-side tables into his bathrooms. He makes them rooms to live in, instead of so obviously functional.

I didn't quite have the space to get a desk into my bathroom, but could, for once, have a huge dressing table (against the window in photograph 34). It is made out of a plain door—the door that was scrapped from the downstairs living room (page 14). All its holes are filled with wood putty, and it, too, has a glass top. It is supported by two simple and shallow cupboards.

B

They are only deep enough to store single rows of jars and bottles. This is because behind the cupboards and across the kneehole is a long radiator, and I had to leave enough room for the air to circulate around it. The top of the dressing table also stops short of the wall so that the warm air can rise from behind it. There are two small drawers above the kneehole.

To add—albeit grudgingly—to the room's Louis XV style (and fake Louis XV style at that), I added more plastic twirls to the dressing table drawers and cupboard doors. I joined the twirls with long strips of molding. (See figure B.)

From the wall opposite the bath I took out two cupboard doors and one wooden separation to build a seat (left side of photograph 34). The back and side of it are lined in mirror like the wall behind the tub. More books are in the shelf above it. Below the seat is space for large books and albums of clippings on decoration. The two doors that I scrapped I cut down and reused to form the cupboards left and right of the window, to make the window appear more central.

Finally, I painted the bathroom. I whitewashed it. I used an ordinary water-soluble household paint, as chalky white as possible. Whereas before there was heavy-handed emphasis on moldings, now the moldings are simply part of the frosting. The bathroom looks remarkably like a wedding cake. I used pink gingham to cover the ceiling of the bathroom/dressing room (page 23), to make the blind (pages 188–90), to cover the cushion on the dressing table chair (page 85) and to cover the seat opposite the bath (pages 217–18).

Adjoining what used to be the bedroom but is now the dressing room plus bathtub was the original bathroom. The only entrance into it, however, was from the stair landing. I now use one of the closet doors to enter it from the dressing room (the door to the right of the dressing table, photograph 34 and figure B). We removed the back of that particular closet and broke through into the bathroom. What was a closet is now a small passageway. The space to the left of it—on the side of the dressing table and enclosed by a scrapped door—I use to hang clothes. (See figure B.) The new opening is narrow, the same width as the cupboard door, and just fits in between the lavatory and the basin of the original bathroom.

Had the original bathroom been in perfect shape, I would have just broken a door through and concentrated on doing it up superficially, despite its size. But the bathtub was not only abysmally small and badly stained, it had to be moved anyway —the pipes below it were leaking. So I grabbed the chance to scrap it. The basin and lavatory, however, I kept.

We built a dividing wall ($2'' \times 2''$s, covered with plaster-board) to separate the lavatory and basin part of the room from the bathtub part. The window was between the lavatory and the tub. Now the dividing wall bisected it. In order to be able to open it from both sides, we made the dividing wall only up to the window ledge. I made a curtain that forms a corner. One part covers half of the window, the other part the opening to the next room. With the curtains closed, I have privacy from the outside and also from the next room. (c)

When the bathtub behind the dividing wall was removed, it was replaced by a washing machine and drier. This is the laundry room. There is only enough space between the wall and the machines to open them. By building another opening in the dividing wall (to balance the one next to the window, only slightly larger), I can reach the sink in the lavatory from the laundry room. I can throw things that need to be hand-washed straight into it. This way I saved having to have another sink in the laundry room. Another curtain closes off the opening when I am not using it.

Above the washer and drier, I keep the linen. I keep it in wire baskets on runners, and to protect it (and hide the baskets), I have hung a curtain across. The ironing board is attached to the wall next to the washing machine. (D) It is a bit constricting ironing in the space available (I have to stand in the open doorway on the stair landing), but it has the advantage that I can reach through into the next room for the water with which to sprinkle the ironing.

The lavatory cubicle is tented, curtained and covered in a pink-red-and-green-flowered print on a white background. The laundry room curtain is in the same material. It blends in color but is decidedly different from the gingham of the bedroom.

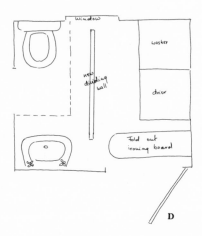

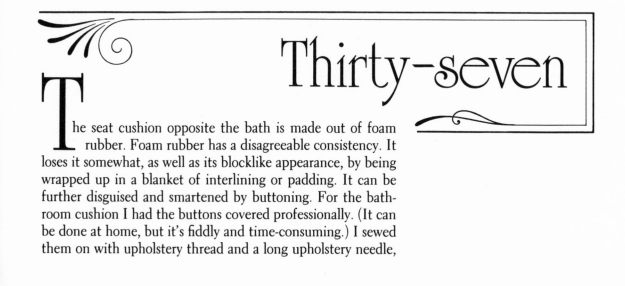

Thirty-seven

The seat cushion opposite the bath is made out of foam rubber. Foam rubber has a disagreeable consistency. It loses it somewhat, as well as its blocklike appearance, by being wrapped up in a blanket of interlining or padding. It can be further disguised and smartened by buttoning. For the bathroom cushion I had the buttons covered professionally. (It can be done at home, but it's fiddly and time-consuming.) I sewed them on with upholstery thread and a long upholstery needle, sewing right through the cushion. On the reverse side of the cushion, I caught the thread with the help of some woolen tufts. I could have used more buttons on the other side, but I wanted to try tufting a cushion.

Tufting is very like buttoning except that the thread that runs through the cushion is held by some strands of wool instead of buttons. To do this, I wind some wool around a small piece of paper. I pull the paper out and catch the wool to the cushion with the same thread that holds the button on the other side. (A) Then I cut the wool as for a tassel (pages 220–21) to make it into a tuft. Hence tufting. Things can also be tufted on both sides, eliminating buttons completely.

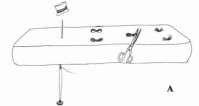

A

Modern fringes that are easy to find shine. It's all right for silk to shine, but silk looks different. It is also astronomically expensive and can usually be acquired only through decorators. As I don't use silk on anything I do—certainly not new silk—silk fringe would be useless to me anyway. I like dull woolen or cotton fringes and braid, which are more difficult to find than the shiny, showy nylon ones. So for the most part I make my own, or doctor up the ones I have or the ones I buy (which, when I find them, tend to be sparse). To make them or enrich them, I use wool yarn, cotton cord or ordinary string.

Years ago I used to buy my woolen fringes and braids from a wonderful firm in downtown New York. They would often feed as many as six different colors of wool into one fringe or braid. A braid of theirs frames the crewelwork alcove and the stair arch in the blue denim dining room in photographs 16 and 17, and a matching woolen rope frames the curved windows.

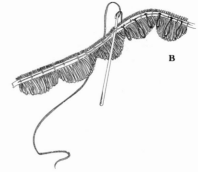

B

The pink gingham bed (photograph 33) has braid that started out from the same establishment. I had it made twenty years ago to trim the curtains in my daughter's room in New York. When we moved to England, I naturally dragged every single possession along. Some proved more useful than others. I used the braid from my daughter's curtains to trim my bed curtains, but first I livened up the baby-room pink by adding some red wool to the white and the two shades of pale pink that made up the original braid. To do this I bought a skein of red wool and a crochet hook. Then I crocheted extra red loops into the pink-and-white braid. (B)

I don't know any fancy crochet stitches. I go in, make a loop and come out again. This artistic maneuver is sufficient to add color and more substance to an existing fringe or braid, and no one looks closely enough to spot the knots and uneven loops.

When she was small, my daughter's favorite toy was a piece of string. Alas, she was more interested in boating knots than in macramé. Finally I found her a toy that combined her passion for string with my longing to make her knots useful. It's called a French knitting doll and comes in the form of a little wooden person with four metal nails in its head. Different colored wools get looped around the nails, pulled up and over each nail with a stick and a multicolored woolen cord mysteriously appears at the other end of the doll. (c)

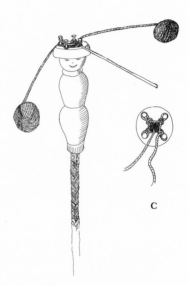

c

This makes the nicest homemade cord I know, but neither my daughter nor I have ever been strong at completing long projects. I've surrounded cushions and hidden staples around upholstered furniture with cord made in this way, but for greater quantity, I have devised my own way of making woolen cord. I buy the wool yarn in any thickness, concentrating more on the right colors than on the right grade of wool. But for a good-sized cord I need about ten strands of wool in an average thickness (that of a strand of spaghetti). Each strand can be a different color, or they can all be the same; there can be two of one, eight of another—any variation is possible. Even if I need a longer length of cord, I don't use strands that are longer than about 12' (which makes about a 10' cord). I don't dare. Longer pieces get knotted up.

I first tie the ten ends together and loop them over some solid object (I use one of the taps on the bathtub in photograph 34). Then I stretch the wool to the other end of the room (in my case, to the other end of the next room through the open arch—see photograph). Holding the wool very taut, I twist it, always in the same direction. (D) While still keeping the cord

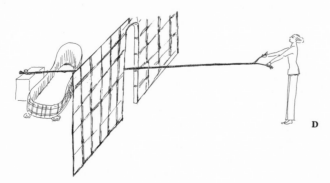

D

taut—otherwise it will untwist or start curling up—I wind thread around the end I'm holding. Then I wind another bit of thread around the end where the wools are looped on the taps. Only then do I cut the wool free of the taps.

I used a cord made in this way for the czar's carriage (photograph 1) and to trim the S-shaped sofa and the banquettes in the California living room (photograph 6).

Wool tassels for curtain tiebacks or to dangle from an end of a bolster (photographs 1, 18 and 54) can be made quickly and easily at home. To make them look right, however, takes quite a lot of wool. They mustn't look skimpy. If they are in a solid color, I find they tend to look too much like just a skein of knitting wool tied together, but in a mixture of different colored wools to match a patterned material, they can be quite successful.

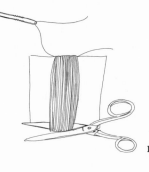

E

To make a tassel, I take a piece of cardboard the length I want my tassel to be and wind wool around it. (E) If I have four colors in it, I wind them one on top of the other or side by side, depending on what effect I want. Then, using a needle with an eye that is large enough to take the wool (or a hairpin if I can't find a needle), I pull a strand of any of the four wools— or all four of them—under the wool at the top of the cardboard and tie a knot. I slip a pair of scissors in at the bottom of the cardboard, cut the strands and remove the cardboard. Now the tassel has to be made to look like one by tying the two bushy bits together. I do this by winding one color—or all four— around the top third of the strands. (F) To use as a tieback, the tassel can be tied or crocheted to a cord in the same colors.

F

People more expert with the crochet hook than I am can crochet a form of snood for the top of the tassel and make it look more as if it was a handmade antique one. In fact, now that I think about it, anyone can do it. A little circle in a chain stitch for the top, loops for the next row and so on until the wound-around wool tie is reached—where another circle in chain stitch (with the loops above it crocheted into it) finishes off the snood. (G) For the best effect, the snood should be in a contrasting color to the wool underneath it.

Antique tassels often had a few knobs—made out of wood and covered—above the actual tassel. I have used various modern oddments to reproduce them, but the most useful were the things I helped myself to from my daughter's toy cupboard:

large wooden beads, through and around which I wound wools; wooden rings, covered in wool or velvet ribbon. Used thread spools can be useful (see figure G) as can tubes that once housed pills or sweets. Ping-pong balls enclosed in tassel tops can work, but winding wool around them can be tricky; it is better to tie the top of the tassel first, put the ball in, and then tie the two parts of the tassle together under the ball.

G

The nicest fringe I made, I made out of string. Not the very untidy kind with pieces sticking out of it, but ordinary, thinnish, supple packing string the thickness of uncooked spaghetti. With a medium-sized crochet hook I crocheted a double row of stitches to form a band. Onto the band I crocheted another row—little loops. I took eight chain stitches for each loop and crocheted it into every fourth stitch of the band. I made about 2′ lengths of this at a time. Then I took a ruler and wound string around it, as much as I could get on it. I tied a knot at the start and at the end so that it would not unravel. The ruler—my ruler at least (an ordinary plastic one)—has a slight shape to it. This leaves space to get the crochet hook under the string. Using a new length of string I crocheted every six or eight strands of string together. In order not to have to cut the string each time, I crocheted a second row of stitches into the chain stitch of each loop. Halfway along each loop I picked up the six or eight strands on the ruler and crocheted them to the loops on the band. (H)

When I had done this to all the strands on the ruler (or to as many strands as fitted onto the 2′ length), I slipped my scissors in at the base of the ruler and cut the strands. What

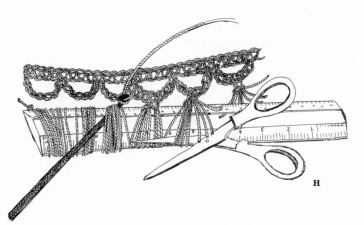

H

was left, when I cut it, looked like a disorganized mop. I had to tie in a "waist" on each tassel—as I did on the single one (see figure F)—to give it shape. The string was slightly too thick to use for this, so I had to "waist" the tassels with some string-colored cotton thread.

The easiest and quickest way, however, to a grand fringe is to buy two or three inexpensive ones and put one on top of the other (see Chapter 4, figure Q), perhaps even adding a different border or ribbon as a top binding. (As with materials, where I have more success in finding what I want in the dress-material section than in the upholstery section, I find better fringes and borders in the clothes-trimming department than in the curtain-trimming one.)

Another nice, grand-looking and inexpensive bit of trim is the rosette. It can be used on curtain tiebacks, bed hangings (Chapter 29, figure B), above a single picture or above a line of pictures. Any material can be used to make a rosette (I like stripes and borders best), but unless it is very thick, the material must be stiffened. I buy either a piece of buckram, which I cut into strips, or the stiffening that is put into belting (obtainable from a dress-trimmings shop). I glue the material onto these. I use one piece of material to cover both sides of stiffening, the seam overlapping on the back side.

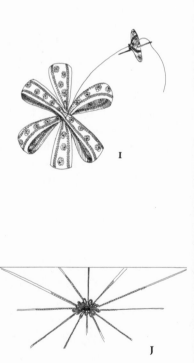

I

The rosette can have any number of loops, but six is usual. I mostly make three double ones and sew them on top of one another. To hide the middle stitches and to make the rosette look more like a flower, it has to have a middle. For this I take a large button and cover it with a circle of the same material. (The diameter of the circle of material must be double the diameter of the button.) I gather the circle, slip the button inside it, pull it tight and take a couple of stitches through the holes of the button. Then I sew the button into the center of the loops. (I)

Large rosettes can also be used to finish off a center of a tented ceiling. For the ceiling of the pink gingham bedroom, I made a rosette that has at least a dozen different-sized loops. (J) In the center of the stiff ribbons (buckram strips covered in the same material as the walls and ceiling), I put a large "button" to hide the staples. As I was unable to find a button the size I needed, I made one by covering the lid of a jam jar with material and gluing that on.

J

Thirty-eight

The barn bathroom (photograph 44) is above the barn kitchen (photographs 26 and 27). When the conversion of the barn began, all that was there were the stone walls and the old beams. There was only a partial roof, and no floor existed between what became the kitchen and the bathroom. (See Chapter 42 for details.) Now there is an upstairs balcony. The bathroom is separated from it—and therefore from the rest of the room—only by curtains. When it's not being used, the curtains are drawn back and the bathroom is in full view. So I wanted it to look as unbathroomy as possible.

A

Had there been more headroom in the kitchen below, I would have had a sunken tub. But I couldn't afford to give up the space. The bottom of the tub would have hung down into the kitchen. I decided to build steps up to the bathtub to make the tub appear sunken and so less visible. Unfortunately, if I had had the steps, there wouldn't have been space enough for an enclosed lavatory between the bath and the fireplace. I had to settle for just one curved step (see photograph 44). The mirrored doors left and right of it are angled. The lavatory cubicle (behind the left mirrored door) is lined in the same brown-and-cream batik as the rest of the bathroom. The lavatory itself is boxed in. (A) The boxing, as well as the seat and lid, I stippled imitation mahogany. (See Chapter 16 for how this is done.)

The mirrored door on the right side of the bathtub hides the hot-water tank and an ample linen closet. The tank is at the back of the closet, and in front of it wooden slats make up the shelves for the linen. The unplastered walls can make things feel cold and damp when the house hasn't been heated for a while, but this way the linen is always dry and warm.

The cold-water tank is above the bath, boxed in. The boxing is made to look like part of the ceiling by having additional upright beams attached to the front of it. It is covered in the same brown-and-cream batik. Eyeball spotlights are sunk into the bottom of the boxing. They are on a dimmer so that the strength of the light above the bath can be adjusted.

Behind the bathtub and under the window there is a wide, low shelf. It holds the taps, a hand shower, plants, soaps and bath oils. I find it increasingly difficult to remember to water all the plants that I like to have around. So I keep whatever plants I have near my bathtub. They look good there, and when I do water them, it is a wave of a jug from bath to plants. If I forget, the steam from the bath keeps the plants going until the time that I remember to water them. The barn inhabitants can do the same—by keeping plants on the ledge by the bath.

There are several things about the workings of a bathtub that I've always found extremely irritating. If the spout and the taps are at the foot of the bath, it means heaving oneself partially out of the water to add more water. If they are on the side and more hot water is wanted, the hot water scorches the body. If a hand shower is attached to any of this and hasn't got its own tap, I invariably get the water in my face: I can never remember to switch back to the spout after using the shower. But if the spout and taps are separate, the spout can be at the foot of the bath, where the toes can pull away to avoid scorching, and the taps can be close at hand to adjust the flow and temperature. I was able to get this arrangement in the barn bathtub. (B)

I was also able to sink a telephone-type hand shower into the wooden shelf next to the tub. When it is not in use, only the head of the shower is visible. It rests on a brass collar, which was originally part of an old doorknob. The hose is hidden under the shelf and pulls out for use. The control for the shower is separate and next to the taps.

B

Personally, I don't like showers. The material-covered bath-rooms that I like aren't really suitable for shower addicts. I know this is a selfish attitude and I have been trying to find ways to compromise. How should I decorate a bathroom that is also a much-used shower and does not have the space for a separate shower cubicle?

I find tiles particularly odious. White tiles are cold and remind me of all-too-clinical hygiene. And colored tiles, espe-cially with matching bath and basin, I find even more awful *and* expensive. Victorian patterned tiles or delft tiles can be lovely, but they are very expensive indeed and hard to come by. If plain tiles are there—as in the bathroom of the New York studio (Chapter 39, figure E)—I leave them and paint them (pages 104–5). There the shower can be, and is, used con-stantly. In the small orange bathroom (photograph 45), the shower is also used constantly and the water sprayed about haphazardly. But since the elephant batik is under a huge piece of plexiglass and the bath surrounded by black glass, not much of the orange material is at risk. (An advantage of using batik in the bathroom is that, being hand-printed, it looks as if it had been sprayed with water from misguided showers for years, even when brand new. This, in fact, is one of the reasons why it's so attractive. It also makes real water stains less visible.)

In the barn bathroom, the shelf behind the tub is the recipi-ent of most of the water sprayed in error from the hand shower. I built it out of marine ply. (Marine ply is plywood made with watertight glues.) I stippled it to look like mahogany (see Chap-ter 16 for how) and sealed the paint with three coats of polyure-thane. We used marine ply for the flooring and the rise of the curved step as well, wetting the wood for the rise and then bending it a little at a time until it bent into the curve we were after. At the foot and at the head of the bath, I stole 6″ from the lavatory space and 6″ from the linen closet to make in-dented bookshelves (photograph 44 and figure B). The shelves are hardwood, also stippled mahogany.

I like a large bathtub. (This wish can, of course, only be gratified if starting from scratch as I did here, not having to adapt to an existing bath and being able to spend the extra that a longer tub costs.) A bathtub, I can't help feeling, should be white unless it can be marble, onyx or plexiglass, but my aspirations don't quite reach to those heights. I refuse, however, to have "primrose" or "avocado," and my dislike of them is not only because of the names.

The best-looking basin for its cost is a white, under-the-counter, oval one (photograph 44 and seen in the mirror of photograph 45). The counter it gets set under must be of hardwood to withstand the water spills. Plexiglass, glass or a thin sheet of marine ply can be used on top of a softwood counter, but then the edge must be properly sealed. Under the basin I usually make a cupboard, either covered in the same material as the room, as I did in the barn bathroom, or painted or grained to look like a wood that it isn't. The cupboard is useful for storing toiletries and cleaning equipment.

If at all possible, I try to find old brass kitchen sink faucets to use on washbasins. If I fail to find old ones, I buy modern chrome sink faucets. A faucet designed for a kitchen sink has a much longer spout than one designed for a bathroom. This enables a person to get his or her head under the spout for hair washing—something that I find very useful.

As the barn was—and remained—only a shell (no attic, inside walls or plaster), it was easy to build a chimney so as to have a log fire in the bathroom (photograph 44). There are few luxuries that are as satisfying as having a fire going while taking a bath, especially in a cold country house. The fireplace surround is brass. I found it, black and anonymous, in my favorite junkyard. I have no idea what it was originally meant for. I used a piece of stone from the local quarry for the mantel shelf above it, and the cement chimney-breast I covered with the same cream-and-brown batik as the rest of the room.

I fixed a bamboo curtain pole on the far side of the beam that spans the bathroom. The ringed curtains (looped back in photograph 44) draw across the room for privacy. The bathroom window has batik-covered shutters attached with piano hinges. (See page 28 for how I do this.) The carpet is a plain brown "wall-to-wall." It covers the floor of the bathroom and the curved step leading up to the tub.

The green country bathroom (photograph 46) was originally a bedroom. It had already been converted to a bathroom when I came to it and had a pale-gray bath, sink and lavatory. As much as I dislike colored bathroom suites, gray is better than "aqua" or "shell pink." The walls were painted gray as well.

The whole battleship-gray effect had only recently been comp-leted. To have changed it simply for aesthetic reasons would have been criminal. There was a lot to be grateful for about the conversion: that the size of the perfectly proportioned room in the Queen Anne house hadn't been reduced; that all the won-derful old features (cornice, shutters, window seats) had re-mained, despite the room being relegated to a bathroom; that the original fireplace hadn't been scrapped.

Gray may not be an inspiring tone to live with, but it is an excellent background color to paint on. Once again, out came the chinoiserie designs (pages 61–62). I used green and white paint only, painting a few twirls and swirls, a bit of trellis and a flowering tree.

The curtains are short and reach only as far as the window seat—something I don't much like. But I didn't have sufficient material to make them reach the ground. The wooden valances were already there—and rather nice valances—so I wanted to keep them, and with blinds they wouldn't have looked right. I had planned to make cushions for the window seats, to cover them in white toweling and border them with the same trel-lised border that is on the curtains. That would have squared off the amputated look of the curtains. (c) But plants estab-lished themselves so happily on the window seats that the cushions never got made.

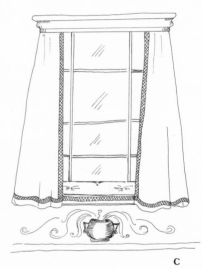

c

The curtain material is printed with a Pillement design—a type of design named after the eighteenth-century painter and designer well known for chinoiserie decorations. The green of the material was, unfortunately, a rather drab green, and I'd used quite a lot of strong chrome green in painting up the walls. The curtains looked comparatively dull. I chose a particular bush in the design of the material, and whenever it appeared, I painted over it in chrome-green artist's oil paint diluted with turpentine. It livened up the curtains speedily.

Over and under the washbasin mirror there are two flower containers (or at least that is what the junkyard owner told me they were when I bought them), a small one and a larger one. The larger one I put over a striplight above the mirror; the smaller one, under the mirror, holds the soap. Both are painted green and white, as is the mirror frame. Above the inverted larger container I couldn't resist painting a little point to make it look like the top of a pagoda.

Covering the lavatory is a white chair—a commode, or what is called a *chaise percée.* Before the days of adequate plumbing it used to hold a china bucket. Any modern lavatory that I am able to cover with a *chaise percée,* I do. A lavatory looks better hidden and a *chaise percée* is a piece of furniture—and often a very well made piece of furniture—that tends to be cheap at the price. (Not many people want them.) A few minor carpentry adjustments to the back of the chair and it can be placed on top of a modern lavatory bowl (See Chapter 36, figure c). After painting the one in the green bathroom white, I picked out lines on it in green.

A *chaise percée* can be turned into a normal chair if it has a seat cushion to hide the lid. (The lid can be nailed down, but it's not strictly necessary.) What gives away that it is a commode is the wooden surround that hides the plumbing. I once bought two well-shaped *chaises percées* very inexpensively. I made white linen slipcovers and chair cushions for them, piped and beribboned in blue. (See pages 46–47 for how this is done.) (D) They made excellent bedroom armchairs.

If at all, a chandelier should be enormous and candle-lit and should go into a ballroom. In any other room in the house, the rather small electrified chandelier that I hung in the green bathroom would have looked pretentious and not all that pretty. But underplayed by being in a bathroom, it looks fine.

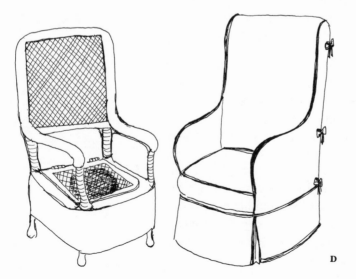

D

Thirty-nine

I was once asked to convert a room into a bathroom that was very much like the room that turned into the pink gingham bathroom (photograph 33)—rows of existing closets. But what was wanted was more like the barn bathroom (photograph 44). I made a plan to have the bathtub crossways, under the window —the same as in the barn. The lavatory I wanted to shut away in one of the closets. I was, alas, working with a plumber who was unable to devise a way of plumbing the lavatory anywhere but against an outside wall.

I have learned, through bitter experience, that there are certain things not worth fighting for. So if a plumber tells me something cannot be done, and I have just finished doing it successfully elsewhere, I won't contradict him. Contradicting him will not only cause irritation; if he hasn't done similar work elsewhere, doing it will be an experiment—and to be at the mercy of a furious experimenter is just not worth it. I either try to find a new plumber, which is time-consuming and frustrating, or I try to adapt my ideas to what he can do. (I have noticed a curious difference between the character of plumbers and carpenters. Carpenters are gentle, charming and inventive. Plumbers, the contrary. Perhaps it comes from the nature of the work. Or perhaps only the holy choose carpentry.)

Not having the space on the outside wall for both lavatory and bathtub, as I wanted, I had to build the tub jutting out into the room. I placed the lavatory to one side, with an angled mirror to partially screen it. As in the barn bathroom, the second angled mirror is a door and hides the hot-water tank. Above the water tank some slatted boards form shelves for linen. (A, *see next page*)

When the bath was boxed in and had steps each side of it, the remaining straight lines of cupboards looked misproportioned and dull. So we cut off part of the room. To do this, Mr. Lewis, the carpenter, enlarged two of the existing closets on the opposite side of the room and made them into angled ones. (B) They have mirrored doors that echo the angled mirrors opposite. One door hides a dressing table, the other a closet. The

A

two closets next in line we removed completely. The opening between the two angled closets and the opening into the next room are the same size. The space between the two openings forms a small "corridor." (B) By lowering the ceiling of the corridor, we made it visually separate from the two neighboring rooms and gained additional storage space, which can be reached through hatches in the lowered ceiling.

There is no door between the bathroom and corridor (nor between corridor and bedroom). The bathroom can be closed off from the bedroom by opening wide the two angled, mirrored doors: They meet and form double doors in the corridor. The rest of the corridor is lined with bookshelves and serves as a miniscule office between the bedroom and bathroom. On one

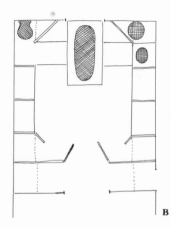

B

side there is work space with a typewriter; on the other side, space for files.

Mr. Lewis surrounded all the bathroom mirrors, mirrored doors and the little office bookshelves with picture framing (page 21). He also put up a cornice between the top and bottom cupboards (page 197). All these plus the office work space, the filing cabinets and even the radiators I painted to look like maple (Chapter 16).

The shelf surrounding the tub is made out of marine ply painted to look like mahogany. There is a narrow picture-frame molding around the edge, painted maple. Brown carpeting covers the steps and the sides of the bathtub. The picture-frame molding hides where the ply is nailed together and where the carpeting ends.

This time the material on the walls is a brown-and-black batik (the same color—but a different pattern—as the library in photograph 55). The swagged window shade is a light-brown (maple-colored) brushed denim. (See pages 188–91 for how to make shades.) Two small, framed openings above the angled mirrors left and right of the bath have blue-and-white pots in them. By chance the design on the pots is the same as the design on the batik: an Eastern flower. The color of the pots is echoed by blue-and-white towels. (The brown needed a contrast.) The pots look quite effective surrounded by the maple framing. The corridor/office is covered in the same batik, both walls and lowered ceiling. The adjoining bedroom is painted blue.

Some photographs of the brown-and-black batik-covered bathroom came out in a magazine. As a result, a debonair bachelor appeared on my doorstep carrying two batik bedspreads. I was branded as a batik stapler. But his batiks were quite different from the East Indian ones I knew and had been working with. These were Balinese, and in very strong colors; one a picture of a green elephant, the other a salmon-colored rhinoceros. My new client wanted them incorporated in an apartment he had just bought. The apartment consisted of one large room, a small bathroom and a kitchen (photographs 29, 45, 47, and 48).

I began with the bathroom (photograph 45). The elephant bedspread exactly fitted the wall behind the bath, but with most of the border removed. I saved the border, and when I covered the three other walls in an inexpensive orange Indian cotton, I used the border to frame the walls and hide the staples. The Indian cotton has exactly the same feel to it and the same color as the cotton of the batik. The border looks as if it belonged to it.

The bathroom had a very high ceiling and no window. A fan, ducted to an air shaft, gave ventilation. Mr. Lewis and I constructed a new, lower ceiling, once again in tent form, but this time the tent is out of mirror.

Mr. Lewis first built a skeleton ceiling out of 2″ × 1″. In the center of the 2″ × 1″ he left a square gap, above which he attached an extractor fan, ducted to the shaft. (c) A mirrored revolving ball now hangs in the center of the mirrored ceiling. We had to put up the machine that revolves the ball before we could put up the mirrors.

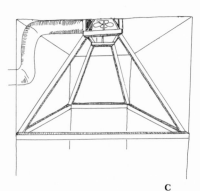

c

Mr. Lewis used the same principle to put up the mirrored ceiling as he used to construct the mirrors in the blue-and-white-tented dining room (photograph 14, description on pages 107–8). First, he nailed eight wedge-shaped pieces of plywood (with their points cut off to accommodate the hole for the fan and mirror ball) to the skeleton ceiling. We then ordered eight wedge-shaped pieces of mirror cut to the size of the plywood, less 1/2″ all around. These we glued to the plywood with a glue made specially for mirrors and tiles. To hold the mirrors firmly in place, Mr. Lewis attached a quadrant molding into the four corner joins, and half-round moldings across the four other mirror joins as well as on top and at the base of the mirrors.

When the apartment was bought, the bathtub was surrounded by rather nice black glass, which we kept. We kept all the old plumbing as well, except for the basin, which was cracked. Mr. Lewis built a new cabinet out of softwood, into which we fitted an undercounter oval basin. The counter around the basin we covered with a piece of black plexiglass, cut to size, to match the black glass around the bathtub. The rest of the cabinet we painted black and lacquered (page 71). The moldings that grip the mirrors in the ceiling are also painted and lacquered black.

Near the air shaft Mr. Lewis found some wasted space behind the partition wall, just big enough for us to fit two mirror-doored medicine cabinets into so that they are flush with the wall. (The bathroom is tiny. It cried out for as much mirror to create visual space, and as much actual space in which to store things, as possible.) One of the cabinets we already had was smaller than the other. In order to use both and make them look balanced without spending on a new, larger mirror door for the smaller cabinet, we made a shelf under the smaller cabinet and lined it with mirror tiles. (D) (See page 90 for more on mirror tiles.)

D

The debonair bachelor wanted atmosphere in his apartment. He wanted it in the living room/bedroom, in the kitchen, in the hall and in the bathroom as well. The row of light bulbs above the basin mirror are on a dimmer. So is the small red spotlight that is directed at the revolving mirrored ball. When *atmosphere* is called for in the bathroom, the lights can all be dimmed, the bright colors of the batik are reflected onto the turning mirror ball and soft lights creep along the orange walls.

The bathroom of the New York studio (main room shown in photograph 50) is about the same size as the green-elephant one. When I started on it, it had chipped and stained white

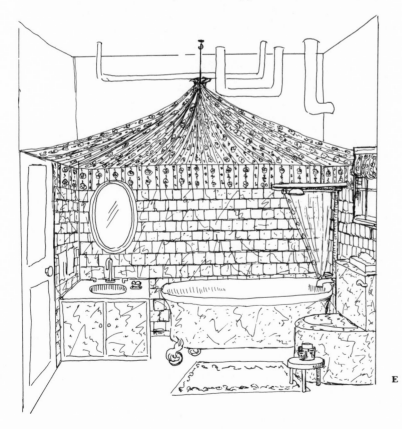

E

tiles on the lower part of the wall, plus a bright-green color above, reaching high up to and over some exposed pipes. It also had a marvelous old-fashioned bathtub on feet, for which the owners apologized, while I thanked.

The studio walls are covered in a large paisley pattern. I covered the bathroom walls in a matching, but smaller-patterned, stripe. (I also glued a strip of the same material to the ordinary plastic shower curtain.) I suspended the material from the ceiling on a string. (E) This way I by-passed the problem of the pipes and at the same time lowered the too-high ceiling. So as to be able to reach the pipes in an emergency, I hung the string onto a hook and did not seam the tenting material together. Should it be necessary to get at the pipes, one can reach in, unhook the string and loosen the material. Then one can crawl, ladder and all, into the tenting as if crawling into a skirt.

The tiles reach quite high on the bathroom wall and I stapled the bottom of the tenting to just above them. Then I *faux*-marbled all the tiles, the outside of the bathtub, the outside of the under-counter basin and all of the lavatory except the inside of the bowl. I did it with brown and rust oil paint to try and make it look like Siena marble. (See pages 104–5 for how this is done.)

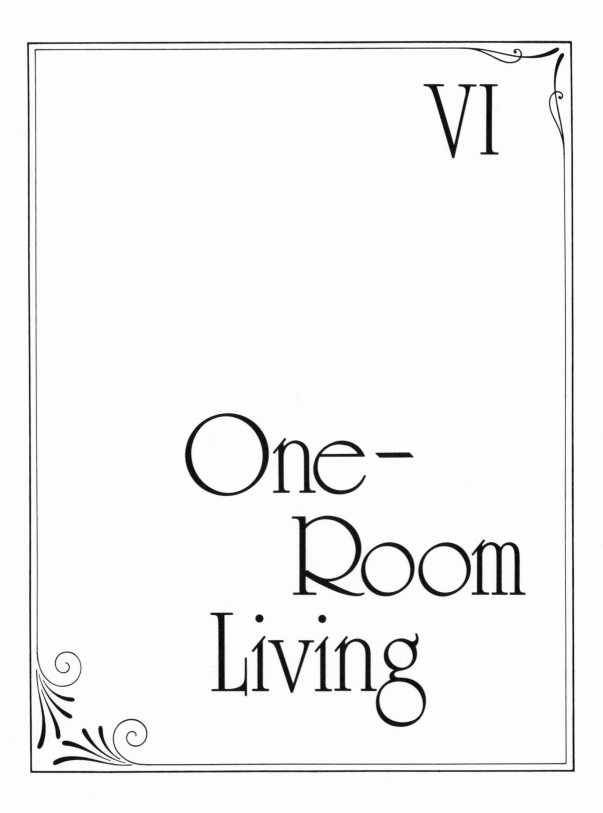

VI

One-
Room
Living

If I ever achieve expertise in one thing (instead of being a dabbler in many things), I would like to become an expert on one-room living. By this I don't mean simply the design of it, but how to live in it. How to have luxury, peace and order in a confined space. How to entertain within it and fit a comfortable home life into it. How not to feel in reduced circumstances just because we will, I believe, find ourselves more and more in a reduced space.

I don't see why someone just able to pay the rent for four walls should only have four walls, with perhaps a naked bulb hanging from the ceiling and a wobbly couch to sleep on. A few hours with a paintbrush can make it into something different—perhaps not spectacular, but different.

The most dramatic room I ever had I spent the least on. (A, *see next page*) Oddly enough, I would be considered less mad now for living in such a place than I was then. Now the criticism would be "too decoratory." Then it was just "mad." To me it looked splendid. In fact, what it was, was as grand as I could manage on what I could afford, which was practically nothing. I based the room on some Greek pottery I had seen in a museum. The style was, I suppose, "Attic." I painted the room terra cotta—a nonshiny brick color. Where there should have been, but wasn't, a cornice, I made one out of black poster paper. I made myself a suitable Greek-looking stencil (see Chapter 10 for stenciling), traced it onto strips of the black paper and cut it out with a utility knife. I glued it around the top and bottom of the room and around the doors and the window. It looked a bit flat and dead. The ceiling was white, so I picked out a white line around the black pattern. I did this in white ink with a drawing pen. Onto the floor (which was pretty grim) I laid a checkerboard of black-and-white plastic tiles. I sawed off part of the legs from the bed—a queen-sized one—to make it sofa height. (This has become my habit with most beds ever since.) I placed it in the center of the room and covered it with a thick-pile blanket. (Ideally I was after goatskin, but that I couldn't afford.) I finished off the blanket—

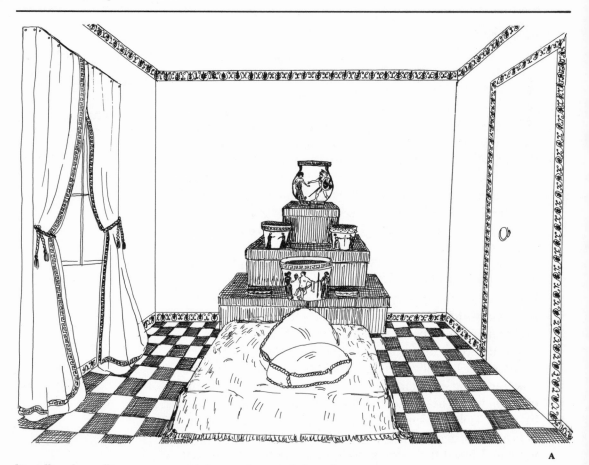

A

literally—by pulling out some of the wool around the edges to make a fringe.

I bought some dust sheets in a sale—the kind painters use to cover the floor when they are working and spilling—and painted their edges with a border, using black laundry markers. I used thumbtacks to fasten the dust-sheet curtains onto the window frame (the staple gun hadn't yet entered my life) and looped them back with a woolen cord (pages 219–20). I built pyramids out of boxes that I had first covered in black paper. In these I stored my belongings. On top of the boxes I placed terra-cotta flowerpots painted up with black figures and Greek motifs (see page 62). That was all there was. It was wonderful. Alas, the pleasure was short-lived. To keep putting things away in the boxes was a nuisance, and when the closet and bathroom overbulged, the rest lay on the floor. A kind aunt, shocked by the mess, gave me a chest of drawers to store the overflow. A friend gave me some chairs to substitute for the floor cushions. The glory of the room was over.

If I were doing a room like that now, the chair problem could be solved without great expense. The canvas folding chair, called a safari chair or a director's chair, can be bought reasonably. It blends in extremely well with most styles, especially if it is the kind with crossed legs. The wood can be painted black, the canvas painted with a pattern or covered with another fabric—glued or sewn to the original one—or the chair can be left as it is.

The debonair bachelor and owner of the tropical studio (photographs 45, 47 and 48) had, apart from his batiks, a collection of hand-carved wooden animals from Jamaica, a collection of nineteenth- and early twentieth-century watercolors—mostly from the West Indies—and a decided preference for bright colors. The bathroom (photograph 45) was certainly colorful, and if the living room/bedroom was to house the rhinoceros batik (see photograph 47), it, too, was well on its way. I decided to make it, and call it, a tropical studio.

The tropical studio is in an old house that had been converted into apartments. Judging by its size, the studio had been the main living room of a rather grand house. In the course of the conversion, the old staircase had been lost, and instead the studio is now approached via a nasty little enterprise through which it is practically impossible to move any but the smallest bits of furniture. What space was saved from the original stairs makes up the bathroom, a minuscule kitchen and a long, thin hall.

Eventually the owner was able to add to this by buying two other rooms and connecting them to the long orange passage —the blue batik bedroom (photographs 37 and 38), which was once probably the dining room; and the rather strangely shaped room, which must have also been part of the stairs, that became the orange room (photograph 54). But that came later. To start off with, I was dealing with a studio.

The room is large and light. It has a fireplace and three windows, the windows grouped together to form an alcove (photograph 48). The middle one is a French window and opens onto a balcony. (B)

I found an Indian cotton material with green, yellow and salmon stripes. The same colors appear in the rhinoceros batik.

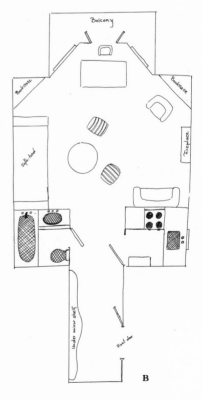

B

I used it to cover the walls. (See Chapter 2 for how this is done.) I decided to treat the batik as a picture and frame it. I used bamboo—cheap and suitable. Most Oriental shops import the thick bamboo canes, whereas the thinner varieties can be bought even in gardening supply shops. Mr. Lewis and I bought masses of it.

Included among our acquisitions were two really thick poles, which Mr. Lewis split with a sharp knife for the frame. The next smaller size we used whole to form the two pyramid bookcases (left and right of the windows, photographs 47 and 48). We used the same size bamboo, but split, to trim the large sofa bed and the edges of the bookshelves and to hide the staples below the cornice and in the corners of the room where the material had been stapled to the walls. A much thinner bamboo (almost a reed and therefore too thin to split) hides the staples around doors and windows, where the material meets the chair rail, and around the built-in furniture.

The window and door frames, the doors and the woodwork below the chair rail I painted a light bamboo color, somewhere between the color of bamboo and parchment. (See chapter 16 for how.) The windows have wooden slatted blinds, which I bought ready-made; I darkened their natural wood color only slightly.

To make the large sofa, which is also used as a bed, Mr. Lewis constructed a 12′ × 4′ platform out of timber. (He used the same system as for the czar's carriage, described on pages 11–12, but he didn't use joist hangers.) At each end he added an extra box, 1′ wide and 1′ higher than the platform. The boxes form the two sides of the sofa. They can serve as armrests or tables, and the one on the right holds a stereo and tape deck (see figure D). The tops are painted the same as the woodwork —a light bamboo color—and the inner sides are padded and covered with the same green, yellow and salmon Indian cotton as the walls and the rest of the sofa bed. I stapled the padding and the material to the top edge and the sides of the "tables," pulled padding and material down and stapled both to the platform. The top and side staples are hidden by bamboo, the bottom ones by the mattress, which I had made to measure. Stereo speakers are hidden behind removable bamboo-covered panels on the base of the sofa.

To screw the long bamboo (horizontally) and the short bamboo (vertically) to the front of the sofa-bed platform, Mr. Lewis had to drill holes through the already split bamboo halves with an electric drill. (Simply hitting nails through the bamboo would have split it further.) To edge the top of the armrest/tables and to hide the staples, he sliced right angles out of pieces of bamboo, mitered the pieces (page 140) and glued those on. (c) Pieces of bamboo cut in the same way edge the tops of the cupboards under the bookshelves.

To make the pyramid bookcases (photographs 47 and 48), Mr. Lewis first built the counter-high cupboards across the two corners of the room. Then he cut and made two boxes out of plywood to form the tops of the pyramids. They appear to be square, but have a hidden right angle at the back that makes them fit into the corners. We secured them just under the cornice. From the front two corners of each box we placed a bamboo pole to the front corners of each cupboard. The poles gave the angles and dimensions to which Mr. Lewis cut the plywood shelves. Although the shelves appear to be held by the bamboo, they are not: the bamboo would never be strong enough. The shelves are supported on steel brackets that are screwed to the wall, the legs of the brackets hidden by the striped material that covers the wall.

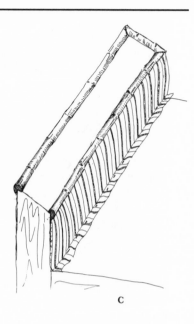

c

The shelves are painted the same as the rest of the woodwork —a light bamboo color—and edged in bamboo. The boxes on the top are covered in material, crossed and framed in bamboo. The cupboard doors are also material-covered. (See pages 120–22 for how to do this.) The left-hand one holds liquor bottles and glasses, and the right-hand one conceals the television set.

The cushions and bolsters on the long sofa bed are feather filled. (See pages 35–36 and 117–18 for how to make them.) Two of them hide bed pillows. The bedcover is more of the striped material that covers the walls, cupboards, cushions and bolsters: two lengths sewn together, lined and tucked in around the bedding. (See Chapter 30 for more on bedcovers.) A second, better-quilted bedcover (pages 123–24) was in the laundry when the photograph was taken.

The bed is longer than any sheets or blankets that can be bought. Made up, the bedclothes end two thirds of the way up the bed. To use the bed, one must peel the cover off and throw

D

all the cushions to the sheetless end. The mountain of them acts as a headboard and an anchor for the top sheet. (D)

The two padded ottomans standing across from the sofa bed are covered in a sarong from the Philippines. The iridescent purple color picks up the background color of the rhinoceros batik on the wall. As the sarong wasn't large enough, I patched the tops of the stools and the undersides of the cushions with some green Indian cotton. A small sofa (Chapter 27, figure c) next to the ottomans is slipcovered out of the same green cotton. (See Chapter 5 for how to make slipcovers.)

The chair in photograph 48 is a Victorian invalid's chair. Not only can it be pushed around on nice brass wheels, but it can be wound upright, be made completely flat and have or lose the footstool (which can be raised or lowered to any level). The arms open and close (fastened by beautiful heavy brass hooks) for easy entry and exit. I covered it in yet another colorful batik from the owner's seemingly inexhaustible supply: a tree-patterned one. The chair may look rather surprising covered in batik, but it blends well with the rest of the room. The batik was quite small. When it ran out, I supplemented it with more of the green Indian cotton for the sides and the back. (See pages 38–39 for how to reupholster like this.)

Between the two bookcases stands a modern desk from Korea. At $800 it was expensive, but relatively inexpensive for the effect it achieves. The room desperately needed some formal, dark and glowing piece of wood that would serve as the tree trunk to all the leafiness of the surrounding fabrics.

The round coffee table in front of the sofa bed (photograph 47) started out as a wooden kitchen table, or perhaps a garden table. It was standing in a junkyard when I found it and bought it—cheaply. I cut the legs down and stippled it bamboo color to match the rest of the room.

I find coffee tables—in fact any low tables—a bit of a problem. They are a twentieth-century invention and there are no examples from previous centuries to copy. (Except, of course, from the Chinese.) There are many good modern coffee tables, but they tend to be extremely expensive. The low table with a center pit for bottles and glasses that stands in the brown living room (see photographs 2, 3 and 5) I didn't make but bought in Italy. I have since made similar ones, which I turn either *faux bois* or *faux* marble, but I skip the center well. I start out with two skeleton tables, the same shape but one smaller than the other, made out of 2″ × 1″. (E) I cover the skeletons in pieces of plywood, cut to size in my local lumberyard. Then I glue the larger box on top of the smaller box. If I am painting the table, I smooth wood putty over all the nail holes before I prime the wood and paint it. This is unnecessary if I am covering the table in mirror tiles (pages 90–91) or material.

E

The long, narrow hall leading up to the studio is also covered in an Indian cotton: an orange-gray-and-white stripe (photograph 29). The chair and picture rails, the door and the door surrounds I painted the color of bamboo, and I covered the staples that hold the material with more of the very thin bamboo I had used in the room itself.

To give the hall an illusion of space, we built a large mirror. For the sake of economy we used the same principle as for the mirror in the blue-and-white tented dining room (pages 107–8, photograph 14), but here we used split bamboo instead of molding. To hold those things that need to be noticed immediately, like keys, mail and messages, we built a long, narrow and curved shelf under the mirror opposite the front door (see figure B|). Mr. Lewis built it out of plywood and edged it in bamboo. To bend the length of bamboo, we spent a lot of time softening it over a steaming kettle.

Further up the hall, on the wall opposite the mirror, two charming West Indian watercolors—part of the client's collection—frame the entrance into the jungle of a kitchen (photograph 29).

Forty-one

The studio apartment in New York (photographs 49 and 50) I am proud of for one reason: the timing of it. I found it, did it up (on a *very* limited budget) and moved in the tenant all within two weeks. The apartment consists of a small entrance, a bathroom (Chapter 39, figure E), a closet and the large room in the photographs. There was no kitchen. Into the tiny hall we managed to squeeze a complete kitchen unit. For $1,300 I got an oven, a sink, four burners, a smell extractor, an icebox and a small cupboard for the pots. Quite enough of a kitchen for a hard-working bachelor's breakfast and occasional dinner.

The most important thing in one-room living is storage space, so that the unsightly mess that makes up daily life can get shut away when a room has to turn from bedroom to living room in a hurry. Downtown, I found an enormous armoire of bird's-eye maple. There seem to be no bargains left in the world, but large pieces of furniture are comparatively inexpensive. (Few people have space for them.) Cupboards especially can sometimes be found at a reasonable price; anyone with space enough for a large cupboard usually has built-in closets and doesn't need one. I bought the huge maple cupboard for $800. One side is now used for extra clothes (there is also a walk-in closet in the hall), the middle houses the television set, the drawers are the linen cupboard and more storage, and the third section serves as a bar and stores plates and glasses (see Chapter 31, figure C).

Beds in studios should be unbedroomy and the kind that can be made up quickly. The New York studio has two sleeping possibilities: the chaise longue to the left of the large maple cupboard and a large wicker sofa opposite the cupboard (unseen in the photograph). If the chaise longue is made up as a bed, the bedding must be removed daily. (I didn't have the time to make a cover for it out of the same material as the mattress.) The bedding can be rolled up, however, pretty quickly and stuffed behind the bentwood headboard.

If the large sofa is being used, life is easier. The sofa is covered in a beige canvas—seat as well as back cushions—and I have made a large extra piece of beige canvas to tuck in around the bedding to hide it (see pages 241–42). To cover the pillows during the day, I made pillow shams (page 123) in the same material as covers the chaise longue and the wicker chair (just visible to the right of the cupboard).

The disadvantage of using the sofa as a bed—even though it is faster to get into at night than remaking the chaise longue —is that it is used to sit on more than the chaise is. And if many people sit on it in the course of the day, it might become so unmade that it might be necessary to start from scratch anyway.

In New York, I love to buy my materials on West 39th Street. Not just because they have the best cheap cottons, but because it's an adventure. To even get inside a shop is an achievement. The sidewalks abound with people carrying bolt upon bolt of fabric, the bolts often obscuring the carriers, who furiously proclaim their existence from inside the cocoon of fabric to whoever gets in the way. In the shops (anyway, in the ones I like) the owners seem to have no idea of what they own and prefer that the customer burrow in case they themselves get lost among their stock.

The material I found on my last foray—in a wholesale dress fabrics shop—was straight out of a design for a Biedermeier drawing room: bunches of dusty-pink roses with brown-and-green leaves twisting into paisley lozenges on a black background (photographs 49 and 50). I often wonder what the dresses made up out of those huge bunches look like, but the walls look fine in it. An additional boon was finding another material in exactly the same colors but with smaller bunches of flowers within a stripe. Out of this second material I cut strips to use as a border to hide the staples below the cornice and above the baseboard. I also used it, uncut, to cover the little hall and the bathroom (Chapter 39, figure E).

The room has quite a heavy cornice. I painted it and the baseboard to match the bird's-eye-maple cupboard. I also "mapled" all the doors in the apartment, the struts of the large window, the radiator cover under it and the bookshelves left and right of it. (See Chapter 16 for method.)

The wall opposite the window already had some plain white bookshelves on it—boards on steel brackets. (A) I mapled the

A

shelves and then put up the material in strips between them, thereby also covering up the legs of the brackets. On top of the shelves I placed two huge fishing baskets, the wicker of which matches the brown in the leaves of the material.

The blinds are out of split bamboo—the cheapest and easiest way to cover a window fast and one which also suits the nineteenth-century style of the room. They don't block out the light too well, however, and one day I plan to make a black canvas Roman shade (pages 188–89) instead, and cover it in white cotton lace.

The furniture for the studio was begged, bought and borrowed in a hurry. The bentwood bed—now the chaise longue —lent to me by a kind relative, was much prettier when it had both its headboard and footboard, but the only space for it was in the corner where it now stands (photograph 50), and there the footboard made it look rather as if prison bars were dividing it from the rest of the room. So I unscrewed one side and stored it. It would make a spectacular bed canopy one day! (B)

The wicker table in the foreground of the photograph is in fact a footstool, minus its cushion, that belongs to the wicker armchair. The Regency stool—also a loan—is painted black and gold (see pages 74–75 for how) and is covered in a bit of green needlework in the Empire style. The borrowed carpet is upside down, with the pile against the floor. (Right side up, the colors were too bright; see page 125.) The spool-back chair—cheap for having torn chair webbing—I bought in the same place as the cupboard. I wove in some new webbing (page 41, figure o) and peeled off the chair's ugly tattered covering. I found the nice faded green cotton lining underneath, and the original buttoning, and decided not to reupholster the chair. Unfortunately, the arms didn't have the lining—nor had I the time to try to turn a piece of new lining into the same worn-out shade and texture as on the cushions. (See pages 195–96 for how to fade material.)

B

I also bought (always in the same shop) a large triple shelf on wheels (see figure A) and a very big mirror with a simple frame. (The plainer the frame on a large mirror, the better in looks and cost, unless, of course, one is shopping in the realms of Adam or Chippendale mirrors. [c])

The triple shelf on wheels (a glorified teacart, sometimes called a livery cupboard) just manages to fit into the tiny hall together with the kitchen unit and whoever is doing the cooking. Provided the guests are already in the room (they don't have space to pass if cook and cart are already there), the person cooking can put the prepared food, plates, glasses and so on onto the cart and push it into the room. There it can serve as a sideboard, and guests can help themselves from it or it can be wheeled around among them. If there are a lot of guests, they have to balance plates on their laps and sit dotted around the room.

C

If only eight people are going to eat, they can sit down at a table. The table is the desk in front of the bookshelves on the wall opposite the window. (A) It's made up of the usual: a pair of trestles, a scrapped old sheet of wood and a cover. (See page 150; photograph 7 shows a table also made in this way.) In this case the cover is a piece of green felt (baize), the same color as a pool table. For dinner it can have a piece of cotton lace

over it. The eight chairs to seat the guests around the table are:
The large wicker armchair at one end, the ram's-head chair in
photograph 50 (also a loan) at the other. Two spool-back chairs
(I later found a second one) divided by the tin trunk (serving
as a plant stand in photograph 50) with a cushion on top of it
go on the side against the bookshelves, and three stools go on
the opposite side—the Regency stool, the wicker "table" with
its original cushion, and a small table from the bathroom, with
another cushion. (D)

The table in the corner of the studio (see photograph 49) is
a card table. (It gets added to the long table for seated dinners.)
It is covered with a paisley shawl that harmonizes beautifully
with the walls. Same curves, same colors. The lamp has the
shape of a Chinese vase, and the lampshade is pleated (page
58). I tried to make the lamp look like some form of green stone
—perhaps even jade—by stippling it. The bottle with the
tulips is actually a wine bottle painted in the same way (pages
105–6).

The pipes in the corner behind the table were already
painted red and green when I started doing up the studio. "Of
course you'll want to box in those pipes," I was told. Not at all.
They go beautifully with the colors of the wall, and I think of
them as some furled-up flags standing in the corner. The room
has high ceilings. Had I boxed in the pipes, it would have taken
time as well as expense. Instead, I indulged myself by buying
two strips of mirror for left and right of the window (photographs 49 and 50). This makes the windows appear larger and
reflects more light into the room.

D

Τhe converted barn (photographs 26, 27, 43, 44, 51 and 52) is rather grand one-room living, but it is nonetheless one room. Though it consists of a living room, kitchen, two bedrooms, two dressing rooms, a bathroom and a downstairs cloakroom, there are no walls, only a few partitions. (A, *see next page*)

When I first saw the derelict barn in the Cotswolds, I became enamored with the color and size of the stone out of which it was built. I wanted to hide as little as possible of the massive pinkish slabs that had been dug out from the local quarry pre-1600. To plaster would have been a terrible pity, and interior walls would have forced that, as well as ruining the proportions of the barn.

The barn is 60' long and 20' wide, with an additional central 20' cube—making it 40' wide in the part that now includes the kitchen.

I decided to build a minstrel gallery on three sides (B) to make it large enough at each end for sleeping alcoves, to connect the two with a walk, to floor in the extra cube addition on gallery level and make a bathroom within it.

My difficulty was with the height of the balconies. It would have been visually more pleasing had they been further off the ground than they are. But had they been higher than 8', it would have left less than the 7' headroom that was needed to walk under the beams on the upper level. The original massive crooked beams are one of the beautiful features of the barn, and I certainly didn't want to interfere with them.

The barn had two openings, large doors opposite each other across the 40' divide. Through these, grain must have been carted. Three other slits in the stone, high up underneath the rafters, could hardly be called windows. Once enlarged, however, they became the window in the bathroom (photograph 44), the window in the "double-decker" sleeping alcove (photograph 43) and a window in the dressing room (to the right of the double-bedded sleeping alcove, photograph 52).

Four additional windows, top and bottom—left and right of

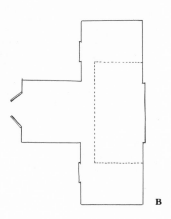

B

A

the kitchen and bathroom—are newly constructed. (Two can be seen in photograph 52.) Also newly constructed—although they mercifully look to be as old as the rest of the barn—are three stone arches, two left and right of the fireplace (photograph 52). The fireplace is also new.

To make the fireplace and arches appear four hundred years old in a hurry happened practically by itself. We used local uncut stone to build them. My helper—an old gentleman well versed in the building habits of the neighborhood—built the new arches on the same principle used to build the walls that line the country roads in that part of England.

The walls along the roads are built without any cement to bind them: The art is in making them hold together. The stones have to be fitted to one another by size and shape, and the wall must have a certain slant—how and where I don't know—to enable it to withstand weather change and water. I asked the builder to build the arches and the walk-in fireplace in the same rough way as he builds the "dry walls"; only this time, of course, gluing the stones together with cement mixed with sand and some lime (to lose the gray appearance of cement).

The fireplace opening is supported by an old beam, bought from a demolition in the neighborhood. The hearth is floored with cut stone, the stone out of the local quarry. The rest of the floor is covered with cement paving stones (page 154).

The balconies (and the flooring of the sleeping alcoves and bathroom) were put up by a serious team of builders. This was on account of the unmanageable steel joists, or beams, that were necessary to support the balconies and that arrived in formidable lengths. Once up, the front edges of the joists were faced with long boards. The boards had to be new; old, weathered ones, which I wanted, were unfindable in that length. To age them a bit, I sanded them and waxed them, rubbing some burnt-umber oil paint into the wax.

The steel joists were dark red. Because we were so short of headroom, I didn't dare attach boards under the joists. This left horrid red pieces of steel showing. I painted them white and then grained them to match the front board (Chapter 16 and photograph 52).

I longed to put two staircases into the barn. Though totally unnecessary and a frivolous waste of money, double staircases have always haunted me. Whether it is because they conjure up entertaining bedroom farces or because the most beautiful staircases I have ever seen are double ones is questionable. In a monastery in Styria, Austria, there is a double intertwining iron staircase of incredible beauty. (c) Although it looks like a modern Giacometti, it was built in the seventeenth century. Two thin, arching balustrades curve into each other, while the treads are hardly noticeable pieces of wood. The stairs are in a library and lead up to a gallery—a second layer of books surrounding the huge room. I imagine that the stairs are double so that one scholarly monk could pass another without interrupting his thought with a politeness.

The staircases I designed for the barn are rather humbler in form, although even there I helped myself to a design from the past—some stone steps in a neighboring sixteenth-century church. The church steps, leading up to the choir loft, take up remarkably little space. That was what I was after: wasting as little space as possible, yet having a separate approach to each sleeping alcove. (One set of stairs can just be seen within the left-hand arch in photograph 52 and in figure A.)

What I would have liked to build were three balconies, each with its own staircase, but not connecting one to the other on the upstairs level. Rather like three separate nests in the same tree. Unfortunately, too fanciful for anyone! Even without considering that there wasn't enough space for three staircases, it would have been a nuisance to have to come down in order to go up again to reach the bathroom. As for my ideal—three sleeping alcoves, each with its own little bathroom—I lacked both space and money.

Directly above the arches on the wall with the fireplace, left and right of the double-bed sleeping alcove, we built two roofless boxes, up to the height of, but not as far out as, the beam. (Had they gone as far as the beam, they would have bisected the window.) The walls are built of 2" × 2" uprights, and the uprights are covered in plywood on one side. Both boxes, front and sides, are covered in an Indian printed cotton. (When I was stapling the material on the side with the uprights, I realized the plywood had been a waste of money. I could have simply stretched material on both sides of the uprights.)

One box encloses the stairs and a curtained coat closet, partly seen through the open door (top of photograph 52). The

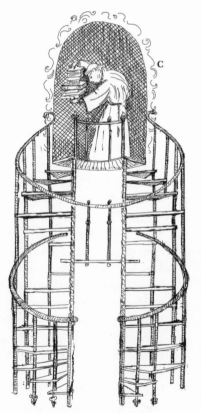

c

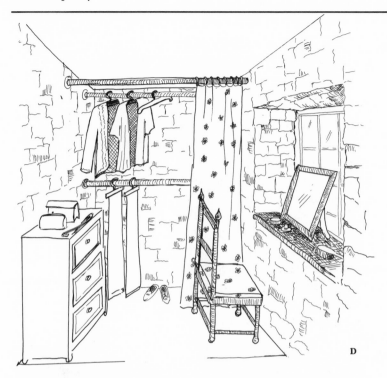

D

second one is a dressing room. It has just enough space for a curtained-off double clothes rail, a chest of drawers and a chair to put in front of the dressing table, which is the window shelf. (D)

The walls of the barn are very thick. I utilized the thickness to make window seats in the new windows, but the old windows—adapted from the original slits—were all too high and had to become shelves. All of them—seats and shelves alike—I made "oak." The only exception was the window shelf in the bathroom, which I made "mahogany" to match the bath and basin surrounds. (See Chapter 16 for how to paint imitation wood.)

An owner of an antique shop complained that a wonderful oak cupboard he had bought in France had arrived with its top completely devoured by woodworm. After he had treated what was left of the cupboard, I bought it and used the doors from it for the doors on the two boxes left and right of the double bed. The back of the cupboard I made into the back and sides of the huge couch in front of the fireplace (photograph 52). I covered the inner back and sides in thin foam rubber, stapled on, and then covered the foam with false suede, also stapled on. The huge 12' mattress, made to measure, has a cover made out of the same rust false suede. (See page 35 for covering a mattress in suede). The mattress rests on a wooden platform made out of a framing of 2″ × 4″ covered in plywood and mounted on castors. (E)

E

To arrange the sleeping alcove above the fireplace, I first filled in the two spaces between the chimney-breast and the boxes with shelves (photograph 52). The shelves are faced with a piece of thin plywood (page 16). The plywood is the same height as the boxes. The Indian printed cotton that I stapled on the boxes also covers the shelves, the plywood and the chimney-breast. Small tents out of material form roofs from the plywood to the stone wall. From the bottom shelves to the floor I hung little curtains out of the same material. (See figure F.) Behind them is space for storage. Huge curtains, still in the same material, are on a curtain rod at the back of the beam and stretch right across the barn to curtain off the sleeping alcove as well as the doors to the boxes. (The curtains, drawn back to the far right side, are unseen in photograph 52.)

What with my dislike of heights there was no way I was going to get up to the top of the chimney-breast to fasten up the canopy and hangings that would hide it. I knew the measurements from the roof of the barn to the gallery floor. I subtracted the height of the boxes, and that gave me the distance between the top of them and the roof. I cut six pieces of material that length. I made a 2' square out of some leftover 2″ × 1″. I nailed a board across it. I stapled the material to it in pleats (page 25) and then I made a sunburst and a *chou* (page 193) for the center of it. Onto the other side of the board I screwed two picture eyes, to which I tied a long string. I asked the builder, who is less cowardly than I, to screw a large hook into the wooden crossbeam of the ceiling, 3' away from the chimney-breast, and to loop my string over it. Then I raised the canopy, with the material hanging off it, by pulling the string. (F) When I had it at the height I wanted—about 3' under the crossbeam, I crept behind the hanging material, hammered a nail to the top of the plywood and wound the end of the string securely around it.

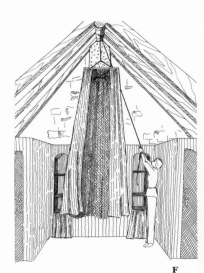

F

The hanging material was longer than necessary, but I could judge how much to cut off only when the front curves of the hangings looked right. When they did, I stapled the material

in occasional pleats around the very top of the plywood walls
and cut off the excess. I covered the staples with carpet tape
(page 21). As I didn't sew the material together, I need only
reach between the lengths to unwind the string and let the
canopy down when it needs dusting, washing or repair.

The sleeping alcove on the opposite side of the barn (photograph 43) is also formed by two boxes. Again, one encloses the
stairs and a coat closet, the other is a dressing room. This
dressing room, however, has no window. The only window on
this side is the rather high one above the two beds. That is one
of the reasons I layered the two single beds. By having one of
them higher than the other, I minimize the space between the
top bed and the window. Also, the beds look more like a sofa
this way, especially when viewed from the ground floor. Had
they stood next to one another, they would have made a low,
large block.

I found some Indian cotton bedspreads that I liked. They
had a wine-colored ground with white, brown and black
flowers. Some had flowered borders while others had borders
with rows of elephants, camels or horses. I couldn't find enough
bedspreads to cover the whole alcove, so I cut up the ones I
could get and pieced them together—some with light-brown
linen and some with an Indian cotton, which I had dyed to
match the wine color of the bedspreads. I covered both mattresses in the dyed Indian cotton, the box springs with march-
ing camels and elephants. I also attached a padded border of
elephants to the stone wall behind the bed to look like the
backrest of a sofa and to protect the person in the upper bed
from lying against the cold stone wall.

I used only one bedspread complete—for the roof of the
alcove. I had to make the roof the height and strange shape it
is in order to clear the high window (photograph 43). It is
constructed out of pieces of 2" × 1": the first three pieces are
attached to the wall around the window, another three form
an arch from one box to the other. Some of the flimsiness of
the front arch was eliminated when the two arches were joined
to each other by two long pieces of 2" × 1". (G) The structure
was made still less wobbly when I stretched and stapled the
bedspread tightly across the top and then stapled some bordered brown linen on the sides.

G

The two side walls of the alcove are also covered in brown

linen and bordered (as are the doors to the two boxes). In the center of each wall I made a small plywood indentation. It is lined in bedspread material and framed with a flowered border. I was going to put shelves up, but when I found a pair of small cupboards that exactly fitted in, I hung those up instead.

The shutters for the window are made in the same way as those in the rest of the barn (photographs 44 and 52, description page 28) and are covered with the central part of a bedspread.

The beds are 2′ shorter than the alcove. On each side of the beds are 1′ wide plywood platforms (covered with cushions in photograph 43) that can be used as night tables. The platforms are not on a level with the beds, but reach only up to the box springs. The platform of the lower bed frames it on three sides; on one side it is the support for the top bed. The other sides are also a useful step up to the higher bed if both are being used. Two makeshift tables—1′ wide and as long as the bed is wide (H)—are slotted in at the head and foot to become the night tables for the top bed. I faced them with a piece of border from the Indian cotton bedspreads and painted all the wood to look like weathered oak, to match the color of the beams. (See Chapter 16.)

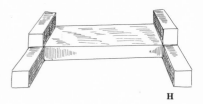

H

A bamboo pole (hidden behind the beam in photograph 43) holds wine-colored curtains, suspended off wooden rings, which can be drawn for a modicum of privacy. They, too, have borders all around.

I had some difficulty getting the banisters for the gallery right. I'm not sure if they are right even now. When I tried out wooden banisters—which I originally wanted to use—they blocked the open look of the gallery no matter how delicate a banister I tried to design. (I) In the end I settled on three rows of ship's rope strung through brass uprights.

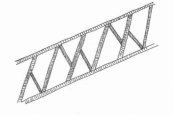

On the ground floor under the double-decker beds, there are two more boxes, but this time the space between them is narrower and they are joined together by the front door, a short corridor and a stone arch. (J) On the right of the front door and off the corridor is the downstairs lavatory, on the left a large coat closet. On each side of the stone arch there is a bookcase, and on the left side, next to the bookcase, a large cupboard. The front of it is the front of an old oak French provincial armoire. I lined the inside of the new cupboard in

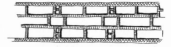

I

J

material (another Indian cotton bedspread) and it is used as a liquor cabinet.

On the right of the arch, another part of the same provincial armoire (the full-length door) follows the bookcase and hides the second pair of stairs. The bookcases, as well as the frame of the cupboard and door, were newly made. I painted them "oak" to match the old wood. (See Chapter 16 for how.)

The shutters for the large window (photograph 51) were painted by my mother. When the barn began to resemble a medieval hall, I longed to further the look with a tapestry. I went from auction to auction, but prices were beyond reason. I moaned and groaned and wondered if it was possible to paint a tapestry. My mother, in a saintlike fashion, did. It took months.

She used large plywood panels and drew lines on them with pencil, horizontally and vertically, so they looked like a piece of canvas. Then she outlined her design on top of it—trees, flowers and animals—and began painting. She painted stitches, little slanting lines across the two corners of each penciled box, just as if she were sewing across them with a needle and wool. Only someone who paints as well as she does, however, would know when and how far to "line" one color before joining it to another.

As my mother didn't have the space (or the strength) to line up the panels one next to the other while she was painting, the transition from one panel to the next is not as smooth as it ought to be. This was my job. Although the barn has been inhabited for the past two years, I have yet to complete that job: to dot the same color from one panel to the next so that it looks like one tapestry and the joins—which are now visible (see photograph)—completely disappear.

The shutters are hung on a track above the window and run in a channel at the bottom. They have two brass handles with which to pull them. Of course, I dreamed of sliding them shut electronically—like a garage door—but that had to remain a dream: too expensive.

The two center panels are cut in half and joined with piano hinges. Each panel is not cut all the way to the top, but has a 4″ piece that remains attached to the other half and to the track. This is done so that when the shutters are open, the two narrow panels can be folded back against the wide stone recess of the window—it frames the window better and gives maximum light. (See figure A.)

At a country sale I bought three pine church pews. One of them fits into the window recess; the wood from the other two was made into the refectory table by an amateur woodcarver and made to appear "oaken" by me (photograph 51 and figure A). Also in the window recess, hidden behind the pew, is a row of four cumbersome space heaters. As many of them can be turned on as the temperature demands. (They can also be used as plate and food warmers when giving a large party.)

Forty-three

The rooms in photographs 53 and 54 could be used for one-room living. The top one is a self-contained guest room (see Chapter 20), the lower one—the orange room—a later addition to the tropical studio.

The orange room has a very extraordinary shape. When it was acquired it came with, and was connected to, the room that became the blue batik bedroom (photographs 37 and 38). The now orange room was used solely for storage, and it had, like the blue batik room, a wall of flimsy plywood closets. It also had a ceiling that was too high, and practically no window. A partition wall separated it from the long hallway of the tropical studio. The new room was to have many uses. It was to be a guest room, a dining room and a storage room. It would have been easier had it had a clearly defined purpose.

We first took down the partition that separated the room from the orange-striped hall. To do this, we had to reduce and partly remove the mirror shelf in the hall. (See Chapter 40, figure B.) We replaced the partition with wide double doors. (One half can be seen in photograph 54.) I covered the doors in the same orange material as the rest of the room. (See pages 120–22 for how to cover doors, Chapter 2 for walls.) They open inward. As they are the same color as the walls and the opening is, at that point, the full width of the orange room, it gives the impression that the room is part of the hall. I wanted this effect to minimize the "white rabbit down the hole" sensation of the long narrow hall on entering the front door. The existing plywood closets and the cupboards above them I also covered in material.

My antique dealer friend, knowing my weakness for old cupboard doors and broken cupboards (page 253), sent me in pursuit of yet another pair of lovely oak French provincial ones with wonderful brass locks. We removed two of the existing plywood closet doors and prepared to hang the new oak ones instead. However, not only were they far too short and narrow, but they had curved tops and the closet opening was straight.

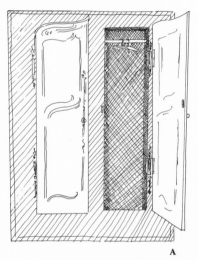

A

The carpenter, Mr. Lewis, made a wide plywood frame with a wide central separation. He hung the new doors onto the two sides of the frame. The oak doors don't close into the frame, but over it, so the curved tops become immaterial. (A) The doors are held to the central separation by magnetic touch catches. I painted the frame and the central separation to look like oak (see Chapter 16). As the doors were hanging next to the surface I was painting, it was easy to get the correct match of color and grain. I painted the same color on the picture rail, on the molding that surrounds the door and window and on the baseboard.

Where the chrome hinges on the existing cupboard doors showed, I painted them orange (cadmium red). I did the same to any visible staples (which I had used to cover doors and walls with material). I used a very fine paintbrush and artist's oil paint straight out of a tube. As the paint wasn't thinned (it can't be to cover metal), it took a long time to dry.

The ceiling seemed very far away. Not only was it high up, but it was covered with the most awful pitted plastic tiles, which had been put up, or so I was told, to muffle the sound of feet from the apartment on the floor above. I felt discouraged just looking at it. I couldn't remove the tiles and risk a crescendo of sound. I couldn't hide them with a sectional flat tent (as in photograph 14) on account of the uneven angles of the room. Too difficult. I couldn't make a pleated tent (photographs 1 and 38) and lower the ceiling on account of the strange window that went all the way up to the ceiling. It was narrow (it must have been the window of the former stairwell) and I couldn't afford to cut out more light by covering part of it.

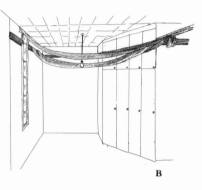

B

The owner of the apartment suggested I make a Bedouin tent. It seems their tents look more like canvas thrown unevenly over poles than the perfectly balanced and fitted tents I know from films, books and Boy Scouts. I started off by stapling a length of material to the top of the window frame just below the ceiling. (B) I stapled another length of material next to it, but lower down, just above the picture rail. I let the lengths droop into the shape of a large hammock and stapled the other ends to a piece of $2'' \times 1''$ that Mr. Lewis had attached for me where the room narrowed (photograph 54).

A naked bulb hung sadly between the two lengths at the approximate center. I took what bamboo poles I had left over from work on the tropical studio (Chapter 40) and used them to lift the material to the ceiling, around the light. I supported one end on the picture rail, which juts out, and jammed the other end into the ceiling. I used as many pieces of bamboo as I had left (six), placing them wherever they fitted in, according to their length. The material balloons out between the bamboo. (C)

To cover the part of the ceiling where the room is narrowest, I stretched a piece of material flat from the $2'' \times 1''$ to the wall. I slotted a bamboo (split in half) from one picture rail to the other under the $2'' \times 1''$ to hide the staples.

C

When Mr. Lewis had secured the pieces of bamboo to the ceiling around the light bulb, it became clear that the central light had to go. I couldn't just cover the bulb with a lampshade and leave it; it would have been too incongruous with the rest of the room.

As I dislike wasting anything that is already there, I decided to use the electrical connection and install a ceiling fan. This would further the tropical illusion throughout the apartment. I searched for a nice, old-fashioned-looking wooden fan. Unobtainable. I had to settle for a metal one and paint it. Although they are well out of reach, I was terrified that at high speed the fan might suck the tent billows into the blades. To avoid even the slightest chance of this, the fan has been doctored to function at low speed only. Having removed the only light source from the room, I now put up two brass extending-arm wall lights with brass shades. (One can be seen on the right of photograph 54; see also Chapter 8.)

The sofa is out of foam rubber and is what is called, I think, a piece of modular furniture. It was the cheapest narrow sofa I could buy that could also be used as a bed. The large foam-rubber mattress unfolds to make it a low double bed. (When it becomes a double bed, it must be leaped on from the door, as it takes up all the floor space.)

I covered the sofa's rather odious, shiny "gold," plushlike covering with a green-and-white-striped Indian cotton slip-cover, piped in white. (See Chapter 5.) To do this, I covered an old fitted bedcover that I already had with the new cotton material. I made the cover for the backrest separately and treated the front ends as if they were a bolster (pages 117–18).

To have a serious meal in the room, a round folding table for six can be placed right over the glass coffee table in front of the sofa. (The glass table can be rather painful on the shins, but it is easier than moving it.)

I bought six modern but secondhand rush-seated and spindly armchairs cheaply. The two painted to look like bamboo (one visible in the photograph) stay in the orange room. The two that look almost Regency because of their being painted black are in the blue batik bedroom (left and right of the sunken-in tallboy, photograph 37), and two are still green—the color they were when I bought them. (One of those, its back covered by a cushion, is behind the desk in the studio, photograph 48.) The two green chairs join the bamboo-colored ones to surround the table when the owner gives a dinner party. Two guests sit on the sofa on those occasions.

Forty-four

When I was arranging the California house, I gave the greatest attention to the library (photograph 55). This was the room in which things would be written that would last. This is where the owner would spend the most time and would have to feel the most content. I may have an exaggerated belief in the influence of surroundings; still, I longed to produce a room not to inspire—that wasn't necessary —but not to disturb inspiration, either.

With three square windows on one wall, a door on each of the other three, a low ceiling and no cornice, it was a far cry from a room one might readily think of as a library.

There were some points to keep in mind before starting. The room is next door to the master bedroom (photograph 40). I couldn't make it too incompatible in style. In case the house should be lent or rented, it might have to be used as a dressing room or guest room. It had to have a sofabed. Some of the bookcases, holding the author's own first editions, would need to be kept locked. This meant doors on the bookcases, and locks on the doors.

With Mr. Lewis's help we built three walls of bookcases. Each bookcase has three sections, and there are three separate compartments to each section. I based the bookcases on a small rectangular mahogany cupboard bought at auction. (A) It is now built in under the central window (just visible in photograph 55), and its drawer is built in below it. The cupboard is glassed in and opens like a flap. Its shape is copied on all the top protruding units on the window side as well as on the other two walls. The original cupboard also serves as the model for the cupboards under the other two windows and the rest of the under-counter cupboards. We made the shape of the baseboard from the shape of the cupboard drawer—and behind it we made useful, secret storage space. The upright cupboards are glassed in as well; all the cupboards in fact are, except for the very flat ones above the windows, where the books help to disguise the ugly shape of the windows.

The molding that we used to make up the baseboard can be

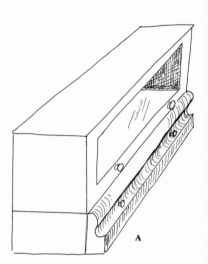

A

seen more clearly on the valance above the bed in photograph 42. We bought it, and the moldings that make up the cornice, ready-made, by the foot, at the local lumberyard.

I made newspaper patterns to get the right lengths and widths of molding and for the sizing of the cupboards (as on page 97). Mr. Lewis mitered (page 140) and directed, and the two students (page 54) hammered and sanded.

On my second trip to California, Fran and I painted the library "maple" and "mahogany" (Chapter 16)—"maple" for most of the cupboards, "mahogany" for some of the baseboard drawers, for some of the below-counter cupboards and for the line of molding around the top of the bookcases. After painting, we French-polished, resanded and waxed (page 103).

The walls are covered in a batik (see Chapter 2 for method) that has the same design as the one in the adjoining master bedroom (photograph 41), but the bedroom batik is yellow and brown, whereas the library one is brown and black. All three library doors are material-covered (see pages 120–22 for how) and so are the shutters (page 28). The day bed (B), which is modern, I bought in Los Angeles. It is finished off in the same way as the bookcases—"maple"—and covered in the same black-and-brown batik. (See Chapter 30 for quilted bedcovers.)

The mahogany "partners' desk" (photograph 55) I bought in New York. It is probably Dutch, late eighteenth century. I have always been intrigued by partners' desks, designed for two

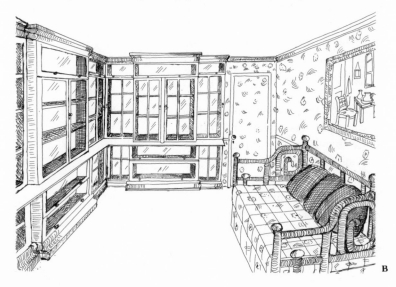

B

people at work, face to face. It makes for a nice piece of furniture, but I doubt if it made for good working conditions. This particular desk had no top, only raw wood, and it was too low. These facts had a certain influence on the price. (Normally, a partners' desk is not an inexpensive piece of furniture.) I had a black tooled-leather top made for the desk. That *was* expensive—more expensive, in fact, than the desk. This is because it is becoming a vanishing art. To tool leather, an artisan stamps a pattern into it and covers it in gold leaf. Had I not considered the desk the most important piece of furniture in the house, I would have made the top myself. I would have had a piece of plywood cut the same shape as the desktop, glued leather onto it and painted on the tooling (pages 65–66).

To heighten the desk and continue the shape of the legs, we cut round disks out of plywood. Each leg is heightened by three disks stacked up and screwed on, two in the same size, the third, a bottom one, a little larger. (c) I sanded down their sharp edges and painted them "mahogany." Had the legs been slightly less thick, I could have used thread spools (page 30) to raise the desk.

c

Another writer friend, with an otherwise lovely house, had a room that was going to waste. "Waste" is not strictly the right word; "overuse" might be better. The room was used for everything. As it was next to the front door, opposite the living room and the only access to the dining room, it had heavy traffic and was used to dump things—many sportive children threw their equipment there when they walked into the house. The room was used for telephoning, for the overflow of books, for filing cabinets; it even had a small refrigerator for cold drinks. All of this, and the room was small: only 8' × 10' (photographs 56 and 57).

Habits of rooms, like the habits of people, seldom change, no matter how convinced of success the person masterminding the change is. There was no way that I, or a different look to the room, would keep the large household from using it in the way to which they had become accustomed.

By lining the walls with bookshelves, however, I might rid the floor of books. By making cupboard space, one filing cabinet could be eliminated and the other painted the same *faux bois* as the bookcases. A chest, built by Mr. Lewis, with a foam rubber cushion covered in a paisley shawl on top of it (to make it a seat as well), became the "sports chest" (photograph 57). With luck, it may sometimes have the tennis rackets and roller skates in it instead of on top of it.

The bookcases had to be shallow. I didn't dare rob the room of more than 6″ on each wall (the depth of an average book), except on the window side. There the depth of the window frame was the guide: It jutted out 9″. Therefore the shelves left and right of it could be 9″ deep—an opportunity to shelve the larger books. We decided not to back the shelves: the room was already green when we began, the dragged paint (pages 68–70) was in good order, and not backing the bookshelves meant a substantial saving on wood. The shelves will soon be filled and books will hide most of the green anyway.

I modeled the bookcases on a small nineteenth-century maple mirror. (D) Mr. Lewis began on the wall in photograph 56. He put up four vertical boards 6″ deep. We used the window opposite as a guide to size and made the central part of the bookcase the same width. The three sections are filled with shelves, the shelves screwed to the vertical boards. To make the cornice, Mr. Lewis screwed a 7″ board to the vertical boards all the way around the room. On top of the horizontal board, just under the ceiling, he attached a curved piece of molding.

Getting the proportions right in a built-in library is extremely important. If the books are to go all around—line the walls—corners become wasted space. (See left and right of the bookcase in photograph 56.) When calculating how to make the divisions in a bookcase symmetrical, it is vital to remember about those corners.

There are also several things to consider when putting up molding in a corner. If a corner molding is the same as a molding on one of the divisions, but doubled—as would be correct (E)—it will look too wide and heavy. If it is used singly and across the corner, it is visually and technically awkward. (F) If it is the same size as the "division" molding, but split in half —a half on each side of the corner—it looks too thin. (G)

The only thing that works for me, I find, is to hold up different-sized pieces of wood, rely on my eye and forget the tape measure. If I don't have pieces of wood to try out, cutting pieces of newspaper into shapes I want to try and taping those up helps. In the little green library, the half-round moldings on

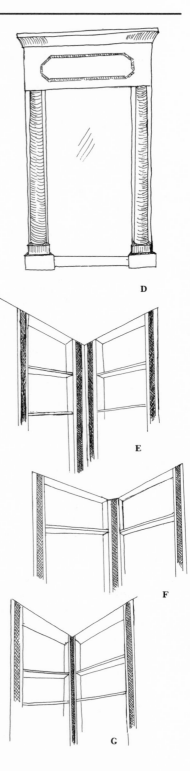

D

E

F

G

the corners are the same size as on the divisions, but they have the advantage that, being backed by two boards; they can be used more easily across the ninety-degree angle of the boards.

All the half-rounds are backed by narrow wooden boards. On the divisions the board extends beyond the half-round by 1″ on each side. The two boards that form the corners are 1″ narrower than the division boards because they overlap the half-round only on one side. (H)

H

A counter-high cupboard juts out an extra 10″ from the shelves at the central part of the bookcase (photograph 56). The dictionaries, which are deeper than the rest of the books, stand on top of the cupboard, where they have more room. They are readily accessible and can also be easily opened on the counter space in front of them. Files are kept inside the cupboard.

I didn't want the cupboard across the whole wall; it would have made the room heavy and bisected the shelves on the left wall. In order to have extra counter space to lay out books for research, we made small pull-out shelves on each side of the cupboard top. (I)

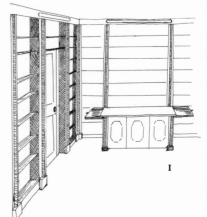

I

The door on the wall to the left of the bookcase is central and posed no problem. There are shelves to the left and right of it, and two shelves above it. The door opposite is not in the center. We left the wall free of tall bookcases and built only the two rows of shelves above the door (photograph 56). This was mainly because I felt the room needed some free wall space and also because I wanted to hang a mirror there to enlarge the room.

The mirror above the telephone table in photograph 56 was also made by Mr. Lewis—a copy of the nineteenth-century model (figure D), only a great deal larger. It is made in the same way as the bookcases. On the original mirror the half-round uprights are tapered. To do this for the whole library would have been rather more expensive than it was to buy the ready-made 2″ half-rounds. To give the slight illusion that they taper, when I painted them I tried to make them darker on top than at the base.

Because I was combining the bookcases with green walls, I didn't make them the strong maple color I had planned, but kept it paler. I don't quite know what wood it is supposed to imitate, so I simply call it a *bois clair*.

The thin oval moldings (see page 21 for how to apply them) centered on each of the four cornice boards and the moldings on the three cupboard doors I painted dark brown. The black armchairs are Regency with green slip cushions piped in pink. (See pages 44–45 and 46–47 for how to cover piping and make slip cushions.)

A trellis made by Mr. Lewis out of 1″ × 1″ pieces nailed together hides the radiator and serves as a backrest on the bench (photograph 57). The same trellis, only this time two layers of it, to support the bottles, makes a wine rack. All are grained—including the refrigerator and the original old shutters—to appear to be out of the same *bois clair* as the bookcases.

Forty-five

Some time ago I rented a house on a river. Without actually spilling over its banks, the river had mysterious ways of coming up in the cellar of the house. Between the house and the river stood a constantly damp barn, no longer in use except for a barrage of pigeons. It was dark and floorless (sand, when not mud) and pretty near roofless.

Although my lease was long, I didn't own the house, so there was, of course, no question of building the swimming pool I longed for. Even if I could have afforded one, which I couldn't, the only available land would have been that between the barn and the river—and there, had we dug a hole even a few feet deep, we'd have met the river.

At a swimming pool firm I saw what looked like a large wading pool, although the firm called it a swimming pool—iron struts within which hung a hideously bright-blue oval rubber sack. The whole thing was only 4′ deep, but 24′ long and 12′ wide—quite adequate to swim in. The price, eight years ago, was under $500.

We erected it in the barn. One step toward my ideal—an indoor swimming pool. A very small step, considering the ugliness of a 4′ tall blue plastic bathtub standing in the center of a dark barn. It was not tempting. I had to make the edifice disappear. A platform around it and terracing up to it were clearly the answer.

The barn, of pale, honey-colored stone, is 50′ long and 20′ wide. A stone wall a third of the way along divides it into two parts. The first thing we did was to chip out an irregular Gothic archway in the wall. (A) Since I was not permitted to change the exterior look of the barn, I was obliged to use such openings —for light as well as access—as already existed. The barn had two shedlike doors of normal height and two huge doors opposite each other, the same as in the converted barn (Chapter 42). I had to terrace my platform so that I could use the original shed doors without reducing their size. Also, they would have to have extra glass doors to let in as much light as possible. The huge doors would have to be glassed in as well. (Not being allowed to change the structure meant no new windows nor digging into the stone to heighten the existing doors.) Eventually I was allowed to gain a little more light by glassing in the wooden tip of the wall just under the roof (photograph 58) and making a small window in the roof to the left of the pool.

At about this stage I realized I would have to floor the whole area. That is the unfortunate thing about all my projects: They breed like rabbits. If I am making the outlay for the roof, doors and windows to weatherproof the barn, then why not a pool usable all winter? After all, the platform would be the ideal hiding space for heating. Furthermore, if the floor was above-ground, the river waters could come and go as they pleased underfoot. So what started out as a rubber wading pool sheltered from falling leaves by a derelict barn turned into a rather grander affair.

Of course, in the end it wasn't cheap, but it was certainly cheaper than building a concrete pool—indoor or out—and a conservatory. When my lease on the house on the river comes to an end and I have to leave, I could, if required to (and as it states in my lease), "return the barn to its original state." Though it would be a shame to dismantle it, it would be a challenge to fold up the rubber sack, remove the windows, stack up the boards and reassemble it all in some other derelict

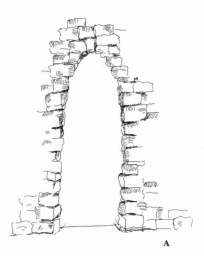

A

place. And if starting over, I would try to avoid some of the mistakes I made.

A tall barn is not economical. Considering the cost of fuel, the smaller the space that needs to be heated, the better. Condensation is practically unavoidable in an indoor pool, especially in cold weather. The cheap cardboard interior roofing I had put on the barn does not take kindly to condensation, and horrid damp spots appear on it. To minimize condensation, the room temperature should be warmer than that of the water. In winter and in a large space, this is impossible nowadays. Even if people are rich enough to do so, they shouldn't, considering fuel shortages. If doing the pool today, I would try to find some additional plastic enclosure to put around the pool and cover it with a low tin or plastic roof. Then I would try to disguise the insulation with paint, lights or plants.

I had to terrace away 4' to keep the pool from looking like a tomb sitting at one end of the barn. (The sides of the pool are 4' high.) I decided to use the original shed door, directly opposite the pool, as the main entrance. This way there is a full view of the pool through the Gothic arch on entering, as well as the longest visual run for the 4' jump.

The terracing begins at the Gothic arch. (B) Before it, the flooring is 4" off the ground. Immediately after the arch, two 8" high steps lead into the main part of the barn, which is now used for sitting and eating (the foreground of photograph 58).

The flooring is built out of 2" × 3" and covered in chip-

B

board (page 12). The platform directly surrounding the pool is out of 2" × 3" and marine ply, a waterproof plywood.

A 12" high box running the length of the platform serves as the first of two rather high, but manageable, steps to the pool's edge. It is also a bench to sit on, and the inside of it has storage space.

Once the platform was up, it seemed only logical to cut two holes in the rubber sack, install a filter and heating system, and hide the machinery under the platform. (The last part of the boxlike seat can be removed to get to it.)

The system was easy to install. The company from which I bought the pool had recommended it in the first place and now deftly attached it. Although the workings of the pool's filter and heating system still remain a mystery to me, they have functioned for the past eight years and been well worth the initial outlay.

The heating for the actual barn is separate: Oil heats the hot water that fills pipes under the platform. Into the floor along the edge of the walls, we drilled a row of holes, through which the heat rises. This follows a principle devised by the Romans which I read about somewhere and which I am proud to have made work. The fact that I can no longer afford to make it work is another matter.

On the left of the barn, two 8" steps go down to an extension (very like the kitchen extension in the converted barn—see page 249—but much smaller). This is now the "conservatory." Half of it is floored in 8" above ground level, and we dug out another 8" below ground level. This part we filled with earth.

The larger of the two huge barn doors is on the conservatory side. For economy (and also because I think it looks better) we glassed in the opening with small windowpanes.

Within the opening of the smaller barn doors opposite, we fitted a pair of sliding glass doors, which open onto the river-bank. They are 24" above ground level. In the summer, when they are open, a wooden box acts as a step to make it easier to get in and out. I was unable to make a permanent step because I kept all the original barn doors, despite the new glazing, and a step would interfere with their closing. When the old wooden barn doors are closed over the new windows and doors, they hide the glass and the exterior of the barn remains unchanged. Also, closing them at night and in winter preserves warmth.

In front of the window on the conservatory side, the earth-filled trench enables me to grow tropical plants. (Jasmine, bougainvillaea, plumbago and gardenia are all doing nicely in the damp air.) In front of the trench I have a wooden peacock, a seat from off an old merry-go-round (see figure B). I removed the benches and filled the peacock with pots of flowers.

When my mother moved from Wales to come and live with my daughter and me in the house on the river, she moved true to form—carrying her hangings. She arrived with yards and yards of a William Morris flowered material that she had used to cover the interior of her Welsh cottage. (The material has lilies and orchids and reminded her of her home before the Welsh one—in the West Indies.) One of her reasons for moving from Wales was that she had covered the outside of her cottage with flowers as well—painted on—and as a result the cottage became a tourist attraction. Wanting a quiet life, she was forced to flee. Now we used the William Morris material to cover the foam-rubber mattresses and cushions on an Indian red-lacquer sofa as well as two thin foam-rubber pads on the boxlike seat in front of the pool and the six rather stiff sofa-bed cushions that I stacked up to make into seats (photograph 58).

I eventually used more of the same material to make the slipcover for the sofa in the green kitchen (Chapter 5 and photograph 23).

The peacock, which had once been painted red, blue, yellow and green for the merry-go-round, I repainted. I denuded it of red and stuck to peacock colors, which are also the colors in the William Morris material. A lucky find was the china—a pre–running-water washing-table set—that also matches. An auction of the contents of an old house produced basin, jug, bowl, chamberpot and soap dishes. I use them all for plants.

To turn the royal-blue plastic sack that is the pool into a lagoon, I sprayed the edges of it with moss-green car spray. (See pages 97–98.) This way the color of the edges isn't so startling and the underwater bright blue makes the pool appear far deeper than the 4' that it is. At the head of the pool a wooden ornamental stag (probably once an advertisement for a pub—the White Hart or some such thing) gives atmosphere to the fern-filled lagooned arbor.

Of course, eventually I was unable to resist using up the space within the first part of the barn before the stone arch.

We built a small bathroom to the right of the main entrance, a small cubicle to house the boiler for the "Roman" heating on the left. In front of the wall of the heating cubicle, we built a sink with shelf space above it, and on the opposite side a small oven with two burners and some cupboard space.

A flight of stairs—more like a rather makeshift ladder—leads up to the sleeping gallery above the bathroom and heating cubicle (see figure B). An existing crossbeam acts as a banister for the gallery. When climbing up to the gallery, one must clamber over the beam, but there was no other way, bar major reconstruction.

The barn is damp, but self-sufficient. It is slowly turning into a jungle. A long trestle table (see page 150 for how to make one) stands against the wall most of the time and occasionally gets moved in front of the long bench and encircled with chairs for a meal. On those occasions I leave the sliding doors onto the river open and make a large fire between doors and river. I cook meat or fish on a spit, potatoes and onions in the hot coals. When I'm lazy and don't have willing wood-collecting and pyromaniacal children around, I cook outside on a hibachi charcoal grill. It is less dramatic, but quicker and easier.

Sometime after the photograph of the barn was taken, I was topping up the pool water and forgot that I had left the hose turned on. I flooded the barn floor and ruined the coconut matting. The flooring around the pool had worried me for some time—it looked too much like a gymnasium. Now I painted the whole floor expanse—around the pool, in the seating area and on the steps—Siena marble (see Chapter 16).

Instead of continually repainting and redoing, I sometimes wonder why I don't just paint up four sheets with well-proportioned windows, sunny views, pleasing pictures and closed doors. I could staple those up wherever I went, lie down on a mattress and imagine the rooms behind the doors. Decorating can become obsessive, but if it does, doing it differently each time is more fun than doing it over and over again the same way. Rather like cooking—and at least no one eats it away quite so fast.

Index

antiques, 13–14, 114–15, 173
appliances
    kitchen, 136–37; painting of, 137,
        142, 152–53, 156–57, 158
appliqué, 185
auctions, 52–53, 114

backgammon boards, 150
balconies, 249
bamboo, 132, 240–43, 256, 260,
        261;
    in blinds, 122–23, 246
    painting to match, 102
banisters
    rope, 256
banquettes, 55, 74–75, 81, 96,
        99–100, 116–17
basins
    bathroom, 217, 226, 232
baskets, 144–46, 246
bathtubs, 212–13, 224–26, 229–31,
        232, 234
    fixtures for, 213, 224
batik, 128
    in bathroom, 225
batten, 14
    for material-covered walls, 18
beams (joists), 10, 198
beds, 169–70
    from banquettes, 81
    covers for, 163–64, 171, 172–73,
        199; on walls, 255
    double-decker, 255, 256
    draped and tented, 161–64,
        166–70, 191–93, 196–98, 199,
        202–4; *lit à la duchesse*,
        162–63; *lit à la polonaise*,
        162, 166–70
    fourposter, 202–4
    lit à l'anglaise, 122–23, 167
    sofa-, 34–37, 122–24, 193,
        241–42, 244–45, 261
    widening of, 167–68
beeswax, 154–55
bias
    cutting material on, 44
blinds

bamboo, 122–23, 246
bolsters, 39, 117–18
bookcases, 198, 241, 256–57, 262,
        265–66
    on chimney breast, 14–16
    in doorframe, 14
    pyramid, 241
    See also shelves
borders, 18, 121, 168–69, 186–87,
        199–200
bottles
    holders for, 119
    painting of, 106
box springs
    covers for, 172
brackets (joist hangers), 11–12
braid, 218–19
brick
    in platform, 11
    walls of, 10, 11–12
buttons
    painting of, 86
    sewing of, 42

cabinets
    kitchen, 151–53, 156, 158
    liquor, 179–80, 259
    medicine, 232–33
cambric, 35–36
canopies
    over beds, 203–4
    on chimney breasts, 254–55
carpets/rugs, 16, 124–27, 226
    in bathroom, 231
    covering of, 126–27
    kilim, 72, 118, 124–25
    on platform, 11
    on stairs, 127
car spray
    painting with, 97–98, 152, 271
ceilings
    fans on, 232, 261
    material on, 23–25, 26–28,
        94–96, 169, 201–2, 260–61;
        chou for, 193; lowering of,
        27, 260–61; rosette for, 222;
        sunburst for, 94–96, 193

measuring of, 26
mirrors on, 232
painting of, 66
chairs, 85, 130, 165
bentwood, 88
chaises percées, 228
folding, 87–88, 239
invalids' (Victorian), 39, 242
mixing styles of, 81–82, 248
reupholstering of, 41, 43–45, 84
side, 87–88
chaise longue, 38–39, 244, 246–47
chaises percées (commodes), 228
chandeliers, 59–60, 228
chimney breasts, 12, 14–16, 107–8,
130, 254–55
china, 81, 91, 271
on walls, 89–90
chinoiserie, 61–62, 227
chipboard (particle board), 12
chou, 193
clocks, 109
closets, 205–6, 208, 229–30
shelves on doors of, 179
collage, 48, 177
columns, 20, 64, 142
tables from, 53, 76, 103–4
commodes, 228
"conversations" (seating), 39–43
cord
woolen, 74, 117, 129, 219–20
corners
closets in, 205–6
molding in, 265–66
shelves in, 96–97, 110–11, 241
cornices, 20–21, 197–98
of material or paper, 199–201,
237
painting of, 62–63, 142
plaster v. wood, 12
crochet, 169, 218, 220, 221
cupboards, 244, 253–54
under bathroom basin, 226
on chimney breast, 14–16
for concealing television, 176
doors as, 215
shelves on doors of, 179
curtains, 21–22, 182–87, 188, 198,
215, 226, 238
bed, 162–63, 166–70, 191–93,
196–98, 199, 202–4
festoons for, 191–92
opening and closing of, 182

on storage space, 205–6, 253,
254
trim on, 185–87
cushions, 35–37, 46–47, 117,
217–18, 271
adding feathers to, 31, 33, 36,
74, 118
covers for, 194–95
foam-rubber, 46
horsehair, 85, 96
slip, 85–86, 124
czar's carriage, 17, 22–27, 195

denim
in curtains, 183–84, 186
on sofas, 128
in tablecloths, 83
on valances, 181
on walls, 129
desks, 242
"partners'," 263–64
as tables, 247–48
doors
bookcase in frames of, 14
as cupboards, 215
double, 13–14, 177–79, 259
as dressing tables, 213–14
locks for, 13–14
material on, 120–22, 208, 259
mirrors on, 223, 231
sliding glass, 270
dressing tables, 175, 206, 213–14,
253
duvet, 170–73
dying, 37, 132, 185
velvet, 18–19

E-Pox-E Ribbon, 115–16, 169

fabric. *See* material
fans
ceiling, 232, 261
extractor, in kitchen, 138
feathers
in cushions/pillows, 31, 33, 46,
74, 118
mock, 162
festoons
for curtains, 191–92
fireplaces, 12–13, 108, 226, 227,
251
barbecue in, 142–43
See also chimney breasts

floors
of cement stone, 154–55, 251
painting design on, 63–64, 126,
272
parquet, 125–26
terracing of, 269–70
tiles for, 237
foam rubber, 11, 46, 85–86, 118,
217
frames, 47, 106–7, 231, 240, 243
molding for, 20–21
fringe, 37, 42, 132, 218–19,
221–22
grand, 222

gesso, 115
gilding, 13, 21, 47, 60, 65, 108,
141
See also Liquid Leaf

hatches (kitchen-dining room),
177–79

iron
sandblasting of, 201
wrought, 132

japanning, 61–62, 119
joists (beams), 10
ceiling, locating of, 198
hangers for (brackets), 11–12

kilim carpet, 72, 118, 124–25

lace, 113–14
lacquer. *See* sealers
lamps, 57, 60–61
shades for, 58–59
laundry rooms, 217
lavatories, 215–17, 223, 228, 229
leather
for covering furniture, 35–36
painting of, 65–66, 106–7, 119,
264
lighting, 9, 56–61, 142
bathroom, 223, 227, 228, 233
chandeliers, 59–60, 228
dimmers for, 60, 223
lamps, 57, 58–59, 60–61
spotlights, 56–57, 233
uplighters, 57
Liquid Leaf, 47, 60, 62, 64, 65,
66, 71, 74, 106, 108, 110,

115, 132, 146
See also gilding
lit à l'anglaise, 122–23, 167
lit à la duchesse, 162–63
lit à la polonaise, 162, 166–70

mantelpieces, 12–13, 105–6
material
  architectural effects with,
    128–32, 199–201
  in bathrooms, 213, 223, 225,
    231–32
  on ceilings, 23–25, 26–28,
    94–96, 169, 201–2, 260–61
  cutting on bias, 44
  on doors, 120–22, 208, 259
  dyeing of, 18–19, 37, 132, 185
  fading or aging of, 132, 195–96
  to hide staples, 21
  around mirrors, 25–26, 106–7,
    175, 206
  painting of, 31, 32–33, 36, 42,
    55, 86, 186, 227, 238
  selection of, 18, 72–74, 185, 245
  and shelves, 20, 25, 122, 180,
    254
  on shutters, 27–28, 207
  on walls, 3, 16, 29, 94–96,
    112–13, 163, 169, 199–200,
    201–2, 205–7, 240–43,
    255–56, 263; application of,
    17–21, 25
mattresses
  and box spring covers, 172
  for sofas, 34–35, 254
measuring
  with string, 26, 30, 99, 184
mesh
  metal, 15
metal, 132
  "antiquing", 64
  mesh of, 15
  painting of, 61–62, 119
  sandblasting of, 201
mirrors, 10, 106–11, 129–30, 231,
  247, 248, 266
  in bathrooms, 213, 214–15,
    232–33
  on ceilings, 232–33
  on doors, 223, 231
  framing of, 106–7, 231, 243
  material around, 25–26, 106–7,
    175, 206

tiles of, 90–91, 233
mitering, 21, 106–7, 140
molding
  over bed, 168, 197
  in corners, 265–66
  curved, 97
  on double door, 13
  around mirrors, 107
  mitering of, 140
  painting nonexistent, 69
  painting of, 70–71
  picture frame, to hide staples,
    20–21
  "pinning" of, 71, 97
  plastic, 212

needles
  curved, 19, 32, 33, 35
  three-cornered, 35

ottomans, 242

painting
  of bottles, 106
  of buttons, 86
  with car sprays, 97–98, 152, 271
  of ceiling, 66
  of columns, 20, 64
  of cornices, 62–63, 142
  of floors, 63–64, 126, 272
  japanning, 61–62, 119
  in kitchen, 137, 141–42,
    151–53, 156–58
  of leather, 65–66, 106–7, 119,
    264
  of material, 31, 32–33, 36, 42,
    55, 86, 186, 227, 238
  of metal, 61–62, 119
  of molding, 69, 70–71
  and paint-mixing, 141–42
  of picture frames, 47
  for special effects, 67–71, 98,
    152–53; "marble," 76, 103–6,
    234; "parchment," 60;
    stippling/distressing/
    dragging/ragging, 66–70;
    "tapestry," 257–58; "tortoise
    shell," 105, 116, 119; "wood,"
    12, 13, 14, 21, 28, 38, 82, 92,
    98, 100–3, 112–13, 132, 156,
    197, 198–99
  with stencils, 62–66
  of wicker, 76, 86–87, 123, 143

paneling
  for kitchen, 139–40
  painting nonexistent, 69
particle board (chipboard), 12
patchwork, 195
patterns
  of newspapers, 97, 195, 263,
    265
  for stencils, 62–64
pillows
  bed, 170–71, 173; shams for,
    123–24, 193–94
  for cushions, 36
pipes
  exposed, 248
piping, 39, 44
  double, 44–45
  painting of, 31, 32–33, 36, 86
plants, 51, 144, 224, 271
plates
  on walls, 49, 89–90, 109
platforms
  construction of, 11–12
  for swimming pool, 269–70
pleats
  in material on walls, 25
  pinch-, 184
plywood, 16, 97
  marine, 225, 226
polish
  French, for wood, 102–3, 145
pots
  glazing of, 116–17
putty, 115

quilts and quilting, 117, 123–24,
  172–74, 195
  for clothes hangers, 181
  covering of, 172–73, 192
  as table covers, 173–74

radiators
  concealing of, 14–15, 214, 258,
    267
reupholstering. *See* upholstering
  and reupholstering
ribbons, 48–49, 109–10, 185–86
rosettes, 222
ruffles, 162, 171, 194

screens, 55, 66, 117, 130
  mirrored, 110
sealers, 60, 65, 68, 102–3, 153

sealers, 60, 65, 68, 102–3, 153
  for unglazed tiles, 139
settee (curved), 74–75
shades (window), 188–91
  bamboo blinds, 122–23, 246
  Holland (roller), 113, 130, 157,
    188, 198
  Roman, 188–89
  Vienna, 189
  See also shutters
shawls, 75–76, 248, 264–65
sheets, 170–71
  as tablecloths, 83
  as wall coverings, 94–96
shelves
  near bathtub, 213, 225, 231
  in corners, 96–97, 110–11,
    241
  on cupboard/closet doors, 179
  material on, 20, 25, 122, 180,
    254
  See also bookcases
showers, 224–25
shutters, 27–28, 206–7, 226, 256,
    257–58
  material on, 27–28
  mirrored, 110
  sliding, 117, 258
sideboards, 97–98, 114
slipcovers, 30, 46–47, 85, 128–29
sofas, 46–47, 128
  as beds, 34–35, 122–24, 193,
    241–42, 244–45, 261
  from cupboard backs, 253–54
  in kitchens, 144
  reupholstering of, 30–37
spotlights, 56–57, 233
springs
  tying of, 41
stairs
  carpet on, 127
  double, 251–52
  handrails for, 131, 132
staples
  hiding of, 20–21, 22, 27, 28, 30,
    37, 39
stencils, 62–66, 237

stereos
  concealing of speakers of, 55
stones, 252
  cement, 154–55, 251
  on kitchen counters, 153–54
storage space, 137, 244
  under banquettes, 55
  in bathrooms, 180, 208, 225–26,
    229–30, 232–33
  closets, 179, 205–6, 208, 229–30
  curtains over, 205–6, 253, 254
  in kitchen, 136, 144–45, 180
  under platform, 12
suede, 35–37
sunbursts, 94–96, 193
swimming pools (indoor), 267–72

tables, 81–83, 98–99, 149–50, 243,
    247–48, 261
  behind beds, 169–70
  from columns, 53, 76, 103–4
  covered, 150, 174–75; in mirror
    tiles, 90–91
  dressing, 175, 206, 213–14, 253
  material covers for, 173–75, 176;
    tablecloths, 83–84
  night, 256
  settings for, 89–92, 147
  from trunks, 118–19
tassels, 220–21
television
  concealing of, 54, 81, 147–48,
    176–77, 179, 241
tiles
  in bathroom, 104–6, 225, 234
  floor, 139, 237
  mirror, 90–91, 233
tinware
  "antiquing", 64
  japanning, 61–62, 119
trays, 76, 148–49
  cloths and napkins for, 148
Treasure Gold, 65, 108
Treasure Sealer, 60, 65
trellis (garden), 15, 267
trestles, 149–50, 174
trompe l'oeil, 69, 152–53, 156–58

trunks, 65, 118–19, 248
tufting, 218

upholstering and reupholstering,
    28–45
  of banquettes, 74
  of chairs, 41, 43–45, 84, 130
  of chaise longue, 38–39
  of settees, 74–75
  of sofas, 30–33
uplighters, 57
uprights, 10

valances, 22, 181–82, 186, 197
  over beds, 162, 191–93
velvet
  in curtains, 21–23
  dyeing of, 18–19
  on furniture, 35
  on walls, 18–21
  washing of, 196

walls
  brick, 10, 11–12
  groupings on, 47–50, 89–90
  material on, 3, 16, 94–96,
    112–13, 129, 163, 169,
    199–200, 201–2, 205–7,
    240–43, 255–56, 263;
    application of, 17–21, 25
  painting of special effects on,
    62–64, 67–71, 186
  partition, 10, 215, 252
  removal of, 10
wicker
  painting of, 76, 86–87, 123, 145
  repairing of, 86–87
windows
  bamboo blinds for, 122–23, 246
  kitchen-to-dining room, 177–79
  material around, 25
  moving frames of, 54
  "raising" of, 54–55
  seats in, 227
  shades for, 113, 130, 157,
    188–91, 198
  shutters for, 27–28, 110, 117,
    206–7, 226, 256, 257–58

About the Author

Diana Phipps was born in Vienna and spent her childhood in luxury, in a castle in Czechoslovakia that had been in her family for eight hundred years. After her parents lost all their properties, as a result first of the German occupation and then of the communist takeover, they emigrated to the United States, where, in reduced circumstances, Diana first began making do. She now lives in England, dividing her time between a Victorian house in London and a Queen Anne parsonage on the Thames in Oxfordshire, and travels frequently to this country. She decorates for herself and her friends both here and in Europe, and still believes that our homes — whether they are forty-room mansions or one-room apartments — should be our castles.

Paint
Liquid leaf (gold
Car spray (can)